MILITARY LOGISTICS
and
STRATEGIC PERFORMANCE

Cass Series: Strategy and History
Series Editors: Colin Gray and Williamson Murray
ISSN: 1473-6403

This new series will focus on the theory and practice of strategy. Following Clausewitz, strategy has been understood to mean the use made of force, and the threat of the use of force, for the ends of policy. This series is as interested in ideas as in historical cases of grand strategy and military strategy in action. All historical periods, near and past, and even future, are of interest. In addition to original monographs, the series will from time to time publish edited reprints of neglected classics as well as collections of essays.

1. *Military Logistics and Strategic Performance*, Thomas M. Kane

2. *Strategy for Chaos: RMA Theory and the Evidence of History*, Colin Gray

3. *The Myth of Inevitable American Defeat in Vietnam*, Dale Walton

MILITARY LOGISTICS and STRATEGIC PERFORMANCE

THOMAS M. KANE
University of Hull

LONDON AND NEW YORK

First Published in 2001 in Great Britain by
Routledge
2 Park Square, Milton Park, Abingdon, Oxfordshire OX14 4RN
711 Third Avenue, New York, NY 10017

First issued in paperback 2015

Routledge is an imprint of the Taylor and Francis Group, an informa business

Copyright © 2001 Thomas M. Kane

British Library Cataloguing in Publication Data

Kane, Thomas M.
  Military logistics and strategic performance
  1. Logistics 2. Strategy
  I. Title
  355.4'11

ISBN 0-7146-5161-3 (cloth)
ISSN 1473-6403

Library Congress Cataloging-in-Publication Data

Kane, Thomas M., 1969–
  Military logistics and strategic performance / Thomas M. Kane.
    p. cm.
  Includes bibliographical references and index.
  ISBN 0–7146–5161–3 (cloth)
  1. Logistics. 2. Strategy. I. Title.
  U168.K35 2001
  355.4'11 – dc21
                                                         00-069446

All rights reserved. No part of this publication may be reproduced, stored in or introduced into a retrieval system or transmitted in any form or by any means, electronic, mechanical, photocopying, recording or otherwise, without the prior written permission of the publisher of this book.

Typeset in 10½/12 Minion by Cambridge Photosetting Services

Publisher's Note
The publisher has gone to great lengths to ensure the quality of this reprint but points out that some imperfections in the original may be apparent.

ISBN 13: 978-1-138-98111-9 (pbk)
ISBN 13: 978-0-7146-5161-3 (hbk)

To my father, Norman E. Kane

Contents

Series Editor's Preface	ix
Acknowledgements	xi
List of Abbreviations	xii
1 The Arbiter of Opportunity	1
2 The Burma Campaign	15
3 Making It Work: America's War in the Pacific	36
4 Making Haste Slowly: Communist Logistics in Vietnam	77
5 The Cold War	124
6 The Revolution in Military Affairs	149
Conclusion: The Foundation of Strategy	171
Bibliography	181
Index	191

Series Editor's Preface

This is a profound book on a much-neglected subject which speaks to core matters of strategy. That is why we, the editors, are delighted to have Tom Kane's *Military Logistics and Strategic Performance* as the first book in our new series on 'Strategy and History'. In our view, Dr Kane advances the understanding of strategy through proper application of historical method. He is respectful of the value of theory, recognizing that the facts will not speak, neatly organized, for themselves. However, he is even more respectful of empirical evidence and, in general, of an inductive spirit in scholarship. Kane is gloriously damning of that genus of speculative general theory which sees 'facts' as the manufactured products of chosen ideas. Readers of this book should profit from, and enjoy, the author's willingness fearlessly to criticize even the grandest of contemporary theorists in political science for a fundamentally irresponsible attitude to evidence. Kane affronts several of the scholarly deities of post-modernity when he affirms the creed that 'we must increase, rather than reduce, the amount of empiricism in our work' (p.178).

Kane is not the first social scientist to write about military logistics, but he is by far the most successful. If this book provided simply a superior set of case studies of better and worse performance in the science of supply and movement, then it would probably not feature in this series. The most valuable distinguishing characteristic of *Military Logistics and Strategic Performance* is, as the title claims, its systematically *strategic* focus. Many doctrine manuals and studies assert the strategic significance of logistics, but none before Kane – including the formidably insightful Martin Van Creveld – has really shown persuasively how the two relate umbilically to each other. Military history is full of examples of great adventures which appeared to triumph over logistical frailty, and of other great adventures which were brought to nought apparently because of those frailties. In short, history yields ever-arguable 'evidence' in abundance to illustrate any position in argument a scholar prefers to take. Kane is one of the few scholars who has grasped that, to have resort to a bastard form of a familiar proposition, 'they cannot logistics know who only logistics know'. The path to better understanding of how to think about logistics does not lie, at least does not only lie, through more and more detailed logistical studies. Such an approach would be akin to the fallacious view that if a medium-sized heap of artillery shells is good for the prospects of offensive success, then a veritable mountain of the same should all but guarantee victory. The key to offensive success is not the mindless maximization of supply, but rather a timely reliability of sufficient supply, yielding the opportunity for the art of strategy to show its magic.

Kane emphasizes the essential unity of strategy, logistics and command. He highlights the significance of context: 'logistics ought to excite us, because it helps to set the stage upon which strategists act, and therefore ranks among the factors which decide the course and outcome of a war' (p. 1). Kane advises, convincingly, that '[t]o provide the resources which strategy requires, logisticians must participate in the making of strategy, not only in the planning phase of a campaign, but every step of the way' (p. 5). Synergism and nuance pervade this sophisticated study. The author does not conceal his ambition, recommending that 'a fresh analysis of logistics needs to encompass all levels of activity from battlefield tactics to national policy without attempting to impose artificial boundaries between them' (p. 8). As if that were not enough, Kane then adds the wise, if complicating, judgement that 'such an analysis must never overlook the fact that, although causes may lead to effects, the process is often part of a larger pattern and is seldom direct'. In other words, while the author argues for the systematic importance of the logistical dimension of strategy, he is fully alert to the peril which menaced the Western Allies in 1915–17, of confusing logistics *with* strategy. The measure of scholarly success of this book lies almost as much in what the author does not claim for his theme as for what he does.

Military Logistics and Strategic Performance offers remarkable value for a volume of such modest dimensions. It can be read with profit as: a major contribution to the debate among (mostly) historians about military logistics launched a generation ago by Van Creveld with his *tour de force, Supplying War*; a valuable addition to the unduly slim library of comparative historical case studies on logistics; or as an exceedingly rare bid to explain how logistics 'works' strategically. In our opinion, the book succeeds admirably in all three regards.

COLIN GRAY
Series Co-Editor

Acknowledgements

My deepest gratitude to Professor Colin S. Gray, Dr Eric Grove, Captain Peter Hore and Professor Philip Towle, all of whom helped immeasurably with the development of this work.

Abbreviations

AA	Anti-Aircraft
ARVN	Army of the Republic of (South) Vietnam
BT	Binh Tram (Military Station)
COSVN	Central Office of South Vietnam
DMZ	De-Militarised Zone
DRV	Democratic Republic of (North) Vietnam
DUKW	A US Army landing craft or 'amphibious tractor'. (The exact meaning of the letters is lost, but may have been a code at the factory that made these vehicles.)
DVN	Democratic Republic of (North) Vietnam
FOFA	Follow-On Forces Attack
GDRS	General Directorate of Rear Services
GPS	Global Positioning System
GSFG	Group of Soviet Forces, Germany
J-STARS	Joint Surveillance and Target Acquisition Radar System
LCI	Landing Craft, Infantry
LCT	Landing Craft, Tank
LCVP	Landing Craft, Vehicles and Personnel
LSD	Landing Ship, Dock
LSM	Landing Ship, Medium
LST	Landing Ship, Tank
NATO	North Atlantic Treaty Organisation
NLF	National Liberation Front
NVA	North Vietnamese Army
OMG	Operational Manoeuvre Group
PAVN	People's Army of (North) Vietnam
PGM	Precision-Guided Munition
PLF	People's Liberation Front
POL	Petroleum, Oil, Lubricants
POMCUS	Pre-positioned Overseas Material Configured to Unit Sets
RAND	Research and Development Corporation
REFORGER	Return of Forces to Germany
RMA	Revolution in Military Affairs

ABBREVIATIONS

RPV	Remotely Piloted Vehicle
RVN	Republic of (South) Vietnam
SADARM	Sense and Destroy Armour
SAS	Special Air Services
SCUBA	Self-Contained Underwater Breathing Apparatus
SO	Special Operations
TG	Transportation Group
TRADOC	Training and Doctrine Command
UCAV	Uninhabited Air Combat Vehicle
US	United States
USAF	United States Air Force
USN	United States Navy
USMC	United States Marine Corps
USSR	Union of Soviet Socialist Republics
VC	Viet Cong
WAAM	Wide Area Anti-Armour Munition
WTO	Warsaw Treaty Organisation

'The main and principle point in war is to secure plenty of provisions ...'
> Vegetius, in T. Phillips, *Roots of Strategy*, p. 67

'Understand that the foundation of an army is the belly.'
> Frederick the Great, in T. Phillips, *Roots of Strategy*, p. 174

'An army marches on its stomach.'
> Napoleon Bonaparte, in A. Partington, *The Oxford Dictionary of Quotations*, p. 490

'There is nothing so common as to find consideration of supply affecting the strategic lines of a campaign and a war.'
> Carl von Clausewitz, in *On War*, p. 137

'Logistics [as commonly defined] would be nothing more nor less than the science of applying all possible military knowledge.'
> Antoine Jomini, in *The Art of War*, p. 253

'Supply and transport are intimately bound up with all military operations.'
> C.E. Callwell, in *Small Wars*, p. 58

'Amateurs study strategy, professionals study logistics.'
> General Omar Bradley, in T. Pierce, *Proceedings of the US Naval Institute*, Vol. 122, No. 9, p. 74

'The battle is fought and decided by the quartermasters before the shooting begins.'
> Erwin Rommel, in J. Lynn, *Feeding Mars: Logistics in Western Warfare from the Middle Ages to the Present*, p. viii

'During the Second World War 80 per cent of our problems were of a logistic nature.'
> Field Marshal Montgomery, in J. Thompson, *The Lifeblood of War: Logistics in Armed Conflict*, p. 4

'Gentlemen, the officer who doesn't know his communications and supply as well as his tactics is totally useless.'
> General George S. Patton, in US Navy, *Naval Logistics*, p. 45

'Indeed, the foundation for the total success of Desert Storm was, in large measure, laid during the previous two months [of logistical preparation].'
> General William G. Pagonis, in *Military Review*, Vol. 71, No. 9, p. 28

1

The Arbiter of Opportunity

To judge by the remarks of experienced soldiers from every era, logistics ranks among the most crucial elements contributing to military success. Yet, for the student of strategy, the subject of supply has become similar to oatmeal and chicken soup. Everyone agrees that it is good for you, but nobody is enthusiastic enough to say much more than that. To paraphrase one dedicated supporter of logistical studies, this topic has the same level of appeal as a post-game interview with a football team's water boy.[1] It is, however, the purpose of this study to show, not only that supply officers perform an indispensable service, but that logistics ought to excite us, because it helps to set the stage upon which strategists act, and therefore ranks among the factors which decide the course and outcome of a war.

This study fulfils two overall purposes. First, it offers historical analysis to expand a neglected field of strategic research. As a book reviewer in the journal *Joint Forces Quarterly* noted, 'for every thousand books published on military strategy, one deals with logistics'.[2] Second, this study closes a gap which has developed between the common sense of military leaders and the findings of academic researchers.

Despite all the sayings which remind us that logistics are important, historians and scholars in the field of political studies have been unable to explain why this is so. The obvious explanation – that soldiers need food and ammunition to carry out their functions – has proven too simplistic to explain the relationship between logistical planning and military success. For these reasons, certain scholars suggest that logistics may be less important than it seems. This study counters their arguments, reaffirms the importance of supply, offers a theoretical explanation of why logistics matters, and then explains, through a series of historical case studies, how commanders have used their logistical resources to win wars.

A PARADOX

How, exactly, does supply affect warfare? The answer to that question is not as obvious as it would seem. Clearly, soldiers who run out of food, fuel or ammunition will cease to fight, and to the German troops who spent December outside Moscow in summer uniforms or the American soldiers of Task Force Smith who faced 33 North Korean tanks with only six rounds of effective armour-piercing ammunition, the importance of logistics would seem straightforward.[3] Over time, however, such calamities tend to affect both sides, and one is hard pressed to think of a war which ended because an entire army ran out of supplies.

Hence, General Nathanael Greene refused a post as George Washington's chief logistician with the sneer 'Whoever heard of a quartermaster in history as such.'[4] Jomini found himself forced to ask, 'Is logistics simply a science of detail?'[5] Martin Van Creveld, whose book *Supplying War* rates as a pillar of academic logistical studies, concludes that efforts to win wars through improved supply systems have been futile at best.[6] When one compares these feelings and findings to the quotations at the beginning of this chapter, it seems that at least one set of authorities must be missing an important point.

The term 'logistics' can mean many things. Those interested in the convoluted derivation of this word might consult Jomini.[7] Recent books on the topic have considered the subject of logistics broad enough to encompass manpower reserves and mobilisation of national industry.[8] Official military definitions differ both between nations and between branches of service.[9] However, for purposes of this paper, logistics is neither less nor more than the business of 'moving, supplying and maintaining military forces'.[10] Both logistical supporters and logistical sceptics have generally concentrated their analysis upon the actual business of getting materiel to the fighting forces, and under this focused definition, the conflict between the observations of a Van Creveld and the sensibilities of a Bradley becomes yet more of a paradox.

GENRES OF GENERALISATION

Although most commentators lament what they see as an absence of interest in logistics, a review of the relevant literature reveals not so much a dearth of material as a lack of direction.[11] The authors who have tackled this subject conflict on the fundamental issues of what a theory of supply should explain. Economists have treated the whole business of logistics as a single factor in calculating the cost of war for an entire nation. Meanwhile, historians and professional soldiers have concentrated on the specifics of individual supply operations. Some have distilled these observations into principles which purport to explain how logisticians can best serve the purposes of the armed forces. Other historical scholars have followed the lead of Van Creveld and sought to identify the points at which logistics serves as a constraint upon military undertakings. In reality, of course, these different problems are all facets of the same gemstone. To understand logistics as a whole, we might do well to look beyond these authors' explicit conclusions and examine their common intuition about the deeper importance of the subject.

During the 1960s, certain economists, notably Kenneth E. Boulding, used logistics as the basis for a general theory of military power.[12] These theorists proposed that armed forces are strongest in the vicinity of their home country, where they have ready access to food, ammunition and other vital materiel. As military units venture away from their own borders, this theory would have us believe, they experience greater and greater difficulties supplying themselves with such things, and therefore they become progressively weaker in combat. These economists referred to the gap between well-equipped units fighting near their home territory and less well-equipped ones fighting far from their bases as the 'loss-of-force gradient'.

Albert Wohlstetter, however, rejected this entire concept in his *Foreign Affairs* article 'Illusions of Distance'. As Wohlstetter noted, the differences in efficiency between sea and land transport may reverse the logic of the loss-of-force gradient. During the Vietnam War, for instance, the People's Republic of China provided logistical support to the Communist forces in North Vietnam while the United States sent supplies to its own forces and those of its allies in South Vietnam. China shared a border with North Vietnam whereas America was on the other side of the Pacific Ocean, but US forces managed to ship four times as much materiel into the war zone by sea as the Chinese could transport the much shorter distance over land.[13] Within an area of operations, Wohlstetter observes, any attempt to measure logistics as a constant function breaks down even more completely, as purely local features such as roads, mountains, plains, airfields and cities determine the accessibility of any given point.

Both the economists and Wohlstetter take it for granted that an increase in logistical efficiency will directly increase the overall fighting power of a military organisation. Therefore, all parties to this debate felt qualified to draw conclusions about the implications of their arguments for high state policy. To Boulding, advances in technology which change the slope and curve of the 'gradient' are a key factor in determining whether small states will survive and how frequently nations of any size will attack each other.[14] Wohlstetter hoped that his rebuttal of the gradient argument would draw attention to the importance of distant events to the safety of the American homeland, and the consequential folly of isolationism. Furthermore, Wohlstetter wished to make the point that it is perfectly feasible for the United States to intervene in distant parts of the world when such actions suit its interests.[15]

Meanwhile, as economists and their critics have relied on assumptions about logistics in theory, historians have approached the subject from the opposite angle. These authors accept national policy concerning war and peace as a given, but follow the day-to-day results of logistical operations in detail. Examples of historical works which explicitly focus upon logistics range from Donald Engels' minor classic, *Alexander the Great and the Logistics of the Macedonian Army*, to the US Army's series on *Global Logistics and Strategy during the Second World War*, to Allan Gropman's recent study of the logistics of that conflict, *The Big 'L': American Logistics in World War Two*, to the popular memoirs of General William Pagonis, who supervised United States logistical operations during Operations Desert Shield and Desert Storm.[16]

Every war involves its own story of supply. Since the volume of historical data on this subject is staggering, both scholars and soldiers attempt to sift the past for lessons that are generally useful to operations in any age.[17] However, there is a crucial difference between the general assumptions of the economists and the general principles of soldiers. Whereas an assumption is something which one must accept, a principle is something which one must apply. Therefore, the advice which historians give to supply officers offers us a clearer picture of what logisticians believe that they are supposed to do.

Logistical operations in the military require many of the same skills as management in any other bureaucracy. For those who wish to master the organisational aspect of logistics, there is an entire body of literature on the subject within the field of business administration.[18] Pagonis devotes part of his concluding chapter to the application of his experience in the corporate world.[19] The author who drew attention to an age-old plague of organisations by coining the term 'Parkinson's Law' was originally writing about naval administration. (In this context, Parkinson's Law reads, 'The smaller the fleet, the larger the Admiralty.)[20] Admiral Eccles explores this concept of a 'logistical snowball' at great length in his book *Logistics in the National Defense*.[21] However, when one exhausts the study of resource allocation within an organisation, one finds that there is still another dimension to the practice of logistics.

For a supply officer, these authors offer no easy measure of success. A logistical organisation cannot fulfil its duty simply by keeping a large volume of materiel flowing to the front line. Units on the attack require a different level of support from units on the defence, and the rhythm of a particular battle may modify supply demands radically. Furthermore, although the consequences of having a unit run out of supplies at a critical moment are grim, there is also such a thing as too much supply. The 'logistical snowball' which Eccles mentioned not only wastes resources, it creates administrative logjams which impede active operations. Logisticians must strike a balance between starvation and constipation.[22]

One might propose that quartermasters require foresight to anticipate the needs of particular forces in battle. Kenneth N. Brown of the National Defense University asks whether this sort of 'responsiveness' may be key to understanding the role of logistics within strategy.[23] However, if 'foresight' means 'prophecy', this may be more than armies should ask of any officer. Each battle is unique. The historical record makes it abundantly clear that no military oracle can divine supply requirements in advance, even for the most carefully choreographed military operation.[24] To provide the resources which strategy requires, logisticians must participate in the making of strategy, not only in the planning phase of a campaign, but every step of the way.

In the felicitous words of Frederick the Great, 'the good quartermaster general cannot fail to make his fortune, since he will gain, by practice, all the skills needed by an army general'.[25] A more recent commentator suggests that the classic 'combined arms' trinity of infantry, cavalry and artillery should include, as a fourth component, supply.[26] Colonel George C. Thorpe argued that an effective military organisation must give its logistical staff the 'power and authority of the initiative' at the highest levels of the army.[27] These observations concur with another point that Eccles raised, which is that the key problems of logistics 'are not technical problems. They are problems of command.'[28]

To determine the identity of Eccles' 'problems of command', one might examine the logistical principles which military organisations teach to commanders. To quote US Naval Doctrine Publication No. 4, the 'most important principle of logistics' is 'providing the right support, at the right time, in the right place'.[29] This prescription is both vague and self-evident, but that in itself indicates the way in which the Navy views the problem. The authors of Publication No. 4 expect supply officers to do their jobs, not by applying precise rules, but by exercising independence and judgement within broad parameters.

For elaboration on this topic, readers may consult the numerous collections of maxims which provide guidance for logistical work.[30] A typical list of such maxims appears in Trevor Dupuy's *International Military and Defence Encylopedia*.

Unity of Purpose
    Corporate effort
    Functional interdependence and integration
    Mutual understanding and confidence
    Co-operation and teamwork

Preparedness
    Foresight and military judgement
    Determination of requirements
    Co-ordination of planning and plans
    Operational readiness

Viability
    Feasibility and credibility
    Sufficiency
    Sustainability
    Dispersion and protection

Economy
> Elimination of inefficiency and waste
> Role-effectiveness v. cost effectiveness
> Rationalisation, standardisation and specialisation
> Integrated support

Responsiveness
> Forward impetus and momentum
> Local, centralised control of resources
> Proactive, as well as reactive, support
> Dedication to duty

Resourcefulness
> Versatility
> Improvisation and innovation
> Self-reliance, self-containment and self-sufficiency
> Development of aptitudes and attitudes.[31]

Few will be surprised to learn that logistics involves preparation or economical management. Terms such as responsiveness, resourcefulness, versatility, improvisation and innovation, however, point to the factors which make this topic interesting. To one author, logistics is a 'bridge between strategy and tactics', whereas to another, it is a link between national resources and strategy.[32] No matter which particular elements of warfare a given writer seeks to connect through the medium of supply, logistical decisions permeate all of the parts of war which Clausewitz identified as art, rather than science.[33]

Clausewitz himself was well aware of this point. In his chapter on Maintenance and Supply, he notes that as warfare became more organised and purposeful, logistics became progressively more important at every level of military activity.[34] Furthermore, he emphasises the link between logistics and operations. 'Operational requirements are dominant and even in the sphere of maintenance and supply call for appropriate arrangements.'[35] Clausewitz goes on to explain how two logistical revolutions – the development of the depot system in the 1600s and the return of foraging in the wars of the French revolution – led to equally radical changes in the strategy, tactics and the political implications of war.[36]

The economists have offered one genre of generalisation while the historians have offered another. Both have concluded that the subject is tantalisingly vast in scope, and all that is missing are the specifics. Here, in *Supplying War*, Van Creveld enters the field with his promise to replace 'vague speculations' with 'concrete calculations' on the role of logistics.[37] He adopts the method of historical narrative with a series of case studies, but focuses on facts which are hard and measurable, such as distances, consumption rates, speed of vehicles and shortages at the front.

When Van Creveld compares the speed at which armies have moved and supplied troops, he finds that practice always has fallen short of what transportation technology would seem to allow.[38] However, what is more significant is that neither technology nor systematic management has improved that situation. Indeed, although the speed of transportation has increased dramatically with the coming of the internal combustion engine, the fuel and ammunition demands of a modern army more than cancel their effects, and the efficiency of logistical services seems to have declined over time.[39] More depressing yet, when Van Creveld examines innovators such as Napoleon and von Moltke, he finds little evidence that their logistical ideas played a key role in their respective strategies, and when he examines supply fiascos such as Rommel's 1942 campaigns in North Africa and the German war with the Soviet Union, he determines that the administrative problems were insoluble.

Like Thorpe, who felt that 'the military themselves know next to nothing about logistics', Van Creveld notes that commanders in great campaigns have organised their logistical efforts giving 'little, if any, thought to the ideal combination which would have carried them the furthest'.[40] However, whereas Thorpe proposed a programme of reform to help commanders organise their supply services more effectively, Van Creveld sees little hope for such an endeavour. Van Creveld is not certain that armed forces are capable of improving the performance of their logistical services in any systematic way. In his words, 'the results of the only comprehensive effort which was made in this direction [were not] particularly encouraging'.[41] In conclusion, Van Creveld can only say that 'the human intellect alone' is not 'the best instrument for waging war'.[42] His *Supplying War* implies that the logistical factors which affect victory and defeat are beyond any leader's conscious control.

This conclusion contradicts all the previous maxims about logistics, strategy and command. Although others have advised strategists to consider logistics at every stage of their work, Van Creveld has suggested that such considerations are futile. Therefore, readers must decide how to integrate the conclusions of *Supplying War* with the rest of the literature on this subject. One must decide whether to reject the maxims of commanders and historians, reject the findings of Van Creveld, or seek some more inclusive theory which takes both into account.

Van Creveld, of course, would have us believe that his predecessors were wrong. Other scholars, in turn, dismiss his thesis out of hand. An assortment of prominent critics have pointed out that, for every conclusion Van Creveld draws, history provides a counter-example.[43] This, however, is not sufficient to refute the arguments of a book like *Supplying War*.

Every incident in the annals of military history is unique. Numerous authors who have studied logistics from a historical point of view have emphasised this point.[44] Therefore, if one wishes to study military operations in any general way, one must find a way to cope with contradictory evidence. One must learn to understand factors, such as logistics in their larger context, so that one can see why similar actions occasionally lead to different outcomes. Those who question Van Creveld must look beyond his examples to address his underlying logic.

Certainly, Van Creveld was justified in asking students of supply to provide a mechanism which explains precisely how logistical conditions affect strategic outcomes. However, if the observations which led up to the mass of 'vague speculations' demonstrates anything, it demonstrates that logistics is a slippery beast that can become important at many levels of a military operation, sometimes as a cause of events and at other times as the consequence of them. Therefore, a fresh analysis of logistics needs to encompass all levels of activity from battlefield tactics to national policy without attempting to impose artificial boundaries between them. Similarly, such an analysis must never overlook the fact that, although causes may lead to effects, the process is often part of a larger pattern and is seldom direct.

Van Creveld pioneered the study of the relationship between military performance and logistics, and he remains the dominant academic voice on that subject. Therefore, his name is destined to appear again and again throughout this study. The author acknowledges Van Creveld's role as a trailblazer, but argues that *Supplying War* missed a number of crucial points. Later chapters will refute Van Creveld's argument in detail.

THE QUARTERMASTER'S CLAIM

The quartermaster's claim upon history may, at its root, lie in the effect of logistics upon timing. At any given instant, supply determines whether or not forces can put a given plan into action. To pick a simple example, tanks cannot advance without fuel. Certainly, an army can overcome supply difficulties, but this will take time. The longer a nation requires to bring its force to bear, the more time its enemies have to seize whatever objectives they consider desirable. Therefore, the supply and movement of military units not only affects what friendly forces can do, it also helps determine what the enemy can do.

What is the value of a moment? That depends upon the skill of the commanders, the strength of the forces and the will of the troops. However, the side which manages to act first has greater freedom to choose the time, place and manner of the battle. The slower side may then have to react to what its opponent has done, instead of pursuing more profitable objectives elsewhere. In other words, speed plays an important role in determining which antagonist will hold the strategic initiative.

THE ARBITER OF OPPORTUNITY

Colonel John Boyd of the US Air Force has underscored the importance of initiative with a theory which portrays speed as the most crucial element of strategy.[45] Boyd notes that, when military units take action, they go through a cycle which begins when commanders observe that a given set of circumstances has developed, develops when the commanders decide on a response and bears fruit when the armed forces put that decision into effect. Those who manage to complete this cycle faster than their enemies can disorient and outmanoeuvre the forces which oppose them. The slower side will find itself perpetually responding to what its opponents did at some previous point, rather than to what its opponents are doing at the moment.

This author does not argue that supply can predict the outcome of battles in any deterministic way. Logistics does not compete with strategy and tactics. Some forces have overcome great material hardships through determination and cleverness. (The *Wehrmacht* springs to mind.) The key point about such situations is that logistical factors helped create the circumstances which made such heroic performance necessary. Logistics helps determine which side will have the most options available, not what those options will be or how effectively it will use them.

Even if logistics affected merely the ability of armies to seize advantages in individual battles, that fact alone would make this topic crucial to the dynamics of combat. However, the effects of initiative reach far higher. Warfare is a phenomenon which can manifest itself in many different ways. There are wars of attrition, wars of manoeuvre, wars of position and guerrilla wars, to name but four. If one side consistently can choose the manner of fighting in individual battles, that side is well on its way to choosing the overall character of the war.

Different nations prefer to wage different types of wars. Indeed, such 'preferences' are often a matter of survival. To pick but two examples of this principle, the dynamics of both world wars in the twentieth century revolved around the fact that while Germany could not afford a long war, its opponents could not afford a short one. The style and tempo of combat determine what warfare will demand from the material resources of a nation, the political base of a government, the technological sophistication of an army, the diplomatic position of a state, the tactical imagination of an officer corps and the moral sensibilities of a people.

One might note, in passing, that different styles in warfare go hand in hand with different styles of logistics. The distance to which units expect to operate from their bases, the speed with which they expect to manoeuvre, the types of weapons they expect to use and a myriad of other factors determine what sort of supplies they require and how they choose to deliver them. The way in which an army expects to use specific units also plays a role. Although the *Wehrmacht* pioneered modern mechanised warfare, most of its divisions relied on horse transport.

Furthermore, when circumstances allow, armies may provide troops with hot meals, advanced medical care, comfortable accommodation and similar luxuries. Both the standards and the details of such comforts differ from country to country. Societies which value human happiness in the civilian world quite logically attempt to make the lives of their soldiers reasonably pleasant as well. Other armies adopt more spartan policies. Nevertheless, in any military organisation, when troops fail to receive what they perceive as basic standards of comfort, morale will suffer.

Even such a hard-headed and occasionally hard-hearted veteran as Carl von Clausewitz observed:

> Anyone who tries to maintain that wretched food makes no difference to an army ... is not taking a dispassionate view of the subject. Ability to endure privation is one of the soldier's finest qualities; without it an army cannot be filled with a genuine military spirit. But privation must be temporary; it must be imposed by circumstances and not by an inefficient system or a niggardly abstract calculation of the smallest ration that will keep a man alive. In the latter case it is bound to sap the physical and moral strength of every man.[46]

Supply organisations may differ in style without differing in their ability to sustain military operations. However, when one side compels the other to fight an unfamiliar style of war, it forces its enemy to conduct an unfamiliar style of logistics as well. Therefore, supply preparations not only help determine the character of a war, they are affected by the outcome of that determination. The fact that cause and effect flow in both directions should not be allowed to confuse our understanding of either process.

One should understand the supply factor as a piece in the strategic jigsaw puzzle. By itself it means little, but one can assemble other pieces around its edges until the overall picture takes shape. Logistics helps determine which side will be able to mount the type of warfare it is best fitted to win. Thus, logistics takes its place in strategy as an arbiter of opportunity.

RESEARCH METHODS

This study develops its arguments through the structured, focused comparison of case studies. Each chapter will examine the relationship between strategy and logistics in a selected military campaign. Four themes will remain constant throughout the study. Each chapter will address four questions about the military campaign under consideration:

1. How have military commanders perceived the relationship between logistics and strategy?

By answering this question, this study will reiterate the point that experienced commanders have found an inseparable link between logistics and military success. Furthermore, this question highlights the fact that generals and admirals use logistical factors in a conscious, proactive way, in order to maximise their advantages over their enemies. Logistics, in other words, is not merely a precondition to military operations, it is an integral component of the art of war.

2. How have logistical factors helped or harmed the strategic performance of armed forces?
By answering this question, this study makes it clear that the intuition of military commanders has a basis in objective fact. Supplies, transportation resources and well-conceived logistical plans allow armed forces to execute strategies which they would otherwise find physically impossible.

3. What factors have given particular forces advantages in logistics?
By addressing this question, this study will explore what 'good logistics' means in practice. Although it would be impossible to cover every possible factor which might influence the supply and movement of armed forces, this study will introduce the more common ones, and provide readers with an intellectual starting point for identifying and analysing others.

4. What logistical problems are associated with particular styles of warfare, and how have commanders addressed them?
Like question three, question four aims to connect this study's theoretical propositions about logistics to the practical problems of specific campaigns. Furthermore, by answering this question, this study provides evidence for its assertion that commanders may use the logistical capabilities of their forces to shape the style and tempo of combat.

The bulk of each chapter will consist of narrative and analysis, to put logistical information in its appropriate strategic context. Each chapter will end with a concluding section, in which the author will list the routine questions and review the answers which an intelligent reader might cull from the historical material.

All wars involve logistics. Since it would be impossible to give a full account of every campaign in military history, this study focuses on five specific cases. The author chose these episodes on the basis of the following criteria. First, the author has attempted to cover wars which took place in an assortment of different environments between an assortment of different types of opponent, in order to demonstrate that the arguments of this study apply to wars of many kinds. Second, the author has focused on the period from the Second World War to the near future. Technology plays a key role in determining both the logistical requirements and logistical capabilities of armed forces. Therefore, although one can learn important lessons about logistics and strategy from the wars of other eras, contemporary examples seem likely to offer the largest number of relevant points for those who are interested in the present day. Third, and finally, the author has selected case studies for their historical significance and impact on current strategic debates. Through this process, the author aims to support his arguments as effectively as possible while maximising the relevance of this study for those whose interests lie in the realm of contemporary strategy, as well as history.

CONCLUSION

The chapters address the following topics. Chapter 2 uses the Second World War campaigns in Burma and India to show how a new logistical technology (airlift) gave the Allies novel opportunities for timely manoeuvre, and hence for the economical use of resources in a secondary theatre. Chapter 3 uses the Second World War in the Pacific as an example of how an effective logistical system allows a power with an advantage in resources to bring superior force to bear fast enough to keep its opponent from winning a victory on other terms. In addition to making this general point, Chapter 3 shows how, contrary to Van Creveld's assertions, planning and analysis can help a military establishment improve its logistical performance. Chapter 4 addresses the war in Vietnam. Using the supply of Communist forces as a case study, the chapter notes that unconventional warfare seems to contradict some of this study's maxims about logistics and timing, but argues that, at a deeper level, the principle that supply serves as an arbiter of opportunity remains valid. Because the Communists were able to sustain both guerrilla and regular forces in the South, and to replace their losses on an indefinite basis, they were able to make the war into a long conflict of the sort which the United States ultimately proved unwilling to sustain. Chapter 5 addresses Western preparations for the war-which-never-was against the Soviet Union in Europe with two purposes in mind. First, the discussion explores the role of logistical perceptions in deterrence. Second, the analysis shows how the problems of supplying forces the size of the Red Army gave Western planners reason to hope that their own advantages in airpower and what is now called information technology would allow them to repulse the more massive forces of the Warsaw Pact.

Some have proposed that, whatever the role logistics played in the past, this topic will be radically transformed or rendered irrelevant by the phenomenon known as Information Warfare. In Chapter 6, the author considers the idea that the so-called 'Revolution in Military Affairs' (RMA) will change the role of logistics in strategy. Although this study argues against the idea that the RMA will eliminate the problem of logistics, the author considers the ways in

THE ARBITER OF OPPORTUNITY

which the supply of relatively small, technology- and information-oriented armies may differ from logistical problems in the past.

NOTES

1. Roger A. Beaumont, 'Beyond Tooth and Tail: The Need For New Logistical Analogies', *Military Review*, Vol. 60, No. 3 (March 1985), p. 10.
2. Joseph E. Muckerman II, 'L is For Logistics', *Joint Forces Quarterly*, No. 16 (Summer 1997), p. 121.
3. Martin Van Creveld, *Supplying War* (Cambridge: Cambridge University Press, 1977), p. 174; J. Thompson, *The Lifeblood of War: Logistics in Armed Conflict* (London: Brasseys, 1991), pp. 109–10.
4. Richard L. Kelley, 'Applied Logistics Principles', *Military Review*, Vol. 57, No. 9 (September 1977), p. 57.
5. A. I. Jomini, *The Art of War*, (trans.) G. Mendell and W. Craighill (Philadelphia, PA: J. B. Lippincott & Company, 1868), p. 252.
6. Van Creveld, *Supplying War*, p. 236.
7. Jomini, *The Art of War*, p. 252.
8. John Tetsuro in J. Lynn, *Feeding Mars: Logistics in Western Warfare from the Middle Ages to the Present* (Boulder, CO: Westview Press, 1993), pp. 217–50.
9. For examples of how different armed services approach this problem, see James A. Huston, *The Sinews of War 1775–1955* (Washington, DC: US Government Printing Office, 1966), p. vii.
10. George C. Thorpe, *Pure Logistics* (Washington, DC: National Defence University Press, 1986), *passim*.
11. For examples of prominent authors repeating this theme, see Lynn, *Feeding Mars*, p. 9, and Van Creveld, *Supplying War*, p. 231.
12. Kenneth E. Boulding, *Conflict and Defense: A General Theory* (New York: Harper & Brothers, 1962), p. 79.
13. Albert Wohlstetter, 'Illusions of Distance', *Foreign Affairs*, Vol. 46, No. 2 (January 1968), p. 244.
14. Boulding, *Conflict and Defence*, p. 79.
15. Wohlstetter, 'Illusions of Distance', p. 255.
16. For examples of works in this genre by a soldier and a scholar, see, respectively: William G. Pagonis, *Moving Mountains* (Boston, MA: Harvard Business School Press, 1992), *passim* and Huston, *The Sinews of War*, *passim*. See also Thompson, *The Lifeblood of War*, *passim*, for an example of a historical work by a man who is both.
17. For an introduction to this field, see Donald J. Bowersox and David J. Closs, *Logistical Management: The Integrated Supply Chain Process* (New York: McGraw-Hill, 1996), *passim* and David Taylor (ed.), *Global Cases in Logistics and Supply Chain Management* (London: International Thomson Business Press, 1997), *passim*.
18. Ibid.
19. Pagonis, *Moving Mountains*, pp. 210–20.
20. Henry E. Eccles, *Logistics in the National Defense* (Harrisburg, PA: Stackpole Company, 1959), p. v.
21. Ibid., *passim*.
22. Thanks to Professor Colin Gray for this turn of phrase.
23. Kenneth N. Brown, *Strategics* (Washington, DC: National Defense University Press, 1987), p. 3.

24. See Huston, *The Sinews of War*, p. 665, and Beaumont, 'Beyond Tooth and Tail,' p. 4. Beaumont emphasises this point by offering an apt quote from the Duke of Wellington, who scorned all military history with the sneer, 'I would as soon describe a battle than a ball.'
25. Martin Van Creveld, *Command in War* (Cambridge, MA: Harvard University Press, 1985), p. 36.
26. Beaumont, 'Beyond Tooth and Tail', p. 10.
27. Thorpe, *Pure Logistics*, p. 20.
28. Eccles, *Logistics in the National Defense*, p. 125.
29. US Navy, *Naval Logistics* (Philadelphia, PA: National Technical Information Services, 1995), p. 13.
30. For similar collections of maxims, see ibid., pp. 13–15, and Kelley, 'Applied Logistics Principles', *passim*.
31. Trevor N. Dupuy, *International Military and Defense Encylopedia* (Washington, DC: Brasseys, 1993), pp. 1498–503.
32. Kelley, 'Applied Logistics Principles', p. 57; US Navy, *Naval Logistics*, p. 12.
33. C. von Clausewitz, *On War*, trans. and ed. Michael Howard and Peter Paret (Princeton, NJ: Princeton University Press, 1976), p. 148.
34. Ibid., p. 330.
35. Ibid.
36. Ibid., pp. 331–2.
37. Van Creveld, *Supplying War*, p. 236.
38. Ibid., pp. 234–5.
39. Ibid., p. 235.
40. Thorpe, *Pure Logistics*, p. 1. Van Creveld, *Supplying War*, p. 236;
41. Van Creveld, *Supplying War*, p. 236.
42. Ibid.
43. John Lynn, for instance, challenges Van Creveld along these lines at Lynn, *Feeding Mars*, pp. 9–25.
44. Huston, *The Sinews of War*, p. 665; Beaumont, 'Beyond Tooth and Tail,' p. 4.
45. Although Colonel Boyd is quite influential in contemporary military circles, he has been content to disseminate his thoughts in briefings and by word of mouth, without publishing any definitive works on his concepts. For a discussion of his ideas, see William Owens, 'The Emerging System of Systems', *Military Review*, Vol. 75, No. 3 (May–June 1995), p. 17.
46. Clausewitz, *On War*, p. 331.

2

The Burma Campaign

Just as logistical factors determine whether or not a warring state will be able to bring its material advantages into play, logistics determines whether or not a general will be able to bring his strategic wisdom into play as well. The campaigns for Burma in the Second World War illustrate this principle. Both the Allies and their Japanese enemies faced extreme logistical hardships in this theatre of operations, but thanks to the large-scale use of aerial transportation, the Allied commanders were able to fight in their chosen manner. This is more than an example of the fact that it is better to have supplies than not to have them. The Allied advantage lay, not simply in having greater quantities of useful resources, but in having the flexibility to deploy those resources in a more effective fashion.

General Orde Wingate's Chindit expeditions are an obvious example of strategic and logistical innovation in Burma, but more prosaic aspects of the campaign illustrate the relationship between logistics and military success at an even higher level of strategy. Burma was a secondary theatre of war for the Allies, and therefore one of the most crucial objectives for the commanders fighting there was to defeat their enemies without the need for massive reinforcement. Indeed, without increased logistical capabilities, such reinforcement would not have solved the problems of the British forces even if it had been available. The fact that Allied commanders could move large units by air allowed them to use their limited forces to maximum effect. The aerial transfer of troops from Arakan to Imphal in 1944 demonstrates the connection between logistical technology and the principle of war known as economy of force.

THE PROBLEM OF BURMA: A QUEST FOR INITIATIVE

In 1941, the Japanese launched general offensives in both southeast Asia and the Pacific. Japan's leaders planned their offensives of 1941 with three purposes in mind. First, they intended to secure their own sources of fuel and lubricants by seizing the oil reserves of the Dutch East Indies. Second, they intended to secure the sea lanes which connected their new acquisitions to the Japanese home islands by capturing strategic positions between the Indies and Japan, such as Malaya and the Philippines. Third, Japanese forces also attacked the American fleet, in order to prevent the United States from interfering with their conquests. To the Japanese and their enemies, the main significance of Burma was its position as a bridge between the Far East and India.

Japan's leaders did not include Burma in their plans for a Greater East Asian Co-Prosperity Sphere, but they did anticipate the possibility that British forces would use Burmese territory as a staging ground for counterattacks against their forces in Malaya.[1] An army in Burma is in a position to advance to the south and east in order to control the Kra Isthmus and cut off the Malay Peninsula. Therefore, when the Japanese planned their attacks on southeast Asia, they included a side campaign to seize portions of Burma, notably the port of Rangoon and the airfields around Tenasserim.[2] British commanders wished to recapture Burma in order to stage exactly the sort of counterattack the Japanese feared.[3]

American commanders valued Burma as well, but for different reasons. To American strategists, Burma was 'China's back door'.[4] The Americans placed great importance on keeping the army of the Chinese Nationalists in the field as an active opponent to Japan. US General John Magruder summed up his country's view of the situation in August 1941 when he stated that aid to China would 'counterbalance' the Japanese army so effectively that its value 'can be measured militarily in terms of army corps'.[5] The Chinese army, however, had retreated to Chunking, deep inland and far from Allied territory. If US forces wished to support their Chinese allies, they had to do so through Burma. To supply Chinese forces by air, US pilots had to fly over the 'hump' of the Burmese mountains, and to send the Chinese war materiel by ground, the Americans had to use the Burma Road, a land route which ran from Mandalay and Lashio in Burma to Kunming in China.

In January 1942, Japan invaded Burma with two experienced divisions, the 33rd and the 55th.[6] Initially, Japanese troops encountered no opposition other than the 1st Burma Division, which was little more than an internal security force.[7] Although the British reinforced this unit with the 17th Indian Light Division, the Indian troops were poorly equipped and had been trained for desert combat in the Middle East, not jungle warfare in Burma.[8] The Allied situation in the air was bleak. Of the 14 fighter squadrons which British commanders estimated that they would need to retain control of the skies, their order of battle included only two.[9] The Japanese brought three more divisions into the battle and by the summer they had swept the Allied forces from Burma.[10] That victory put Japan's forces in a position from which they might easily have staged an invasion of India.

When one reviews the series of Allied defeats which led to the loss of Burma, the Japanese appear to have been invincible and this sort of belief certainly took hold among the Allied troops who found themselves deployed in this theatre. Fear of the 'Japanese superman' ate at men's minds, and officers were equally pessimistic.[11] When Admiral Lord Louis Mountbatten met with senior Army, Navy and Air Force commanders, they offered him the collective opinion that their troops could not fight the Japanese in the jungle, that the monsoon season would prevent all combat on land and in the air for five months of the year, that they disapproved of any special operations such as those proposed by General Orde Wingate, and that they had no interest in the offer of US railway battalions to improve their lines of communications.[12] In conclusion, the commanders rejected Mountbatten's suggestion that they should visit front-line units in order to restore morale. Britain's defeat, however, was far from inevitable. The collapse of the Allied defence stemmed, not from some intrinsic inferiority in the British armed forces, but from poor preparations and poor strategy. Even in terms of manpower and equipment, the Japanese did not always hold the advantage. Despite Japan's command of the air, the losses of British forces to air attack were, in the words of their commander, 'surprisingly small'.[13] Indeed, in March of 1942, when General Sir William Slim took command of Britain's Burma Corps, he found himself in a position of superiority.[14] At that moment, the combined forces of the two British divisions actually possessed more material strength than their opponents.[15]

Slim summed up the reasons why Burma became a disaster as follows:

> To me, thinking it all over, the most distressing aspect of the whole disastrous campaign had been the contrast between our generalship and the enemy's. The Japanese leadership was confident, bold to the point of foolhardiness, and so aggressive that never for one day did they lose the initiative. True, they had a perfect instrument for the type of operation they intended, but their use of it was unhesitating and accurate. Their object, clear and definite, was the destruction of our forces; ours, a rather nebulous idea of retaining territory. This led to the initial dispersion of our forces over wide areas, an error which we continued to commit, and still worse, it led to a defensive attitude of mind.[16]

The failure of British commanders to seize the initiative affected tactics in the same way that it affected strategy, with similar effects upon morale. Slim continues his analysis:

> Tactically, we had been completely outclassed. The Japanese could – and did – do many things which we could not. The chief of these and the tactical method on which all their successes were based was the 'hook'. Their standard action was, while holding us in front, to send a mobile force, mainly infantry, on a wide turning movement round our flank to come in on our line of communications. Here, on the single road, up

which all our supplies, ammunition and reinforcements must come, they would establish a 'road-block', sometimes with a battalion, sometimes with a regiment. We had few if any reserves in depth – all our troops were in the front line – and we had, therefore, to turn about forces from the forward positions to clear the road-block. At this moment, the enemy increased his pressure on our weakened front until it crumbled. Time and time again the Japanese used these tactics, more often than not successfully, until our troops and commanders began to acquire a road-block mentality which often developed into an inferiority complex.[17]

The onset of the monsoon season brought Japan's onslaught to a halt, and since the Japanese had already conquered all of the objectives they had set for themselves, they did not attempt to launch another offensive.[18] Therefore, Slim received the opportunity to regroup his units. The remains of Burma Division were in no shape to fight, but the 17th Indian remained on the line.[19] Over the summer, the British augmented their forces on the Burma front with the 70th Division and the 50th Armoured Brigade, both of which consisted of European troops, along with the Indian 7th, 5th, 20th and 23rd divisions.[20] The 14th Indian Division and the 26th Indian Division defended India's south-eastern coastline.[21]

Although the US Army did not contribute any large combat formations to the reconquest of Burma at this time, the American General Stilwell brought two divisions of Chinese troops into India for use in the Burma theatre.[22] Stilwell hoped that, given time, he could train and equip these troops to approach or meet American standards of combat effectiveness.[23] Eventually, he intended to use them for an offensive to reopen the Burma Road.[24] The United States Army Air Forces (USAAF) flew all 13,000 of these troops over the Hump, from Kunming to India, and one should note that, even at this early stage of the campaign, Allied airpower was making it possible for Allied generals to contemplate operations of a character which would otherwise have been impossible.[25]

The reinforcements and border troops improved Slim's position somewhat, but his forces were still stretched thin. Malaria weakened all of these units, equipment of all sorts was in short supply, and the lack of motor transport hampered their mobility.[26] Despite such handicaps, this force had to face the Japanese army across a land border, defend a 700-mile coastline against landings and protect its lines of communications against sabotage by the increasingly aggressive Indian nationalist movement.[27] The complete lack of naval support made these tasks all the harder.[28]

In the autumn of 1942, the Allied commanders resolved to strike back into Burma. Their plans called for a land advance in the coastal region known as Arakan along with an amphibious assault on Akyab island, but the strategic objectives of the campaign had more to do with initiative and morale. In the words of Slim:

> This, our first offensive in the theatre, was never intended to accomplish more than the very limited objective of taking Akyab. Its most important effect would not be the minor improvement in the tactical situation that the possession of Akyab would give, but the moral effect that any successful offensive would have on world opinion, on our allies, and most important of all, on our own troops.[29]

The British launched the Arakan campaign with great publicity and fanfare, perhaps to maximise the moral effect of its anticipated success.[30] Unfortunately for them, the campaign was a fiasco. In January 1943, the attack stalled around the area of Donbaik, and in March, large Japanese forces moved through the supposedly impenetrable mountains on the British flank to surround the invasion force. The British lost two brigades in the initial fighting.[31] At this point, General Noel Irwin, the British army commander, personally took command of the situation and sent an entire division of reinforcements to regain control of the battlefield. In April, however, the Japanese outflanked the British a second time, and by this point, it was clear that the entire invasion force was in danger of catastrophe. To save themselves, the Allied units in Arakan had to retreat, and Irwin sent Slim to oversee the withdrawal of the invasion force. By May, the survivors of Arakan had pulled back to the positions in India whither the Japanese had chased them the previous year.

A study of the Arakan campaign reveals numerous reasons for the British defeat. Irwin's personal dislike for Slim apparently led the Army Commander to make a series of highly questionable decisions.[32] The terrain was also abominable; British troops found themselves at a great tactical disadvantage. The following passage illustrates this point:

> This first Arakan campaign was conducted upon so narrow a terrain that its topography may be dealt with in a few words. Arakan is a land of steep little hills covered with jungle, of paddy-fields, scrub and swamp. In such country advancing troops can walk over an enemy who is lying doggo and never be aware of him until they get a grenade or a burst of machine-gun fire in their backs ... North of Akyab [in one of the regions where the British invaders intended to mount their attack] the Mayu Peninsula sharpens to a tip called Foul Point. The Mayu Peninsula is split by the steep 1,500-foot spine of the Mayu Range, flanked by low-lying foothills, so that on neither side are the strips of flat land more than a few hundred yards wide. Since these flats themselves are intersected by innumerable tidal creeks, the difficulty of deploying even a brigade for attack will be realised.[33]

The fact that the Japanese had been able to fortify their positions with exceptionally well-constructed bunkers compounded the malign effects of this terrain. As a strategic analyst, however, one must ask why the British chose to attack under these terrible conditions in the first place. The answer appears to be that no better options were available. The same conditions which caused British forces to crumble in 1942 were still at play in 1943. Slim's criticism of Allied generalship was more telling than ever, but it had also become obvious that there were enduring material factors which prevented British commanders from achieving a higher standard of military artistry.

A quotation from Sun Tzu becomes appropriate. '[T]hose skilled in war can make themselves invincible but cannot cause an enemy to be certainly vulnerable. Therefore it can be said that, one may know how to win, but cannot necessarily do so.'[34] Slim, not to mention Wingate and others, had known for some time that the Allies needed to seize the strategic initiative. The situation in Burma, however, made this impossible by ordinary means. For the British to act on their knowledge, they had to find a new way of fighting.

THE IMPEDIMENTS TO STRATEGY

The British suffered an assortment of handicaps in southeast Asia. One such stumbling block was lack of information. The British had no intelligence organisation among the Burmese people, and the prevalence of forest canopy made aerial reconnaissance a poor substitute. Allied forces were also woefully short of people who spoke Japanese, and that limited the value of prisoners and captured documents.[35] Disease took a severe toll on Allied troops. Furthermore, the geography of Burma made it much easier for Japanese forces to defend their conquests than for British forces to re-take them. This factor deprived the British of strategic options and forced them to fight the war on nearly unwinnable terms.

Mountain ranges and deep rivers traversed Burma from north to south, and the few roads which existed tended to follow the valleys on north–south routes.[36] Before the Second World War, most British officers had assumed that any invasion of Burma would come from the direction of China, and therefore, they had laid their military roads along this same north–south orientation.[37] All of these transportation arteries converged on the port of Rangoon. Thus, when the Japanese captured that city, they forced the Allies to do almost entirely without roads.

The fact that the Japanese had also conquered southeast Asia compounded the Allies' problems. Since British forces could not operate from Siam or Indochina, they had to approach Burma from India, along an east–west axis, 'against the grain', of Burma's transportation network. When the Allies needed roads or railway systems, they generally had to build them. Furthermore, Burma's mountain ranges split the British forces into three isolated fronts, a fact which compelled commanders to launch counterattacks along narrow, easily blocked routes. When one examines these facts, it becomes easier to see why the Allies launched the Arakan offensive in the location they did.

This was not a struggle in which the Allies could simply bring in new divisions and overwhelm their enemies with troops and materiel. Due to the campaigns in Europe, north Africa and the Pacific, such reinforcements were not available, but even if the Allies had possessed more resources, numbers alone were not the key to victory in Burma. Even in 1942, there were occasions in which the strength of the British army equalled or exceeded that of its enemy, but this did not halt the Japanese advance.[38] During the Arakan Campaign, the British commanders launched their offensive against a sector of the front in which they possessed a significant numerical superiority, but nevertheless, in the words of Slim, 'Seventeen [Allied] battalions have been chased about by possibly six [Japanese].'[39]

Indeed, the Allied commanders often confronted situations in which they could not support all of the troops which they possessed. In the summer of 1942, although they feared that the Japanese would press their invasion into India despite the monsoon, the British had to withdraw units from the centre of the Burmese front because they did not have the transportation resources to feed more than 40,000 troops in that region.[40] Japan's success at cutting Allied lines of communications created analogous problems at the operational and tactical levels of combat. Slim noted that often, even when replacement troops were available, Japanese road-blocks prevented them from reaching the places where they were needed.[41]

Likewise, one cannot attribute the pattern of Allied defeats entirely to tactics. The Japanese certainly made better use of the terrain than did their opponents, but any army can learn new ways to fight, and Slim has received well-deserved acclaim for his success at training troops to operate in the Burmese environment.[42] One should never forget that the jungle was as alien to the typical Japanese soldier as it was to troops from any European army. The fact that the Japanese maintained a tactical advantage had less to do with any inherent superiority in jungle warfare than with their success at positioning themselves to fight the types of battles they wanted to fight in the types of terrain which favoured their efforts.

To reverse their streak of defeats, the British commanders needed to break out of the geographical trap. On a strategic level, they needed to find a new battlefield. As long as they had to push their troops and supplies overland across the 'grain' of the Burmese terrain, they would be limited to ponderous, predictable manoeuvres. On an operational level, they needed a more effective way to concentrate their forces. The combination of terrain and Japanese roadblocks made it difficult for the British to feed their units into battle at the right time and place. On a tactical level, they needed a way to overcome the outflanking 'hook' manoeuvres in which Japanese units slipped into their rear area and cut off their supplies. These were the problems which Allied commanders needed to address if they were to regain the initiative in Burma. Ultimately, all of these problems were problems of logistics.

THE CHINDITS: INNOVATIVE LOGISTICS, INDIRECT RESULTS

Aircraft could carry supplies above Japanese roadblocks and over Burmese terrain. As early as 1942, Slim recognised the possibility that aerial supply could overcome many of the logistical and stratetical problems of Allied forces, but since large numbers of planes were not available at the time he downplayed this idea, in order not to arouse false expectations among his troops.[43] As transport aircraft grew more plentiful, however, the British became able to undertake novel operations. Even as the first Arakan Offensive suffered its dismal failure, the Allies began to experiment with a new form of long-range penetration tactics which took advantage of aerial resupply to carry the war to the Japanese.

The British general Archibald Wavell had a fondness for guerrilla operations, and as the Japanese forces advanced in January 1942, he asked for the advice of Orde Wingate, a man whose personality and experience made him ideal for unconventional warfare.[44] Wingate came up with a plan to carry Japanese envelopment tactics a step beyond their own practice.[45] He suggested that the British could manoeuvre large formations of troops deep into the Burmese jungle without the need for the 'vulnerable artery' of traditional lines of communication.[46] Radios would allow troops to communicate with their commanders, and aircraft could deliver supplies 'like Father Christmas, down the chimney'.[47]

Accordingly, Wavell authorised Wingate to organise the 77th Indian Infantry Brigade for deep penetration missions and in July of 1942, these troops began training for jungle warfare. Wingate named his units the 'Chindits', after the mythical lions which guard Burmese temples. That winter, the Allies developed a plan to reconquer Burma in which Chinese and British forces would attack the Japanese from all sides with a front-line strength of over 16 divisions, plus substantial reserves.[48] In support of this grand offensive, the Chindit brigade would infiltrate enemy lines and cut the main railway line between Japanese forces in north and central Burma.[49]

The invasion plan disintegrated when Chiang Kai-Shek decided not to provide the ten divisions he had initially promised for the reconquest of Burma. At that point, Wingate offered to have his brigade carry out the raid behind Japanese lines on its own. Although there was no way that a single brigade could engage large Japanese forces in open battle, the Chindit commander saw six reasons why he should go ahead with the attack. First, he wished to test his ideas about penetration operations; second, he had trained his men for an operation in early 1943 and he feared that any delay would cause both physical and psychological deterioration; third, the invasion would help the Allies learn how much support they could expect from the Burmese; fourth, the raid would distract the enemy enough to prevent a Japanese offensive toward Burmese troops in the Fort Hertz area; fifth, the raid would demand attention from Japanese troops who might otherwise conduct infiltration operations of their own, and sixth, the attack would confuse and disrupt any Japanese plans for a general offensive.[50] Wavell accepted Wingate's argument, and on 13 February, the Chindits set out on their raid, which went by the codename Operation Longcloth.

Wingate intended to cut the railway line between Myitkyina and Mandalay, sever the supply lines of the two Japanese divisions in northern Burma, harass all enemy forces in the Shwebo area, northwest of Mandalay and, if possible, destroy the railway between Mandalay and Lasho as well.[51] The Chindits achieved all of these objectives except for the last one, but in the process they suffered losses and hardships which are remarkable even by the exacting standards of warfare. Of the 3,000 men who set out with Wingate's expedition, roughly one-third did not come back.[52] Since the Chindits had no way to evacuate casualties, they had to abandon their wounded in the jungle.[53] The 2,182 survivors returned to India in June with their bellies caved in from hunger, and many of them had severe cases of malaria and beriberi as well.[54]

The concept of aerial resupply worked according to plan. Wingate's use of airdrops allowed the Chindits to march over 1,500 miles through the 'green hell' of central Burma.[55] Within the first four days of the operation, the Royal Air Force had already provided Wingate's troops with 70,000 pounds of supplies.[56] Not only did aerial support give the Chindits the strategic ability to carry out this entire operation, it gave them the tactical ability to abandon equipment when they needed to move quickly, confident that they could resupply themselves by air.[57]

Wingate believed that Longcloth had been a great success, and both Roosevelt and Churchill shared his enthusiasm. The next year, the Allies launched a significantly more ambitious expedition known as Operation Thursday. In this raid, three brigades of Chindits penetrated deep into Japanese territory and set up permanent bases known as strongholds, at which they could build airfields and receive regular supply flights.[58] These bases were intended to give the British troops a more reliable source of commodities such as ammunition and fresh water, while also making it possible for them to evacuate casualties. The Burmese terrain made it possible for the Chindits to defend their bases even in the middle of nominally enemy-held territory.

In 1944 Wingate took his concept of aerial mobility a step farther and actually deployed the majority of his troops by air. Whereas the men of the Longcloth expedition had marched into the jungle on foot and received only their supplies by air, two of the three brigades which participated in

Thursday travelled to their areas of operations by aircraft and glider.[59] Therefore, Wingate was able to catch his enemies off guard with both the size of his forces and the speed with which they reached their strongholds. In two days of flights, the Chindits managed to deploy all of their supplies and equipment, along with 2,000 of their mules and 1,200 of their men.[60] During this period, their enemies did not manage to mount any serious response.[61]

In later years, Japanese commanders recalled that they had felt awe, fear and a certain amount of confusion when they saw formations of British aircraft ferrying men and material to the jungle bases.[62] This blow to the morale of Japan's troops came at the moment when the Japanese were planning an offensive into India. Major-General Tazoe of the Japanese army called on the high command to postpone this attack in order to deal with the Chindit threat.[63] His superiors rejected this advice, but the fact that a man of his rank would take such a potentially embarrassing step indicates the extent to which Wingate's operations disturbed his enemies. Even before the serious fighting began, Operation Thursday had already achieved a psychological victory.

The Chindits went on to wreak havoc behind Japanese lines, but it is difficult to establish the role which they played or might have played in the final victory over Japan. There is no definitive way to measure the effects of such raids on the outcome of a war. To complicate matters further, Wingate died in an aeroplane crash on 24 March, 1944. The general who inherited command of the Chindits, W.D. Lentaigne, had always opposed Wingate's ideas, and he allowed the American General Stillwell to use the long-range penetration groups as shock troops in standard infantry attacks, notably in the campaign to capture the northern Burma town of Moguang.[64] This caused needless deaths among the Chindits and squandered any advantages their special training, experience and operational concepts might have given them. At the end of the summer, Lord Mountbatten dissolved the long-range penetration groups.[65] Both Wingate's ideas and his personality have always been controversial. Many have agreed with Slim, who concluded that the Chindit operations were a misuse of resources.[66] When the official historian of the British Army commented upon Operation Longcloth, he offered the even harsher judgement that 'the operation had no strategic value'.[67] Although the Chindits had caused considerable damage to enemy forces, both by their own actions and through co-operation with the Royal Air Force, they did not inflict enough harm at the tactical and operational levels of war to justify their expense. To evaluate the Chindits fairly, however, one must consider their achievements at a higher level of strategic analysis.

In 1942, Slim noted that the Japanese were formidable as long as they were allowed to follow their projects undisturbed, but were thrown into confusion by the unexpected.[68] 'When in doubt as to two courses of action,' he concluded, 'a general should choose the bolder.'[69] Slim was to expand upon this point in his well-known memorandum on the lessons of the Burma campaign. 'By mobility away from roads, surprise, and offensive action we must regain and keep the initiative.'[70]

The Chindits embodied Slim's principles of warfare, and it was air supply which allowed them to do so. As the historian Louis Allen has observed:

> There was nothing particularly fantastic about the real basis of Wingate's notions. It was air power. British defeat in Malaya and Burma had been at the hands of numerically inferior forces because the British were road-bound. If their L of C [line of communication] was cut – a standard, reiterated Japanese ploy – then they seemed incapable of fighting back. So they always fought with one eye over their shoulder, fearful of enemy road blocks, of being cut off from hospitals and supplies. In an age of air transport, Wingate saw that this could change radically. Most of what lorries could bring up, aircraft could carry in, or if they could not land, could drop by parachute. At one stroke, this destroyed a soldier's dependence on a land L of C ... it sounds so terribly trite now. It is only so because men like Wingate made it a practical reality.[71]

Wingate originally intended his raiders to fight in support of a conventional invasion of Burma. Since the Allies never launched a large-scale attempt to reconquer Burmese territory in conjunction with a Chindit raid, the long-range penetration operations were, without question, an 'engine without a train'.[72] Nevertheless, Wingate's logistical innovations allowed him to take aggressive action at a moment when the Allies had failed to seize it in any other way. Not only did the Chindits help restore British morale, they helped push the Japanese commanders into decisions which led to their ultimate defeat.

At the end of 1942, the Japanese held an advantage, and they were willing to remain on the defensive and exploit it.[73] The Chindit raids pushed them into abandoning this initially successful strategy. To quote from the British Official History:

> As a result of the [first] Chindit operation, the Japanese commanders and their staffs in Burma ... began to realise that their assessment of the capabilities and battle efficiency of the British–Indian troops, based on their comparatively easy victories in 1941–1942, was incorrect. They could therefore no longer uphold the view that, provided the main tracks across the frontier were held, infiltration into Burma could be prevented and that any offensive on a large scale across the Assam [India]–Burma frontier by either contestant would be impossible unless the main roads were repaired and improved. Headquarters 15th Army immediately set to work to review the problem of the defence of upper Burma and came to the conclusion that the British, having evolved new tactics, might repeat the operation on a larger scale in conjunction with

a major offensive. They thereupon decided that, in the circumstances, an offensive–defensive policy was sounder and more economical than a purely defensive one; a decision which was eventually to lead to disaster.[74]

IMPHAL: ON CHOOSING A BATTLEFIELD

In early 1944, as Wingate prepared for Operation Thursday, Slim and his colleagues considered the ways in which they might engineer the general defeat of the Japanese forces. The British did not have enough landing craft to stage an amphibious invasion of Burma, and therefore, if they wished to retake the country, they had to attack overland, probably from the north.[75] Although the Allies had scheduled such invasions in both 1943 and 1944, they had been forced to abandon their plans on both occasions, partially due to Chinese recalcitrance, but also due to the immense difficulty of mounting an offensive across the local terrain.[76] The problem of logistics came to the fore once again, since no matter how much strength the Allies massed for such an operation, there were strict limits on the number of troops they could actually sustain on a supply line which had to run through the mountains of northern Burma.[77]

Since the Allies could not project the bulk of their strength into northern Burma, Slim wished to break the Japanese army before the invasion began.[78] In other words, he wanted to fight the battle for Burma in India. Fortunately for Slim, the Japanese complied with his wishes and attacked him on his chosen battleground. As noted above, the Chindit raids had convinced Japan's leaders that they needed to launch a new offensive against the British. America's naval success in the Pacific also helped to force Japan's hand. The Japanese leaders needed to raise the dead or face defeat in a war of attrition, and they hoped that, if they could overrun India, they might still be able to impose a peace settlement upon the Allies.[79]

Slim reviewed the terrain in order to identify the most advantageous place at which to make his stand against the Japanese. The 800 square miles of the Imphal Plain stood out to him as the most appropriate location for the Allies to concentrate their forces. General Sir Geoffry Scoones, the commander of the troops which would be directly responsible for the defence of Imphal, came independently to the same conclusion.[80] In order to reach Imphal, British combat units had to withdraw from their positions along the Burmese border, but Slim was willing to pay this price.

In a classic paradox of warfare, Slim's withdrawal upon Imphal allowed him to act upon the principles of aggressive action which he had prescribed for his forces. For the first time in the war, the Allies enjoyed favourable terrain, prepared positions and robust lines of communications. The Japanese could not circumvent the Allied forces, since the Imphal Plain was the only region of passable terrain between India and Burma.[81] Furthermore, the Japanese were under great pressure to win the battle quickly, before the monsoon made it impossible for them to supply their troops.[82]

To quote from Slim's memoirs:

> In war it is all-important to gain and retain the initiative, to make the enemy conform to your action, to dance to your tune. When you are advancing, this normally follows; if you withdraw, it is neither so obvious nor so easy. Yet it is possible. There are three reasons for retreat: self-preservation, to save your force from destruction; pressure elsewhere which makes you accept a loss of territory in one place to enable you to transfer troops to a more vital front; and lastly, to draw the enemy into a situation so unfavourable to him that the initiative must pass to you. It was for this third reason that I voluntarily decided upon a withdrawal.[83]

It is one thing to choose a battlefield, but it is another thing to avoid regretting the choice. Despite the advantages of fighting a defensive battle at Imphal, there was also an appreciable chance that Slim's decision could have led to disaster. The British had dispersed their bases in the area over a wide swathe of jungle terrain which afforded protection against air attack, but made them difficult to defend against an attack by land.[84] Most of these camps were located in narrow valleys, which meant that attacking troops would have the opportunity to fire down upon them at point-blank range.[85] Furthermore, the Allies had approximately 70,000 construction workers in the area of operations, men who consumed supplies but had no weapons or combat training.[86]

Worse, all of the British roads ran from north to south or, in Slim's words, 'parallel to the Japanese front and at no great distance from it'.[87] Due to the low ratio of troops to frontage, the Allied commanders had to leave 82 miles of their lines completely undefended.[88] The jungle terrain was ideal for the infiltration tactics which Japan's troops had used so effectively in earlier campaigns, and the Allied lines of communication were vulnerable. In sum, the Allies faced tactical disadvantages: the logistical burden of extra mouths to feed, the near-certainty that their supply lines would be cut and the likely possibility of encirclement. If the British defences at Imphal had collapsed under this pressure, the Japanese would have been in a position to drive on into India.

Just as air supply had allowed Wingate to liberate himself from the constraints of land-bound logistics, so it allowed Slim to liberate his much larger forces at Imphal from the threats to their lines of communications. Air transport would keep units supplied, and in what may have been an even more revolutionary development, air transport allowed Allied commanders the flexibility to deploy fresh divisions into positions which, by the standards of earlier decades, would have been considered to be under siege. The art of strategy can be described as the art of concentrating one's own strength against the enemy's weakness. When one considers the possibilities of aerial redeployment in light of this epigram, one sees how the air forces allowed British commanders to meet the Japanese attack with far greater confidence than their position on the ground would otherwise have inspired.

During January and February of 1944, when, in Slim's words, 'almost every unit in the Imphal plain moved', the British selected the two all-weather airfields at Imphal and Palel as 'strongpoints' or 'keeps' in their defensive scheme.[89] One notes that Slim expressed his strategic ideas in almost exactly the same terms that Wingate used when he based his second Chindit expedition upon the 'stronghold' concept of aerial supply. Whether this parallel use of language was intentional or not, the two commanders were using air supply in much the same way. Slim wished, at this stage, to reinforce Imphal with the British 5th division, then engaged on the Arakan peninsula, but he had to give up this plan due to congestion on the railways.[90]

The Japanese began their offensive in the first week of March 1944.[91] In the words of historian Louis Allen, 'Imphal was not a single engagement but a complex series of battles lasting five months, ranging from the banks of the Chindwin to the road beyond Kohima, well inside Assam.'[92] This situation indicates the fact that the Japanese had managed to attack before the British completed their attempt to concentrate their dispersed forces at Imphal. Slim's strategy of decisive victory on the strategic defensive was off to a bad start, and the Allies faced the danger of defeat in detail.

Slim, in his memoirs, divided the Imphal campaign into four phases. The first of these was the period of concentration, which was followed by a battle of attrition in which the Allied forces wore down the Japanese to the point where they managed to stage a counteroffensive and, finally, a pursuit.[93] One notes that, in a campaign of this nature, the period of concentration is, in fact, the point at which the battle is lost and won. This is the point at which one side manages to achieve the superiority of forces which allows it to prevail in the test of strength which follows.

The Japanese understood the importance of preventing the Allies from concentrating their troops. Lieutenant-General Shozo Sakurai, commander of Japan's 28th Army, undertook an offensive in the Arakan peninsula to tie down Allied troops there and prevent them from joining the main battle in the north.[94] Britain's commanders, on the other hand, had already deployed their forces in order to achieve superior strength in the areas they considered decisive.[95] Even in the early stages of the battle, the Allies relied on air supply to compensate for the speed of the Japanese advance. As the British 17th Division withdrew toward Imphal, for instance, it received all of its supplies by parachute.[96]

Nevertheless, the Japanese swept forward, as they had done so many times in the past, and on 29 March, they had surrounded Imphal.[97] Over 155,000 British troops and 11,000 animals were encircled there, and from that point until June 22, they had no way to receive supplies other than by air.[98] Meanwhile, the Japanese managed to besiege another contingent of British troops at Kohima, to the south. Indeed, for a period in April, the soldiers in that city received even their water by airdrop.[99]

By the time these sieges took place, however, Slim had mustered sufficient aircraft to sustain his men. Early in March, he had requested additional transport aircraft from the American air forces, which had been engaged in the attempt to ship supplies to China over the 'hump' of the Himalayas. Given the fact that, if Imphal and Kohima fell, the 'hump' route would become impassable, this made sound strategic sense, but since the aircraft were American, nobody in the theatre had the authority to divert them. On March 13, Admiral Mountbatten broke the chain of command in order to assign 30 of the American Dakota aircraft to Slim's forces, and took personal responsibility for the act.[100]

Slim also brought new troops into the campaign. The 5th Division had become essential, and since the rail lines, which had previously been too congested to transport the unit, were by then occupied by the enemy, he had to move the entire force by air. Between 19 March and 29 March the Allies ferried the Division 260 miles from its combat positions in Arakan to the front at Imphal.[101] This effort involved the British 194th Transportation Squadron, along with 20 Commando aircraft borrowed from the Americans, and required a total of 760 sorties.[102] Despite the fact that the 5th Division had no training in aerial deployments, the British official historian reports that there were no significant mishaps.[103]

Due to the extreme situation of the British troops in Kohima, Slim diverted the 5th Division's third brigade, the 161st, to Manipur, where it could assist in that battle.[104] For tactical reasons, Slim found the decision to divide his forces troublesome.[105] One must note, however, that the flexibility of air transport allowed his troops to execute the operation without difficulty. The ability to redeploy brigade-sized forces at will over such distances in the face of an attacking enemy was, to say the least, remarkable in military history.

According to official records of the siege, aircraft supplied the troops at Imphal with 423 tons of sugar, 5,000 live chickens, 5,000,000 vitamin tablets, 1,300 tons of animal food, 800,000 gallons of fuel, 919 tons of grain, 27,000 eggs, 12,000 bags of mail and 43,000,000 cigarettes, in addition to all the munitions and vehicles they required for the battle.[106] This amounted to 540 tons per day (480 for the ground forces and 60 for Royal Air Force units on the scene).[107] During the month of March, the air forces also extracted 22,000 non-combatants from the combat zone, allowing the Allies to replace them with fighting troops,[108] Aerial operations allowed the Allies to extract 10,000 of their wounded troops too from the siege zone, a fact which unquestionably improved morale.[109]

Aerial resupply remained important even after the siege had technically ended. During April and June, as the monsoon made all supply operations in the theatre difficult, the air forces removed another 13,000 casualties from Imphal, flew in another 12,550 replacement soldiers, evacuated a further 43,000 non-essential personnel from the combat zone and delivered another 18,800 tons of supplies.[110] The air forces made it possible for the British to overcome their poor beginning and dominate the concentration phase of the Imphal battle, and then to sustain their troops during the phase of attrition. Meanwhile, the air forces continued to play an important role in supplying troops on the secondary Arakan front, and also in the support of Wingate's Chindits, whose raids on enemy communications were slowing the Japanese attack on Imphal by a definite, albeit not measurable, amount.[111]

Just as Slim had hoped, the Japanese army broke itself against the British defences, and the Allies were able to advance into Burma against a crippled foe. By August, all Japanese forces in the theatre were in retreat, and in May of the following year Allied troops entered the Burmese capital of Rangoon without a battle. To summarise the Burma campaign, one might observe, along with historian David Rooney, that:

> Without the contribution of the air forces, in flying in the reserve divisions from the Arakan, in supporting Kohima, and in supplying 150,000 men during the siege of Imphal, there is no doubt that Kohima would have fallen, Imphal would have been lost and the war in the Far East would have taken a totally different course. Perhaps Mutaguchi would have made his triumphal March on Delhi.[112]

FINDINGS

1. How have high-level commanders perceived the problems of logistics?
Wingate described the land-bound lines of communications which the British used early in the war as a 'vulnerable artery' and an impediment which prevented commanders from deploying their forces to best advantage.[113] Slim was also acutely aware of these problems, and he went on to note that they affected every aspect of British performance, from tactics, operations and strategy to the spirit of the commanders and the morale of the troops.[114] Both generals, in other words, perceived logistics as the chief factor which limited what their forces could do. The reverse side of this statement, however, is that logistics can also be the factor which makes new kinds of military activities possible. In that spirit, Wingate and Slim developed an innovative way of supplying their troops and used it to carry out operations which they would not otherwise have been able to carry out.

2. *How have logistical factors helped or harmed the performance of armed forces?*
Japanese commanders took advantage of the vulnerability of Allied lines of communication to drive back British forces early in the war. The British then found themselves in a position where, due largely to their poor lines of communication, they were unable to launch any kind of operations except for weak advances along predictable routes under unfavourable tactical conditions. Through the use of aerial supply, Wingate's Chindits were able to break out of this pattern and attack Japanese forces at times and places which would otherwise have been impossible. Later, at Kohima and Imphal, Slim was able to redeploy large forces by air and to reduce their dependence on overland supply routes on at least a temporary basis. Throughout the campaign, logistics was not only the factor which sustained forces in the field, it was the factor which determined the range of options which the commanders of those units had available to them.

3. *What factors have given countries logistical advantages?*
The Burma campaign provides two answers to this question, one tangible and historically specific, the other intangible and timeless. Obviously, it was the industrial and technological acumen of the Allied nations which allowed the British and Americans to deploy enough transport aircraft to support Slim and Wingate in Burma. In the same vein, the Burmese terrain made aerial transportation particularly useful. Nevertheless, Slim and Wingate's victories were not merely a matter of material resources. Other commanders might have used the same forces in radically different and probably far less effective ways. It was their creativity, their will to seize the initiative and their ability to marry strategic and operational ends with logistical means which allowed Slim and Wingate to win the battles of the Burma campaign.

4. *What logistical problems are associated with particular styles of warfare, and how have commanders addressed them?*
The logistical problem of the Burma campaign was that of figuring out how to mount flexible, aggressive, large-scale operations in the Burmese countryside. Slim and Wingate solved this problem through the use of aerial transportation, and the main body of this chapter describes their methods in detail. In review, one must note that their techniques were extremely risky. When Wingate sent his long-range penetration groups behind enemy lines and forced them to depend on fortified airstrips for supply, he was putting them in essentially the same position that the Germans found themselves in at Stalingrad and the French found themselves in at Dien Bien Phu. Later, when Slim allowed the Japanese to surround his forces at Imphal and Kohima, he placed his entire army in a similar situation.

Why were Slim and Wingate's operations successful when Stalingrad and

Dien Bien Phu were such monumental disasters? One can never answer such questions with certainty. Likely factors include the forces involved and the landscape. The Japanese had neither the aircraft nor the ground-based anti-aircraft weapons to stop the British resupply efforts, and the jungle terrain made it difficult for their ground forces to overrun the airstrips. Ultimately, one might say that luck played an important role. However, one must also give credit to Slim and Wingate for their judgement in determining that their units were capable of fighting on while surrounded by enemy forces, their clarity of thought in seeing that the opportunities outweighed the dangers and their courage in going ahead with these operations despite the risk.

CONCLUSION

The mountains and jungles of the Burmese countryside made even the most routine manoeuvres logistically difficult, and therefore, they magnified any logistical advantage into a war-winning capability. One must also note that the Allies could not have supplied the Chindits or resisted the siege of Imphal had it not been for the fighter pilots of the Royal Air Force who established air superiority throughout the theatre of operations. Although the details of this campaign are historically unique, the lessons it teaches about the relationship among factors such as technology, supply techniques, and operational capabilities are eternal. The fact that supply played an exaggerated role in the Burma campaign makes it easy to identify the points at which logistics enters the strategic equation. Logistics governs the battlefield, not only at the lowest levels of strategy, where it determines whether or not soldiers receive food and bullets, but at the highest, where it determines what armies can do. The example of aerial supply in Burma demands that we reconsider models which measure the effectiveness of transportation technology in narrow terms of speed, distance and tonnages. We must, therefore, question Van Creveld's attempt to evaluate the effectiveness of logistical technology by comparing the rate at which armies advance to the theoretical speed of their vehicles.[115] The importance of air supply in Burma lay, not in its ratio of potential speed to actual speed, but in the fact that it allowed troops to conduct entirely new types of operations. The importance of logistics lies not in administrative efficiency but in tactical, operational and strategic effectiveness.

NOTES

1. Louis Allen, *Burma: The Longest War 1941–1945* (London: J.M. Dent, 1984), p. 6.
2. Ibid., pp. 6–7.
3. For a discussion of the disagreement between American and British planners, see M.C.

Pande, *Allied Air Logistic Supply and Air Transport Operations During the Burma Campaign (1944–45)* (Upavon: Tactical Doctrine Retrieval Cell, 1994), p. 3.
4. Southeast Asia Command, *The Campaign in Burma* (London: Her Majesty's Stationery Office, 1946), p. 12.
5. Charles F. Romanus and Riley Sunderland, *Stilwell's Mission to China* (Washington, DC: Department of the Army, 1953), p. 30.
6. David Rooney, *Burma Victory: Imphal, Kohima and the Chindit Issue, March 1944 to May 1945* (London: Arms & Armour Press, 1992), p. 13.
7. Ibid.
8. Ibid.
9. Sir William Slim, *Defeat Into Victory* (London: Cassell, 1956), pp. 5–6.
10. Staff Group 10C, *Imphal–Kohima – Encirclement: 14th British Army and 15th Japanese* (Ft Leavenworth, KS: USACGSC, 1984), p. 6.
11. For discussion of these factors, see Slim, *Defeat Into Victory*, p. 181.
12. Rooney, *Burma Victory*, p. 24.
13. Slim, *Defeat Into Victory*, p. 42.
14. Ibid., p. 28.
15. Ibid.
16. Ibid., p. 118.
17. Ibid., p. 119.
18. See Rooney, *Burma Victory*, p. 18, and S. Woodburn Kirby, *The War Against Japan, Volume II: India's Most Dangerous Hour* (London: Her Majesty's Stationery Office, 1958), p. 308.
19. Kirby, *The War Against Japan, Volume II*, p. 239.
20. See Rooney, *Burma Victory*, p. 20, and Slim, *Defeat Into Victory*, p. 126.
21. Slim, *Defeat Into Victory*, p. 127.
22. Ibid., p. 144.
23. Ibid.
24. Ibid.
25. Ibid.
26. Ibid., p. 127.
27. Ibid.
28. Ibid.
29. Ibid., p. 151.
30. Southeast Asia Command, *The Campaign in Burma*, p. 31.
31. Rooney, *Burma Victory*, p. 21.
32. First, Irwin refused to assign Slim to the invasion, although Slim's outfit included a corps headquarters which would have been invaluable in directing the operations of the nine Allied brigades which took part in the attack (Rooney, *Burma Victory*). During later stages of the campaign, Irwin sent Slim to report on the status of British units, but he refused to give his rival authority to correct the errors he uncovered. Only when Japanese victory had become inevitable did Irwin order Slim to take command.
33. Southeast Asia Command, *The Campaign in Burma*, p. 31.
34. Slim, *Defeat Into Victory*, p. 101.
35. Ibid., pp. 28–9.
36. Rooney, *Burma Victory*, p. 13.
37. S.P. Rodgers, *The Influence of Combat Service Support on Operations During the Burma Campaign 1944–45* (Upavon: Tactical Doctrine Retrieval Cell, 1994), pp. 12–13.
38. Slim, *Defeat into Victory*, p. 28.
39. John Keegan, *Churchill's Generals* (New York: George Weidenfeld & Nicolson, 1991), p. 311.

40. S. Kirby, *The War Against Japan, Volume II: India's Most Dangerous Hour* (London: Her Majesty's Stationery Office, 1958), pp. 238–9.
41. Slim, *Defeat Into Victory*, p. 29.
42. See Rooney, *Burma Victory*, pp. 20–22.
43. Slim, *Defeat Into Victory*, p. 143.
44. Southeast Asia Command, *The Campaign in Burma*, pp. 34–5.
45. Ibid.
46. Ibid.
47. Ibid.
48. Kirby, *The War Against Japan, Volume II*, p. 307.
49. Ibid., p. 209.
50. Ibid., pp. 309–10.
51. Allen, *Burma*, p. 127.
52. Ibid., p. 147.
53. Rooney, *Defeat Into Victory*, p. 148.
54. Allen, *Burma*, p. 147.
55. Rooney, *Burma Victory*, p. 108.
56. Allen, *Burma*, p. 128.
57. Ibid., p. 132.
58. Rooney, *Burma Victory*, p. 121.
59. Ibid., p. 126.
60. Ibid.
61. Ibid.
62. Allen, *Burma*, p. 316 and Rooney, *Burma Victory*, p. 326.
63. Rooney, *Burma Victory*, p. 327.
64. Ibid. pp. 134–40.
65. Ibid., p. 140.
66. Slim, *Defeat Into Victory*, p. 546.
67. Kirby, *The War Against Japan, Volume II*, p. 327.
68. Slim, *Defeat Into Victory*, p. 121.
69. Ibid.
70. Ibid., p. 143.
71. Allen, *Burma*, p. 120.
72. Ibid., p. 147.
73. Kirby, *The War Against Japan, Volume II*, p. 328.
74. Ibid., p. 328–9.
75. Slim, *Defeat Into Victory*, pp. 285–6.
76. Kirby, *The War Against Japan, Volume II*, pp. 291–308 and S. Woodburn Kirby, *The War Against Japan, Volume III: The Decisive Battles* (London: Her Majesty's Stationery Office, 1961), pp. 58–70.
77. Slim, *Defeat Into Victory*, p. 286.
78. Ibid.
79. Ibid., p. 285.
80. Ibid., p. 292.
81. Ibid., p. 286.
82. Ibid., p. 291.
83. Ibid., p. 292.
84. Ibid., p. 287.
85. Ibid.
86. Ibid.
87. Ibid.

88. Ibid.
89. Ibid., p. 293.
90. Ibid.
91. Allen, *Burma*, p. 191.
92. Ibid.
93. Slim, *Defeat Into Victory*, p. 296.
94. Allen, *Burma*, p. 191.
95. Rooney, *Burma Victory*, p. 59.
96. Slim, *Defeat Into Victory*, p. 303.
97. Rooney, *Burma Victory*, p. 63.
98. Kirby, *The War Against Japan, Volume III*, p. 321 and Rooney, *Burma Victory*, pp. 68–9.
99. Slim, *Defeat Into Victory*, p. 316.
100. Ibid., p. 306.
101. Kirby, *The War Against Japan, Volume III*, p. 235.
102. Ibid.
103. Ibid.
104. Slim, *Defeat Into Victory*, p. 306.
105. Ibid.
106. Rooney, *Burma Victory*, p. 64.
107. Kirby, *The War Against Japan, Volume III*, pp. 321–2.
108. Ibid., p. 320.
109. Rooney, *Burma Victory*, p. 64.
110. Kirby, *The War Against Japan, Volume III*, p. 327.
111. Rooney, *Burma Victory*, p. 64. Those who wish to judge the effects of Operation Thursday on enemy operations might note that, during the opening phases of Japan's offensive, in response to a question from his superiors, the Japanese general Motozo Yanagida wrote that the Chindit raids on his supply lines would make it impossible for him to capture Imphal within the three weeks their plans had allowed. This statement brought Yanagida both private humiliation and official disfavour, but he felt that he had no alternative but to make it. Later, in an irony of history, he was to discover that his commander had not actually asked for his opinion on the prospects for seizing Imphal. Yanagida's admission was unnecessary, but his concern over the Chindit operations was quite serious. Ibid., p. 37.
112. Ibid., p. 69.
113. Southeast Asia Command, *The Campaign in Burma*, pp. 34–5.
114. Slim, *Defeat Into Victory*, p. 118.
115. M. Van Creveld, *Supplying War* (Cambridge: Cambridge University Press, 1977), pp. 234–6.

3

Making It Work: America's War in the Pacific

One sees the relationship between logistics and strategy on a grand scale in the Pacific campaigns of the Second World War. In this war, US forces overcame great challenges of supply and movement in order to thwart Japan's grand strategy. Therefore, the Pacific campaigns demonstrate the central thesis of this study in a particularly comprehensive fashion. The logistical innovations of the US Navy and US Marine Corps allowed American forces to seize and hold the initiative at every level of a protracted war.

The scope of the Pacific War makes this historical episode particularly useful as a case study. Whereas other conflicts may have turned on relatively narrow issues, the war against Japan tested US logistical capabilities over a broad spectrum of ways. American forces fought on the land, on the sea and in the air, in varied climates and locations, for a period of almost four years. In some cases, US forces possessed advantages in intelligence, technology, training or numbers, but in other cases, they did not. Therefore, if one can draw any conclusions from a study of the Pacific War, one may claim that they have been rigorously tested under a wide variety of conditions.

This chapter also addresses a neglected area of logistical studies. Other authors in the field, beginning with Jomini and continuing to Van Creveld, have tended to concentrate exclusively upon land operations.[1] John Lynn added some balance to the literature with the publication of his anthology *Feeding Mars*, which includes essays on maritime logistics in the 15th and 16th centuries, along with a study of Britain's ship-building industry in the First World War.[2] The study of the Pacific War found here not only brings the literature up-to-date by studying a more recent naval conflict, but shows how amphibious landings and joint operations with air forces add new dimensions to the problems of supply and movement at sea.

This chapter begins with a discussion of Japanese grand strategy in the Pacific, in order to put the US reaction in its proper perspective. From that point, the chapter goes on to investigate the way in which the logistical branches of the American armed services prepared for a Pacific War. The narrative continues with an examination of how these preparations allowed the US Navy to meet the test of battle, and of how American forces supplied their first counterattacks in the Pacific. Following sections describe the process by which American commanders learned from early mistakes. A section entitled 'Pouring It On' demonstrates that US logisticians succeeded in their attempts to perfect a system which would allow them to bring the industrial might of their nation to bear against Japan. In conclusion, the chapter discusses key points from the historical sections in the context of the four basic questions which shape this study.

THE STRATEGIC SIDESTEP

Those who look at the Second World War with the benefit of hindsight should not allow the fact that the Pacific War ended with the unconditional surrender of Japan to make them forget that the Japanese leaders began the war with a rational, albeit desperate, plan to win. The essence of this plan appeared in the memorandum in which General Haijime Sugiyama informed the Emperor of the Pearl Harbor attack. Japan's military leaders had gambled that they could establish an 'invincible position' in the Pacific, which would buy enough time for their diplomats to 'influence the trend of events and bring the war to an end'.[3] A summary of Japan's military objectives appears in the 15 November, 1941 Draft Proposal For Hastening the End of the War Against the United States, Great Britain, the Netherlands and Chiang', which appeared as an attachment to the proceedings of the 69th Liaison Conference between the Japanese General Staff and the cabinet of Japan's civilian government.

> Our Empire will engage in a quick war, and will destroy American and British bases in Eastern Asia and in the Southwest Pacific region. At the same time that it secures a strategically powerful position, it will control those areas producing vital minerals, as well as important transportation routes, and thereby prepare for a protracted period of self-sufficiency.[4]

One should note what the Liaison Conference emphasised in its Proposal. The Japanese commanders did not rely on any momentary coup such as the Pearl Harbor raid to win the war for them. Rather, they hoped to establish a position which they could defend for an indefinite period of time. The military component of this plan emphasised the capture of bases, along with the domination of crucial sea lanes. Japan's leaders hoped that if they could deprive the United States and its allies of ports and airfields, the sheer size of the Pacific region would exhaust the US armed forces as they attempted to take back what they had lost.[5]

In short, the Japanese hoped that they could make an American reconquest of the Pacific logistically unfeasible. Japan's leaders hoped that the United States government would eventually tire of the campaign and accept a negotiated settlement. Did this plan have any realistic chance of success? Many commentators seem to feel that the American people would never have settled for anything less than total victory after the outrage of Pearl Harbor, although, in other contexts, it remains perennially fashionable to argue that Americans have no patience for long wars. Ultimately, however, the question is moot, because the American fleet managed to strike back with great celerity, despite Japan's initial successes. The US Navy (USN) developed both the transportation resources and the logistical doctrine it needed to sidestep the grand strategy of Imperial Japan.

This passage, written in 1929, sums up the challenge which the United States armed forces had to overcome in order to achieve that result.

> Problem (4) viz, the defense of outlying territories, particularly the Philippines, Guam, and Samoa, opens up the whole question of Pacific strategy ... Here it suffices to repeat that the American Navy would be almost powerless to prevent the conquest of the Philippines and Guam in the event of war with Japan. Once lost, they might possibly be recovered by an almost superhuman effort. This would involve an amphibious campaign exceeding in magnitude and difficulty anything of the kind that has previously been attempted. It would necessitate the building of an entirely new fleet of warships and auxiliary craft; the conveyance of an army and its impedimenta across the Pacific, the greater part of the route lying within the sphere of enemy naval action; the seizure of intermediate and terminal bases, which would probably be found in a state of defence; the holding of such bases against determined counterattack; the guarding of communications thousands of miles in length; and finally the development of offensive operations in the advanced war zone on a scale sufficient to force a decision.[6]

BLUNDERING TOWARD PREPAREDNESS —
I: THE NAVAL SUPPORT SERVICES

The logistical system which allowed the USN to defeat Imperial Japan took shape in the 1920s and 1930s, as US naval forces absorbed the lessons of the First World War.[7] For naval logisticians, the interwar years were not a particularly dramatic episode of military history. The issue of maritime logistics did not inspire many deep theoretical debates, and few individuals emerged distinguished on account of their unusual logistical foresight.[8] (The military thinkers who developed the US Marine Corps' amphibious doctrine stand out as a conspicuous exception.) Nevertheless, when one reviews the events of this era, one finds a large number of instances in which logistical planners made the correct decisions. The system, in other words, worked.

If the USN had not adopted a new and superior system of supply in the early 1940s, Japan's strategy would have been considerably more successful. In 1924, when the United States armed forces officially adopted the plan known as Orange as their strategy for war with Japan, fleet commanders assumed that they would not be able to fight unless they had access to port facilities within the operating radius of their ships.[9] In public, US officials wished to maintain the impression that they planned to defend all of their Pacific territories, but military leaders tacitly recognised the fact that, given the peacetime weakness of their forces, it would be impossible for them to hold the Philippines and Guam against Japanese attack.[10] Therefore, while the original war plans called for American forces in the Pacific to operate from a 'Western Base' in Manila, a revised version of Orange which appeared in 1935 conceded that the United States would have to seize the Marshall and Caroline island chains as naval staging areas before it could even contemplate offensive operations against Japan.[11] Soon afterward, in order to keep the rest of Plan Orange viable, military commanders developed secondary war plans which called for the US Army to assemble forces for the invasion of these islands within 45 to 60 days.[12]

There was clearly an element of fantasy in these schemes, and the naval historian Duncan S. Ballantine dismisses them with the following words: 'Most certainly, the Army could not have mounted such a force, and the Navy could not have transported it.'[13] Other authors suggest that even the commanders who developed this strategy were well aware that it would take years to capture the island chains.[14] When the war came, the US Marine Corps (USMC) did not land in either the Marshalls or the Carolines until February of 1944. If the US Navy had been forced to rely upon the land-bound logistical system it used from 1929 until 1940, it would have been crippled for the first two years of the Pacific campaign.[15]

There was, however, another way to sustain maritime forces. Ships could resupply other ships at sea, as the British Navy demonstrated with its use of 'victualling sloops' during the Seven Years War.[16] During the First World War, the USN developed the techniques it needed to provide other vital services at sea as well. In Queenstown, for instance, the Navy of that conflict used a pair of ships as floating work platforms.[17] Therefore, personnel at the Queenstown station were able to repair and maintain destroyers, despite the near-absence of port facilities.[18] These developments made it possible for naval forces to carry a substantial portion of their supplies and maintenance equipment with them, in the same fashion that modern land forces carry much of their vital equipment in trucks.

By the Second World War, the idea that ships could sustain ships in twentieth-century naval campaigns was hardly new. A civil engineer named

A.C. Cunningham proposed that the US Navy establish a 'mobile base' of logistics vessels in 1904.[19] Following the First World War, when the USN moved the bulk of its assets to the Pacific, naval commanders organised a pool of vessels known as the Base Force fleet train for this purpose.[20] In the Basic Readiness Plan of 1924, US military planners announced their intention to use mobile bases of this nature as their primary means of supporting naval forces at sea.[21] Although the USN returned to the policy of depending on conventional ports in 1929, these ideas did not die out.[22]

The concepts of fleet logistics did, however, remain dormant for some time. To a naval officer of the 1930s, when the United States had its major vessels stationed in home ports, the problems of sustaining operations in remote parts of the Pacific must have seemed a bit unreal.[23] The Navy did not have the funds to develop new support capabilities.[24] In 1940, when President Franklin Roosevelt declared a state of national emergency, money suddenly became available, but logistics forces had to compete with all the other branches of the Navy for vessels and trained personnel.[25] Naval officers understood the need for new logistical assets, but they had no way to know exactly how many ships and other assets their support services would need.[26]

Admiral Worrall Reed Carter sums up the spirit of the period as follows:

> [T]he idea of fleet logistics afloat was becoming more and more firmly rooted; only time was needed to make it practical, as our knowledge and experience were still so meager that we had little detailed conception of our logistic needs. Even when someone with a vivid imagination hatched an idea, he frequently was unable to substantiate it to the planning experts and it was likely to be set down as wild exaggeration.[27]

Meanwhile, in October 1939, the United States deployed a force of 16 destroyers, eight cruisers and one aircraft carrier to Hawaii.[28] Although the Navy had a base at Pearl Harbor, this move severely stretched its logistical capabilities. In March of 1940, Admiral J.O. Richardson, the Commander in Chief of the US Navy, wrote that he did not consider the basing of the fleet or even a substantial portion of it at Hawaii to be 'a remote possibility'.[29] The Chief of Naval Operations, H.R. Stark, responded that it had become politically necessary to base the fleet in an advanced position, and added that the move would give the Navy an opportunity to identify and solve its supply and support problems.[30]

Just as Stark had hoped, the Navy learned how to overcome its supply difficulties. Base Force carried fuel, munitions and other goods from the continental United States to Hawaii, much as its successor organisations would deliver such material to ships and ports in the combat zone.[31] Logisticians quickly learned that Base Force needed more ships, but nevertheless, in June of 1941, Richardson's successor, Admiral H.E. Kimmel, was able to write 'Many of the deficiencies of this base disclosed by the prolonged stay of the

US Pacific Fleet ... either have been or are now in the process of correction.'[32] The lessons which the Navy learned in this operation impelled it to develop the support it needed to send forces across the breadth of the Pacific.

As a historian and a strategist, one should not oversimplify the logistical system which won the war in the Pacific. Base Force and the Service Squadrons which succeeded it did not eliminate the need for harbours, nor did their advocates claim that they could. Rather, they extended the reach of the fleet into otherwise inaccessible parts of the ocean. Furthermore, they made it possible for the Navy to service large numbers of ships at relatively undeveloped ports at short notice. From Pearl Harbor itself to Noumea, Darwin, Roi, Naha, San Pedro and other anchorages, seaborne and land-based support services would work together to sustain the war effort in the Pacific. In the words of Admiral Spruance, 'each had its advantages, and neither alone could do the job'.[33]

BLUNDERING TOWARD PREPAREDNESS –
II: THE LONG-RANGE SUBMARINE

While logisticians considered the problems of fleet support, different people whose interests and responsibilities lay in completely different areas independently made decisions which would also become important to the US armed forces in their attempt to seize the initiative against Japan. Luck played an important role, as naval strategists took actions which would turn out to be more farsighted than they could have realised. The submarine service, for instance, adopted long-range, low-maintenance vessels as the mainstay of its force. These new boats minimised the logistical requirements of sub-surface operations, giving the US Navy new strategic options in the Pacific War.

American naval strategists first became interested in the concept of such submarines in 1912, when the Submarine Flotilla Board requested a 1,000-ton vessel with enough speed and range to keep up with the battleship fleet.[34] Later that year, the US Naval War College conducted a series of wargames in which they determined that vessels of this type could play an important role in battles between fleets of capital ships. According to this scheme, submarines would press ahead of their side's surface ships in order to take positions in front of the enemy fleet. The underwater boats would act as a mobile minefield, which could move to whatever location would cause the most disruption to the enemy formation.

In the First World War, the submarine emerged, not merely as an adjunct to the battle fleet, but as an instrument for cutting off the enemy's commerce. US officials renounced the right to practice this sort of warfare when they signed the Washington Naval Accords of 1922, which forbade submarine attacks against civilian shipping.[35] Nevertheless, naval planners remained interested in the idea that submarines would be valuable in fleet actions.[36] Furthermore, as American commanders considered the problems of reconnaissance at sea, they decided that submarines would prove valuable as scout vessels.[37] Both tasks required fast boats which would be able to operate at long ranges with minimal logistic support.

Therefore, although European submarine designers placed little emphasis on range, US defence planners made this factor a primary engineering consideration.[38] The consequences of this became apparent on 7 December, 1941, when it was possible for President Roosevelt to order US submarines to counterattack against the Japanese no more than six hours after he received word of the Pearl Harbor raid.[39] US forces abandoned their prewar scruples and directed the submarine commanders to carry out unrestricted warfare against enemy commerce, rather than limiting themselves to combat with other warships.[40] Whatever the moral ramifications of this policy, the existence of a logistically lean submarine fleet allowed the US Navy to put the President's decision into effect.

This strategy of anti-commerce warfare took some time to achieve its full potential, due to the abysmal quality of American torpedoes and the overly cautious doctrine of US submarine commanders.[41] Nevertheless, American submarines sank 180 Japanese ships during 1942 alone.[42] In 1943, the USN corrected the problems in its undersea fleet, and the next year, the number of sinkings rocketed to 600.[43] The Japanese Navy found itself forced to establish its main fleet base in the Dutch East Indies, not for strategic reasons, but because this was the source of its oil.[44] US submarine warfare had made tanker traffic too uncertain for the Japanese Navy to operate from Japan itself.[45]

BLUNDERING TOWARD PREPAREDNESS – III: AMPHIBIOUS TACTICS

The US Navy, as noted above, depended upon its ability to secure ports within the war zone. Therefore, in January 1920, US Chief of Naval Operations Robert E. Coontz advised Commandant George Barnett to develop an expeditionary force for campaigns to capture and control island bases in the Pacific.[46] At this time, the Marine Corps had not yet adopted assaults against defended beaches as its particular speciality.[47] Amphibious descents were a poorly understood area of warfare, and the disastrous failure of the Gallipoli operation in the First World War had led most commanders to view such enterprises as wasteful and potentially foolhardy.[48] Furthermore, as Barnett observed, the Marines did not have either the funds or the personnel to develop a beach landing capability.[49]

Barnett's successor, John A. Lejeune, saw the importance of amphibious warfare, both to United States strategy, and to his own corps. In 1920,

Lejeune instructed his brilliant, hyperenergetic staff officer Earl Ellis to study the requirements of amphibious war in the Pacific.[50] Ellis produced a study known as Operations Plan 712 *Advanced Base Operations in Micronesia*, in which he set out a plan, which, as he predicted, was to 'serve as a guide for the co-ordination of all peace activities and training of the Marine Corps'.[51] Thus, the USMC became a facilitator of naval logistics. By the same token, the USMC took on unique logistical requirements of its own.

The leaders of the Marine Corps understood that beach assaults would entail special problems of supply. Their most obvious problem was that of simply getting heavy equipment from ships to the shore without a harbour. To complicate matters further, they knew that the Marines would often have to conduct this operation under fire. One notes that, in this area, the challenge of logistics overlaps with the tactical challenge of moving troops onto a defended beachhead.

In order to address these problems, the USMC Equipment Board, headed by Brigadier-General Emile P. Moses, adopted a number of specialised vehicles, equipped with light armour and designed to operate in shallow water. Key examples include the shallow-draft 'Eureka' boat invented by Andrew J. Higgins and the armoured, troop-carrying amphibious tractor invented by Donald Roebling.[52] The latter vehicle was especially noteworthy for its caterpillar treads, which allowed it to crawl over sandbars, coral reefs and other subsurface obstacles on its way to a beach.[53]

In addition to new equipment, amphibious landings required new doctrine. In 1934, under the direction of Colonel Ellis Miller, the instructors of the Marine Corps Schools produced a work titled *Tentative Manual for Landing Operations*, which summed up their findings on the subject.[54] This study divided the problem of conducting an attack on a hostile beach into six component parts, one of which was logistics. The *Tentative Manual* focused on the importance of 'combat loading' supply ships so that troops could access their most important equipment as quickly as possible.[55] Key points included:

- Supply handlers should pack goods in the order of 'first used, last loaded,' so that the most urgently needed supplies will be near the top of a ship's hold.[56]
- Supply handlers should divide vital supplies among different transports, so that the loss of one vessel does not cripple the entire force.[57]
- Supply handlers should store materiel belonging to the same units in the same parts of a ship, so that there is no confusion about who owns what.[58]

In hindsight, these maxims seem obvious, and, perhaps, somewhat mundane. Surely, a reader might respond, instructions to stevedores do not rate as deep military insight. Therefore, it is important to note that the concepts of 'combat loading' ran against established rules of practice, and were, for that reason, innovative ideas in their time. The Marine Corps guidelines often contradicted traditional principles of cargo handling, requiring, for instance, that quartermasters pack heavy things such as ammunition and heavy weapons on top of lighter, more fragile supplies.[59] Combat loading also prevents handlers from making maximally efficient use of the space in a ship's hold. In the Guadalcanal campaign, to pick one typical example, the necessities of combat loading forced the crew of the transport *Libra* to set sail with only a third of the cargo their ship would normally have carried.[60]

In the 1930s, the idea of 'combat loading' was new to warfare. The British, for instance, had not practised it during their largest amphibious landing of the First World War, the Dardenelles Campaign.[61] This incident did, however, demonstrate the reasons why the Marine Corps concepts were important. Numerous supply ships arrived in the theatre loaded in such a way that vital materiel was completely inaccessible. British commanders eventually had to send these ships back to the harbour at Alexandria to be repacked.[62] This delayed the landing by several weeks, and robbed the invasion force of its opportunity to take the defenders by surprise.[63]

The faculty of the Marine Corps School understood that large organisations such as military forces do not change their method of operation simply because somebody has a good idea. Therefore, the *Tentative Manual* proposed institutional procedures to insure that the future amphibious forces would practice 'combat loading' in a uniform fashion. The Marine Corps guidelines specified that a specially trained transport quartermaster should supervise the loading of each ship.[64] This officer received orders, not from a naval officer or a logistical bureaucrat, but from the commander of the troops who would be going ashore.[65]

The *Tentative Manual* made the American armed forces aware of the logistical demands of an amphibious assault and provided highly detailed information on how to meet them.[66] There were some lessons which the Marines would only learn in combat, but thanks to their efforts in the 1930s, they entered Second World War with both the training and the doctrine to land on hostile beaches. One cannot quantify the value of these preparations, but one can note that amphibious assaults are notorious for the amount of skill and planning they require.[67]

In autumn of 1940, General Holland M. Smith organised training exercises in which he tested the Marine Corps' amphibious doctrine under the most realistic conditions he could devise.[68] The Navy transported the Marines to the beaches in a fleet resupply ship, an obsolete destroyer and a decommissioned battleship, the *Wyoming*.[69] Since these vessels could not enter shallow waters, the Marines had to make a prolonged journey by boat from their ships to the beach. Furthermore, only 12 experimental landing craft were available, so most of the troops had to go ashore in ordinary ship's boats.[70] Ammunition and uniforms were also in short supply, as were trucks to carry materiel from point to point on the beachhead.[71]

The Marines lacked both equipment and the means to transport it. These were problems of logistics, and if the 1940 landings had been real, numerous marines would have died as a consequence. Over the next two years, Smith campaigned so vigorously for funds to remedy these problems that he earned the nickname 'Howling Mad'.[72] US war planners began a concerted effort to produce the gear required for amphibious warfare in 1942, although the largest modernisations in American landing capabilities did not take place until the final quarter of that year, after the Marines were already in combat.[73]

BLUNDERING TOWARD PREPAREDNESS – IV: JOINT PLANNING

In the Pacific theatre, where every land operation had a naval component, the success or failure of army and navy commanders to co-ordinate their plans had a pronounced importance in every aspect of warfare. Since ground troops depended directly on sea lines of communications for their supplies, the efficiency of joint operations was particularly important in the field of logistics. Operations such as the Guadalcanal campaign demonstrated both the truth of these statements and the problems which plagued collaborative planning in the early 1940s.[74] Nevertheless, the high commanders of the United States Armed Forces were aware of the fact that their next war would require an unusual degree of joint administration. This is not an area in which US planners can claim to have possessed extraordinary foresight, but they can claim to have possessed basic competence.

Until the creation of the Joint Chiefs of Staff in 1942, the US Army and Navy relied on a body known as the Joint Board to co-ordinate their activities.[75] This organisation could only make decisions through complete consensus among its members, and therefore, on important matters, it was often unable to act.[76] The prospect of war in the Pacific, however, galvanised this body into action. In 1937, for instance, the members of the Joint Board unanimously took the momentous decision to rescind War Plan Orange in favour of more realistic (and pessimistic) assessments of the requirements the USA would face in a war against Japan.[77]

One year later, the Army Chief of Staff, General Malin Craig, added a third dimension to joint planning when he commissioned a board to study the relationship of strategic air power to land and sea operations in the Pacific.[78] The board's findings gave considerable attention to the ways in which aircraft could help defend the logistical bases which allowed ground and sea forces to operate.[79] Craig's successor, General George C. Marshall, requested revisions in the Air Board's report, which, among other things, placed additional emphasis on the other point of the triangle – the support requirements of the air forces themselves. Marshall called on the board to pay more attention to the bases which air forces would need to carry out the missions their report foresaw.[80]

MILITARY LOGISTICS AND STRATEGIC PERFORMANCE

THE MOMENT OF TRUTH

When the war actually came, the US logistical services had two main challenges left to face. One was an immediate shortage of equipment and the other was a chronic problem of administration. Only time would allow American factories to produce the necessary materiel, and only combat experience would allow American commanders to identify and solve their organisational difficulties. Nevertheless, the preparations described in earlier sections allowed the US armed forces to seize the initiative in almost every aspect of military operations within the first year of the Pacific War.

By 1941, the commanders of the US Navy were intellectually prepared for the logistic challenges of war in the Pacific, but their material preparations were less impressive. The American naval strategies of the 1930s had emphasised the need for advanced bases, but the USN had not constructed any naval facilities west of Pearl Harbor, and US diplomats had renounced their country's right to fortify islands in the western Pacific under the terms of the Washington Treaty of 1922.[81] Likewise, the fleet had not yet procured the logistics ships it would need to service its fighting vessels at sea. Although the Navy's move to Pearl Harbor had demonstrated the importance of Base Force, the fleet train consisted of only 61 vessels in 1941.[82] In the words of one admiral, 'oilers were almost as rare as carriers', and the few tankers which were in service were so busy ferrying fuel to Pearl Harbor that they could not even train for the task of refuelling warships at sea.[83] The shortage of maintenance vessels was even more acute.[84]

The inadequacy of the 61-ship Base Force becomes clear when one compares the growth of the fleet train to the growth of the combat elements of the Navy. In peacetime, when the Navy had no certain way to predict its logistical requirements, defence planners tended to invest in more tangible symbols of military power, such as warships. Between 1925 and 1940, the number of destroyers, cruisers and aircraft carriers in the US Navy increased well over twice as rapidly as the number of logistics ships. In 1940, President Roosevelt authorised the construction of 125 combat vessels but only 12 support ships.[85] The experience of war, however, altered these priorities considerably. By 1945, the Base Force alone had mushroomed to 315 vessels, and the total number of ships involved in naval logistics numbered in the thousands.[86]

One can argue, in fact, that the Pearl Harbor raid did little to upset the US naval strategy in the Pacific. It was the lack of base facilities and supply vessels which prevented the USN from sending warships to intervene in the Japanese conquests of Wake, Guam, New Britain, New Guinea, the Philippines and the Dutch East Indies.[87] American strategists, however, recognised the causes of their weakness and lost little time in their attempt to rectify the situation. Although the admirals of the US Navy had underestimated the number of support vessels their fleet would require, they understood the fundamental nature of their logistical problem. In the words of Admiral Worrall Reed Carter:

> The original planners had done their best, but it was not until the urgency for auxiliaries developed as a vital element of the war that we fully realised what was needed, and met the demand. Merchant ships were converted whenever possible, and this, with concentrated efforts to provide drydocks and other special construction, produced every required type in numbers which would have been considered preposterous only a short time before.[88]

The lack of supply ships forced US Admiral Chester A. Nimitz to use his forces parsimoniously. Although prewar plans called for him to deploy the entire USN in two large groups, a Scouting Fleet and a Battle Fleet, there were not enough tankers to support detachments of this size.[89] The shortage of cruisers and aircraft made these large fleets even less viable.[90] Therefore, rather than confining the entire navy to operations near home ports, Nimitz divided his forces into task forces, each centred upon a large aircraft carrier.[91] The admiral relegated his fuel-guzzling battleships to patrol and escort duties between Hawaii and California, where they could obtain supplies from the land.[92]

The smaller detachments, of course, had smaller logistical requirements. With support from oilers, individual task forces could operate well beyond the range at which warships could draw supplies from land bases. Therefore, by January 1942, US naval commanders felt ready to strike into Japanese waters. In order to relieve pressure on the British and Dutch contingents which remained in the southwest Pacific, Admiral Nimitz proposed carrier-based air raids on the Gilbert and Marshall islands.[93] Senior naval officers opposed this plan on the grounds that it was too hazardous, but Nimitz received permission for the operation.[94]

Nimitz deployed two units for this raid. The first, Task Force Eight, consisted of the carrier *Enterprise*, the cruisers *Northampton*, *Salt Lake City* and *Chester*, seven destroyers and the oiler *Platte*.[95] The second, Task Force Seventeen, consisted of the carrier *Yorktown*, the cruisers *Louisville* and *St Louis*, five destroyers, and the oiler *Sabine*.[96] These task forces refuelled from their oilers three times on their journey to the target area on 17, 23 and 28 January.[97] The raids took place on 1–2 February, and the ships refuelled at sea for a final time on 4 February.[98]

Over the following months, these raids became standard practice. Carrier task forces attacked Wake Island, Marcus Island, Rabaul, New Guinea, and in April, Tokyo itself.[99] Without underway replenishment from logistics ships, none of these operations would have been possible. With each raid, the US Navy improved the logistical techniques it would later use to support its general advance into the Central Pacific.

None of these raids destroyed significant portions of the Japanese armed forces, and therefore, some historians have questioned their strategic significance.[100] In response, one must observe that even when the results of an operation are intangible, it is always useful to take the offensive in war. The carrier attacks of early 1942 ended a four-month period in which the Allied nations experienced nothing but one military catastrophe after another.[101] No one can deny that these assaults boosted national morale in the United States.[102] Furthermore, the raid on Tokyo caused the Imperial Japanese Navy (IJN) to send all its available ships to sea, in a clumsy attempt to prevent future attacks of that nature.[103]

Every ship which the IJN deployed to stop raids became unavailable for other operations against Allied holdings. Perhaps more importantly, as the Japanese high command sent new orders to the fleet, they generated a vast amount of radio traffic, which Allied intelligence officers managed to intercept.[104] Analysis of these signals alerted the commanders of the US Navy to the fact that their enemies had dispersed their forces.[105] In many instances, Allied commanders knew exactly where the Japanese vessels were located.[106] Therefore, in the months ahead, Admiral Nimitz was often able to concentrate superior forces against his opponents.[107] Although the Japanese Navy of early 1942 was stronger than the American fleet on paper, these events allowed the US commanders to concentrate their ships against one portion of the IJN at a time.

Among other things, this intelligence bonanza confirmed earlier evidence which indicated that the Japanese intended to capture the harbour of Port Moresby, on the island of Papua New Guinea.[108] If the Japanese had seized this port, they would have obtained a base from which to bomb Allied ships in the adjacent Coral Sea. They would have gained control over the airfields the Allies needed to launch bomber raids against the Japanese bases at Truk and Rabaul. Furthermore, if the Japanese had captured this harbour, they would have acquired a position from which to cut off the sea lanes to northern Australia. Ultimately, Port Moresby could have become the staging area for a Japanese invasion of that continent.

In late April, Allied cryptoanalysts decoded enemy signals which revealed the Japanese planned to launch an amphibious attack against Port Moresby in less than two weeks.[109] Nimitz resolved to intervene, and therefore he made a Herculean effort to get as many ships into the area as possible. Thanks to his earlier decision to split the US fleet into logistically supportable task forces, he managed to have the carriers *Yorktown* and *Lexington* in the area by the end of the month, along with their supporting vessels.[110] A detachment of oilers refuelled both task forces on the first and second days of May, two days before the American ships encountered the Japanese fleet in the battle of the Coral Sea.[111]

Both sides claimed victory in the Coral Sea battle, but although the USN lost the *Lexington*, the Japanese were unable to land troops at Port Moresby. The United States was able to build more aircraft carriers, but the Japanese were never able to attempt an amphibious assault at that location again. Although Japanese troops were already ashore in the northern jungles of Papua New Guinea, they never managed to capture the port. Furthermore, the Japanese carriers *Shokaku* and *Zuikaku* lost so many men and aircraft that they were unable to participate in the battle of Midway, and historians estimate that their absence reduced the strength of the Japanese forces at that crucial engagement by over one-third.[112]

The battle of the Coral Sea was a test of American maritime logistics, and the USN passed, although barely. One must remember that the American forces fought this battle approximately 1,300 miles from their bases, and over 400 miles from their nearest emergency anchorage.[113] If Admiral Nimitz had not made the decision to divide his battle fleet, it is unlikely that the USN could have participated in the engagement.[114] Without the oilers, *Yorktown* would have entered the battle short of fuel, and *Lexington* would never have arrived. Under these circumstances, the Japanese would almost certainly have won a complete victory.

On the other hand, with more support ships and more logistical experience, the US Navy might have suffered fewer losses and run fewer risks. The Japanese chose to withdraw from the Coral Sea on 8 May, after the loss of the small carrier *Soho*, but if they had stayed, *Yorktown* would have been perilously low on fuel and unable to obtain more.[115] On the other hand, if the American forces had possessed enough tankers to support its entire fleet, it might have been able to deploy its battleships in this engagement as well.[116] Furthermore, if US commanders had had fleet tugs on the scene, the USN might have salvaged the *Lexington*.[117]

Meanwhile, the US commanders mustered both land and sea forces in the southwest Pacific. During the first quarter of 1942, approximately half the troops and one-third of the cargo the Army shipped overseas went to that region.[118] The reasons for this build-up were twofold. First, the United States had tacitly accepted responsibility for the task of protecting Australia from invasion, and second, many US commanders, notably Douglas MacArthur, were eager to begin an offensive there as quickly as possible.[119]

THE CAMPAIGN OF INFRASTRUCTURE

The campaign for the southwest Pacific began as a campaign of infrastructure. In order to move sufficient quantities of men and materiel this distance, the American transportation fleets required maintenance and oil. Since the US forces had not acquired enough support vessels to sustain a major land-sea offensive without harbours and depots, they had to establish a series of island refuelling stations to connect Australia with the American west coast. The US Army and Navy worked jointly to build these bases.

The Pacific build-up began in December 1941, when US commanders decided to build a refuelling station on the island of Bora-Bora in the Society Group.[120] The Bora-Bora operation, known by the code name of Bobcat, revealed many of the planning and administrative problems which still plagued the US logistical apparatus. As early as January, for instance, communications between the different services broke down. Army commanders believed that the operation would begin on 27 January while naval commanders believed that it would start on 25 January and several weeks passed before anyone resolved the discrepancy.[121]

More serious problems developed when the Navy proved unable to provide three of the six transport ships it required for the operation.[122] The Maritime Commission located vessels to fill this gap, but one of these ships, the *President Tyler* turned out to be in a poor state of repair, and the other, the *Arthur Middleton*, required 1,500 tons of new ballast before it could sail.[123] The 1,400 troops of an Army anti-aircraft detachment, meanwhile, arrived at the Charleston port of embarkation with their equipment uncrated, despite explicit orders to the contrary.[124] Army and Navy logisticians alike failed to label the crates they sent to Charleston for transportation on to Bora-Bora, and the detachments which both services sent to assist the port-quartermaster were so inexperienced that they turned out to be more of a hindrance than a help.[125]

Bobcat reached Bora-Bora on 17 February, and there, the problems only became worse. In the confusion at Charleston, stevedores had packed the ships in a haphazard fashion, and when the task force reached the south Pacific, it proved all but impossible to unpack vital supplies. The admiral in charge of Bobcat's naval escort discovered that 'the ships could not be unloaded without the floating equipment and the floating equipment could not be assembled without unloading'.[126] Furthermore, none of the three replacement ships located by the Maritime Commission had come equipped with slings or cargo nets, and nobody seemed to have noticed this deficiency before the convoy reached Bora-Bora.[127] Commander Carl H. Sanders, the commander of the transport fleet, estimated that his men could have completed their mission a month earlier if the ships had been properly loaded.[128]

The officers who organised Bobcat had based their plans on a French survey from the nineteenth century.[129] These 100-year old maps failed to warn them that the water supplies on Bora-Bora were completely inadequate or that the coastal road, which was vital for defence, could not support heavy vehicles.[130] To complicate the water shortage further, the troops arrived just as the dry season began.[131] These matters occupied the American troops for another six weeks.[132]

When the soldiers of the Bobcat expedition were finally able to begin work on the refuelling station which their commanders had sent them there to build, they discovered yet another error in planning. The Bora-Bora base was supposed to feature a naval fuel depot. Planners had assumed that the troops would situate the petrol tanks on a convenient 'coastal flat', but no such 'flat' existed.[133] Lofty peaks covered the entire island of Bora-Bora, and the ground became steep less than 150 yards from the surf.[134] The US troops had to blast niches for the fuel containers into the sides of cliffs, and therefore, it was early June before the first tanks were in place.[135]

Operation Bobcat took over twice as long as its planners had anticipated. The string of fiascos made it impossible for troops to emplace guns or construct fortifications for several months, and if the Japanese had launched an attack during that period, Bora-Bora would have presented an easy target.[136] As it was, however, no such catastrophe materialised, and Bobcat provided American commanders with valuable lessons about the weaknesses in their procedures.[137] American forces repeated some of the mistakes from the Bora-Bora operation as they established bases on the islands of Efate and Tongtabu, but their planning skills improved as time went on.[138] Unfortunately for thousands of marines and sailors, the US armed forces had not fully absorbed their lessons in time for the Guadalcanal campaign.

THE TURNING POINT

The American naval victory at Midway made it possible for US forces to contemplate a true offensive in the Pacific. In the spring of 1942, the US high command was reluctant to devote resources to such an effort. The leaders of the Allied nations hoped to launch an invasion of Europe known as Operation Sledgehammer that summer, and equipment for amphibious operations was in short supply.[139] Then, in July, the Allies abandoned their plans for Sledgehammer, and General MacArthur won permission to attack the Japanese in his theatre.

MacArthur was fortunate that the Allies made this decision when they did, because the campaign in the southwest Pacific was a contest in which the side that struck first was likely to win. Port Moresby remained vulnerable to an attack from enemy troops already ashore on New Guinea, and furthermore, the Japanese had started to build airbases on the islands of Tulagi and Guadalcanal in the Solomon Islands.[140] These airstrips would have increased Japan's airpower throughout the region. In addition, they would have allowed Japanese planes to bomb US ports in New Caledonia and the Fiji Islands.[141] Therefore, it was imperative for American forces to drive their enemies out of the region before these things came to pass.

Admiral Ernest J. King of the US Navy summed up the situation as follows:

As you know, it has been my conviction that the Japanese will not stand still ... and will not let us stand still. Either they will press us with an extension of their offensive, seeking weak spots in order to break our line of communications, or we will have to be pressing them. It is urgent, in my opinion, that we lose no time in taking the initiative ourselves.[142]

Initially, MacArthur hoped to stage an immediate attack on the main Japanese port at Rabaul.[143] Rabaul, however, lay well beyond the range of Allied air bases, and American forces would have had to rely on carriers for air support.[144] Naval authorities felt that their carrier fleet would suffer unacceptable losses in such a campaign, and therefore, they compelled MacArthur to accept a more cautious strategy, in which US forces would capture island bases in the southern Solomons from which to provide air support for the final battle in the north.[145] As their first objective, the American commanders picked Tulagi, along with several smaller islets in the region.[146] They selected the First Marine Division to carry out the attack.

Although the Solomons offensive was officially called Watchtower, the officers involved in the project quickly nicknamed the affair 'Operation Shoestring'. The Guadalcanal landings involved improvisation and hasty planning in every area, particularly that of logistics. When Admiral Nimitz issued the orders for Watchtower, on 27 June, he left less than five weeks for supply officers to plan the logistics of the campaign.[147] Nimitz did not add Guadalcanal to the list of objectives until a week later, when Admiral Kelly Turner became concerned about reconnaissance reports which indicated that the Japanese were building an airfield there.

The lack of time began to cause logistical problems almost at once. When the orders for Watchtower became official, the First Marine Division was already embarked on ships bound for the southwest Pacific. Since the quartermasters had not expected the troops to go straight into battle, they had not 'combat-loaded' all of the transports.[148] Therefore, 12 of the ships had to stop at Wellington in New Zealand, where stevedores unloaded and repacked their holds.[149] The quay at Wellington could only accommodate five ships at a time, and this led to further delay.[150] In the process, the First Marine Division had to leave 75 per cent of its vehicles, a third of its rations and half of its ammunition behind.[151] The work at Wellington delayed Operation Watchtower for seven days.[152]

In the Solomons campaign, the USMC would finally put the administrative side of its amphibious doctrine into action. (The moment of truth for the tactical side of USMC planning came at Tarawa, where the marines had to wade ashore under enemy fire.) The Marines had attempted to solve the logistical problems which General Smith identified in the landing exercises of 1940, but their measures remained makeshift and incomplete. For transportation across the Pacific Ocean, the USMC relied largely upon chartered civilian vessels, and would continue to do so until late 1943.[153] These ships, of course, could not approach the shore. Therefore, commanders had to transfer their forces from the transports to smaller landing craft, and this process proved difficult, dangerous and time-consuming. One Marine described the process as follows:

> In those days you went down a sort of landing net, a webbing made out of stout rope which they would otherwise use to load cargo. They put these nets over the side and we'd use them as a rope ladder to go down into the Higgins boats. Even with a fairly medium-sized sea the Higgins boats would go up and down, and to try to get down that swaying cargo net with about eighty pounds of equipment on your back without killing yourself or getting jammed between the Higgins boat and the ship was quite a stunt.[154]

The Higgins boats themselves remained in dangerously short supply. Marine commanders managed to acquire 475 landing craft for the Solomons invasion, a number which proved sufficient, but barely.[155] This shortage inhibited training and meant that the sinking of even a few boats would have represented a serious loss for the force.[156] If the Marines had encountered defended beaches on Guadalcanal, the deficiencies in their landing equipment would have resulted in heavier casualties and put the entire operation at risk.

On 7 August, troops of the First Marine Division began the invasion of the Solomons. There was fierce fighting on several of the smaller islands, but the Marines met little opposition on the beaches of Guadalcanal. Within a day, they had captured the partially-completed airfield, along with food, construction equipment and the 'Tokyo Ice Factory' – a refrigeration plant which turned out to contain hundreds of cases of beer.[157] The assault was a success, and USMC amphibious doctrine had proved to be tactically sound. However, less than 48 hours had passed before the Japanese counterattacked by land, air and sea. During the months which followed, the Marines paid a high price for the problems of administration and transportation which still plagued the US Armed Forces.

Japanese air attacks disrupted the Marines as they attempted to get their supplies ashore. The fact that the Navy had only agreed to provide air cover from its carriers for two days made it crucial for the Marines to unload as much as possible before the bombing grew even worse.[158] Despite the importance of this project, marines often proved unco-operative, and although the operational orders for the invasion authorised logistical officers to demand assistance from unoccupied troops, of which there were many in the area, no one actually took advantage of this opportunity.[159] One marine describes the scene on the beaches as follows:

> Untrained coxswains brought rations to beaches marked for fuel, or medical supplies were mixed in with ammunition. Sailors could not

help, because, as they rightfully maintained, it was their job to bring material ashore and the Marines' to get it off the beach. Many marines not committed to action might have helped, but they merely watched their comrades of the shore parties melting under the strain. 'Hell, Mac, we're combat troops,' they sniffed. 'You unload the goddam stuff.'[160]

In fairness to the combat troops and their commanders, one should note that the fighting Marines were preparing to repulse a Japanese counterattack which could have come at any time.

Sailors delivered materiel to the shore faster than the ground troops could unload it, and by evening, there were 100 boats on the beach along with 50 in the water, all waiting to be processed.[161] Stacks of crated supplies littered the beaches, and General Alexander Vandegrift, commander of the Marines on Guadalanal, noted that if Japanese bomber pilots had managed to set these towers on fire, 'the consequences might well have been incalculable and ruinous'.[162] Due to congestion, the shore parties repeatedly had to halt the movement of supplies from the ships to the shore in order to reorganise the crates on the beaches. During the two days they had available, the Marines only managed to devote about 24 hours to unloading the logistics vessels.[163]

The attempt to move supplies onto the Guadalcanal beachhead proved the importance of specialised amphibious transportation equipment. Marine shore parties could have worked much more efficiently if more of their boats had been fitted with ramps. Instead, they often had to manhandle supplies crate by crate over the gunwales of obsolete craft.[164] Amphibian tractors, on the other hand, proved invaluable in the logistical effort. Although there were fewer than 100 of these vehicles on the island, Vandegrift's operations officer noted 'they saved our life, there is no doubt about that'.[165]

Admiral Richmond Kelly Turner diagnosed the cause of the Guadalcanal unloading problems as follows, 'There were two primary reasons for the failure to completely unload. First the vast amount of unnecessary impedimenta taken and second a failure on the part of the 1st Division to provide adequate and well-organised unloading details at the beach.'[166] Peacetime exercises had repeatedly demonstrated the need for larger shore parties and more efficient systems of unloading ships, but nobody had heeded these warnings.[167] The fact that Marine commanders had chosen a cautious landing plan and seized only a relatively small beachhead added to the congestion.[168]

Meanwhile, in the early morning hours of 9 August, a Japanese naval detachment under Admiral Gunichi Mikawa attacked the US naval task force which was supporting the Guadalcanal operation and devastated it. Several Japanese officers urged Mikawa to destroy the undefended American transport ships and shell the Guadalcanal beachheads as well. The admiral, however, was afraid that American carrier aircraft would arrive with the dawn, and he decided to withdraw his ships from the area.[169] This was a stroke of pure good fortune for the Marines, because unbeknown to Mikawa, the US carriers had already withdrawn.[170] Nearly all the supplies available to the Marines were either stacked on the beach or still in the holds of the ships. If Mikawa had listened to his subordinates and attacked the beaches, there would have been nothing to stop him from destroying everything the division possessed.[171] The surviving Marines would have had neither food nor ammunition, and the Japanese troops on Guadalcanal would have made short work of them.

Mikawa had missed his opportunity, but Admiral Turner decided that he could not risk keeping undefended transport ships in the area any longer.[172] Despite a Japanese air attack, Allied seamen worked throughout the morning of 9 August to get as much of their cargo onto the beachhead as possible.[173] It was, however, too late to unload the ships completely. That afternoon, the logistics ships sailed away to safety. Although the Marines had managed to unload about 90 per cent of the materiel in the combat transports which actually carried them to the beaches, the other support vessels departed with over 75 per cent of their cargo still in their holds.[174] The invasion troops found themselves stranded on Guadalcanal with roughly half of their food supplies, and almost none of their artillery, radios, radar gear, heavy weapons or heavy equipment.[175]

Although the Marines had to expect attacks by Japanese ground troops at any time, they had almost no materiel with which to fortify their positions. The withdrawal of the transport fleet left them without a single land mine, and both entrenching tools and barbed wire were in short supply.[176] For the Marines to receive reliable air support, they needed to complete the half-finished airstrip, but the only construction equipment they had was a bulldozer which they had captured from the Japanese.[177] Without captured food, the Marines would soon have starved; with it, they were able eat two small meals per day.[178] As for ammunition, the Americans on Guadalcanal only had enough for about four days of heavy fighting.[179]

The Marines had gained the upper hand when they landed, but they had lost it again when they failed to get their supplies onto the beaches in time. It took six months for American forces to complete the conquest of Guadalcanal. Throughout this period, especially during the early weeks, the dearth of supplies provided as big a problem for the Marines as did the enemy.[180] Historians have commonly summarised this campaign as a race between the Japanese and American naval forces to get men and materiel onto the island.[181] To paraphrase one naval officer of a later generation, the heart of the Guadalcanal campaign was logistics.[182]

Almost a week passed before a group of fast American destroyers managed to slip past the Japanese blockade and deliver the first shipment of further supplies to Guadalcanal.[183] Over a month passed before the Marines had accumulated enough food to resume a normal diet.[184] Japanese ships and aircraft made every possible effort to interrupt US convoys to the island. These air and sea battles took a decisive turn in America's favour after 20 August, when the Marines managed to deploy combat aircraft on the Guadalcanal airfield.

Vandegrift describes the arrival of the planes as the 'major turning point' in the operation.[185] After that point, US forces generally found it possible to move men and equipment by water during daylight hours.[186] Nevertheless, the Americans were unable to establish a regular system of resupply for units on Guadalcanal until November.[187] Despite the fierce battles which raged around Guadalcanal, the Japanese were by no means the only factor which interfered with US efforts to keep the Marines supplied.

The fundamental problem with US logistics at Guadalcanal becomes clear in the following passage by Admiral George Dyer, a member of Admiral King's staff:

> There was no real planning ... about what would happen one week, three weeks or six weeks after the troops had landed. After the marines had gone ashore at Guadalcanal, no one at the highest level had figured out where the next thirty days' rations or the next thirty days' supply of ammunition, or anything was going to come from, or how to get it there way across the Pacific.[188]

In order to ship goods to the Far East, US forces depended on their chain of island way stations, and these installations were not equipped to support an operation as large as the Guadalcanal campaign. Throughout the Pacific Ocean, there was a shortage of fresh water.[189] There was also a shortage of men to fuel ships and handle cargo.[190] Army commanders who saw their duty in terms of protecting the islands from Japanese attacks had requested combat soldiers for their garrisons, but most of them had failed to man their bases with enough trained service troops.[191]

Espiritu Santo and Efate, the bases closest to Guadalcanal, were nothing more than protected anchorages, without fuel or docks.[192] Noumea, the main support installation for the Guadalcanal operation, had only a few berths for ships available, and military commanders had to share them with the French Nickel Company.[193] (Army authorities feared that, without the Nickel Company, the island's economy would permanently collapse.) Inevitably, this port suffered from extreme congestion, and the inability of the Army and the Navy to co-ordinate their efforts made the problem intractable.[194] At various points during the Guadalcanal Campaign, there were between 86 and 91 cargo vessels floating idly in Noumea Harbor.[195] This inefficient use of ships interfered with the flow of supplies to units everywhere in the Pacific. As Noumea became unable to receive new shipments, cargo vessels earmarked for the southwest Pacific but unable to set sail began to clog harbours as far away as California.[196]

Meanwhile, at the air force base on the island of Santo, fliers discovered that they had no dock facilities with which to unload drums of aviation fuel from transport ships.[197] Troops there had to push fuel drums over the sides of ships, haul them to shore with cables, and roll them to the airfields by hand.[198] When one considers the fact that each B-17 needed 50 drums of fuel per mission, the scale of this effort becomes clear.[199] The colonel in command of the installation and his air crews hauled drums for 20 hours during a fierce thunderstorm in order to fuel aircraft during a critical period of the Solomons campaign.[200] Air power was critical to the battle for Guadalcanal, and situations like this undoubtedly reduced both the availability of planes and the performance of air crews.[201]

Nevertheless, despite all the small things which US forces got wrong, this was a campaign in which the Americans got the big things right. If the Japanese had taken full advantage of the American mistakes, the US forces would have suffered a catastrophe at Guadalcanal. This disaster, however, did not come to pass, and therefore, one may count the Solomons campaign as a strategic victory for the United States. The official historian of the US Army refers to the Guadalcanal Campaign as the 'turning point' in the war against Japan, and notes that from December 1942 onward, Allied planners were able to plan their operations in the Pacific entirely in terms of offensive action.[202] In those terms, Guadalcanal was an American triumph, and it is appropriate to note that if the US forces had not planned for long-range logistics in a Pacific War, developed a system of amphibious warfare, won the battle of the Coral Sea, followed up with a decisive victory at Midway and established a string of island bases from California to Australia, Vandegrift's troops would never have reached the Solomon Islands in the first place.

MAKING IT WORK

The lessons of 1942 concerned the importance of planning, co-ordination and routine. Poor preparation and poor logistical teamwork had caused US forces to run unacceptable risks at Bora-Bora and Guadalcanal. Furthermore, if American commanders wished to achieve either initiative or strategic agility in their reconquest of the Pacific, they could not afford another Operation Shoestring. In the early 1940s, the process of producing and distributing the variety of goods required in a major military operation required from 18 months to two years.[203] The pace of events in the theatre of operations, of course, was considerably faster.

The official historians of the US Army noted that, if the Allied high command had been forced to organise all its campaigns in the same spur-of-the-moment fashion which characterised early operations in the Pacific, the invasion of North Africa, which actually began in November 1942, could not have taken place until some time in 1944.[204] 'Lead time, in other words, was far longer than planning time.'[205] One does not need to perform a detailed historical study to note that a world in which the Allied armies moved this sluggishly would have been one in which the *Wehrmacht* made them pay very dearly indeed.

The Army historians went on to note an important principle of logistics: 'The process of fashioning, mobilizing and distributing the tools of warfare had to begin ... long before the specific purposes for which the tools were to be used could be known.'[206] Therefore, even as the Marines fought on Guadalcanal, the Navy took steps to improve its support procedures. In September 1942, naval authorities hired the management engineering firm of Booz, Allen and Hamilton to study the logistical apparatus of the US Navy.[207] This firm was supposed to issue its final recommendations on 15 March 1943, but due to the urgency of the problem, naval officers requested interim reports in November and December.[208] As a civilian agency, Booz, Allen and Hamilton was able to approach the problem of logistics on a purely functional basis, unencumbered by traditional notions of naval organisation. The Booz report concluded, in part:

> (1) ... Logistic situations and possibilities have not been fully or properly represented to F1 (The Cominch) Planning Section in their strategic planning and in their makeup of operational plans. (2) Under these circumstances there has been no real integration and co-ordination of logistic plans with strategic plans. In such a situation, strategic plans may be made that are not logistically feasible, or it may take so long to determine logistic feasibility that the value of strategic planning is seriously impaired.[209]

Furthermore, the Booz report found that, due to conflicting responsibilities within the naval logistics bureaucracy, it was difficult for higher-level departments to make general long-range plans.[210] This meant that lower-level departments, in turn, had to plan operations on an ad hoc and unco-ordinated basis.[211] In order to solve these problems, Booz, Allen and Hamilton recommended the reorganisation of the Navy's administrative services. Their plan called for an independent logistics bureau, which nevertheless had close communications with combat commanders.[212]

As the war continued, numerous other administrative reforms followed the Booz report. In April 1943, for instance, Admirals Nimitz and Halsey instituted Joint Logistical Boards, in which Army and Navy officers shared authority over planning.[213] In May, the Navy strengthened its central Office of Naval Operations in accordance with the principle stated by Admiral O.C. Badger, who said 'Decentralized effort is effective only when the various agencies are provided with guidance sufficient to promote intelligent use of initiative.'[214] A year later, in April 1944, Admiral E.J. King established a Logistics

Organisation and Planning Unit (LOPU) to conduct continual analysis of logistic procedures.[215]

Unlike warriors, administrative reformers seldom enjoy the satisfaction of a final victory. The US Armed Services continued to study and improve their logistical services until the end of the war and beyond. Throughout this process of review and reorganisation, a number of recurrent themes emerged.[216] There was, for instance, a chronic tension between the importance accorded to central planning and the requirements of low-level organisations, which needed the flexibility to address unforeseen events. The different branches of the armed forces never completely solved their problems of inter-service rivalry and poor communication. For those interested in logistics and strategy, however, the theme which emerges most clearly is the one which the historian Duncan S. Ballantine summed up as follows: 'Logistic plans should be the link, in short, between the definition of strategic aims and intentions and the execution of plans for the procurement, assembly and delivery of material.'[217] This was the ultimate goal of all the reforms, from the Booz report onward.

MATERIAL IMPROVEMENTS

In addition to improving their administrative procedures, the commanders of the US armed forces made a number of material improvements to the logistical services. By 1943, American docks had begun to produce ships in staggering quantities, and the support forces received their share of the new vessels. The number of logistical ships available for action in the Central Pacific, for instance, increased almost five-fold, from 77 to 358.[218] This made it possible for the Navy to support major fleet actions and amphibious assaults by water, without the need for nearby bases, and without the risky improvisations of the Coral Sea and Guadalcanal. Admiral Nimitz launched the first major offensive to be supported entirely by the fleet train in November 1943, when he used a detachment of logistics ships known as Service Squadron Four to support Operation Galvanic, the invasion of the Gilbert Islands.

The technology of amphibious transportation improved dramatically after Guadalcanal. By the end of 1942, the production of landing craft and amphibious tractors had increased by a factor of twenty.[219] Furthermore, British designers had invented several entirely new types of amphibious vehicle.[220] Key examples included the infantry landing craft (LCI), which had space for almost 200 men and over 30 tons of cargo, the tank landing ship (LST), which could disembark vehicles directly onto the shore and the dock landing ship (LSD), which could provide ready-made dock unloading facilities for other boats.[221] An LST could also carry secondary landing craft, known as tank landing craft (LCT), medium landing craft (LSM) and vehicle and personnel landing craft (LCVP).[222]

There were problems with these vessels. The smaller landing craft were not entirely seaworthy, and all of these vessels were vulnerable to aircraft. Indeed, some crewmembers joked that the initials LST stood for 'large, stationary target'.[223] Sailors solved the first problem by lashing the little landing craft to the larger LCIs and LSTs for voyages across the Pacific.[224] The Navy also modified these craft to carry anti-aircraft guns, along with batteries of 4.5-inch rockets for use against beach emplacements.[225]

All of these vessels were larger than the boats which Marines had previously used for landings. When the sea was calm and the water off the beach was deep enough, the new ships could deliver troops, vehicles and supplies directly to a hostile shore, eliminating the difficult and time-consuming step of transferring men and equipment into small boats.[226] These new landing vessels found immediate service as Marines and Army forces continued to work their way up the Solomon Island chain, toward the Japanese port at Rabaul. When beach conditions permitted their use, they greatly simplified the problem of getting supplies to shore.

ON THE BEACH

The officers who planned Operation Galvanic had attempted to learn from Guadalcanal. No one could escape the conclusion that the Navy had committed a gross error when it withdrew its carriers before the Marines could finish unpacking their ships. In Galvanic, naval commanders committed themselves to providing more protection for the transport fleet, and shore parties were acutely aware of the need to get the ships unloaded before their enemies could intervene.[227] Nevertheless, US forces suffered one more fiasco before they perfected their techniques for getting supplies ashore on a hostile beach. On 20 November, 1943, when US Marines attacked the island of Betio in the Tarawa atoll, they found that their procedures still did not provide troops with the equipment they needed fast enough.

At Tarawa, US commanders gambled that the morning tide would be high enough for their amphibious vessels to pass over the reefs which lay just beneath the waves off the beaches. The gamble failed, and landing ships had to discharge both their troops and their cargo in chest-deep water half a mile from shore.[228] Japanese fire remained light early in the day, but as the third wave of Marines came ashore, the island's garrison began to defend itself in earnest, and the landing became a bloodbath. Although the transport commander had exhorted his men to keep supplies moving ashore, the boat crews could do nothing but circle in the lagoon and wait for the tide to rise.[229] There was a pier on the beach, and a few support craft managed to unload there, but shore parties had to pass the supplies from the ships to the pier to the combat troops by hand.[230]

One cannot blame the logisticians for the tide. Indeed, given the circumstances, they did an admirable job of getting cargo ashore. However, the support troops failed to anticipate the needs of combat soldiers on a contested beachhead. The Marines required water, ammunition, artillery pieces, medical supplies, and, on the first day, very little else. Although the principles of combat loading were well known in theory, these vital supplies were not always the first things to reach the beach.[231] Furthermore, Marines on the shore had no effective way to communicate with the shore parties, and therefore, they had no way of requesting the goods they really needed.[232]

'Without the amphibian tractor,' General Holland Smith stated, 'it is believed that the landing at Tarawa would have failed.'[233] These vehicles were able to cross the coral reefs, and therefore they were invaluable for both combat landings and logistics. The Marines went to Beito with 125 amphibians, but needed far more.[234] As the fighting grew fierce and combat units needed to land reinforcement troops, supply operations simply had to wait.[235]

After Tarawa, as Marines and US Army commanders planned the invasion of the Marshall Islands, they subjected their logistical procedures to yet another round of reform. Admiral R. Kelly Turner made a personal inquiry into supply operations and assigned officers from his staff to organise the shore parties.[236] Among other things, Turner insured that sailors and shore parties would have a chance to train together and on the same ships they would use in combat.[237] This training proved quite valuable. Marine logisticians and sailors had a great deal of difficulty working together during rehearsal exercises off San Clemente Island, but they had managed to solve their problems almost completely by the invasion itself.[238]

US forces adopted more technical reforms as well. Logisticians drew on the experience of past invasions to develop a palletised system of processing ammunition, which led to quicker handling.[239] The Marines more than doubled their allotment of amphibious tractors to 325 per division.[240] Army units contributed 100 amphibious vehicles of their own model, the DUKW.[241] The DUKWs proved able to carry artillery pieces directly to shore, thus solving one of the major problems of Tarawa.[242] Army logisticians also introduced a more radical system of combat loading known as 'hot cargo'.[243] This procedure called for the invasion fleet to arrive at the Marshalls with 40 DUKWs already loaded with water and ammunition.[244]

Thanks to these measures, among other factors, the invasion of the Marshalls became what one historian called 'the perfect assault'.[245] The quartermasters managed to unload supplies for over two divisions without unexpected delays.[246] There was a shortage of storage space on the beach, but logisticians managed to solve this problem by commandeering an LST as a floating warehouse.[247] Shore parties also stored thousands of barrels of fuel by corralling them in cargo nets just offshore.[248] Within 12 days, the support ships were completely unloaded and ready for another operation: the final assault on Rabaul.[249]

MILITARY LOGISTICS AND STRATEGIC PERFORMANCE

POURING IT ON

From 1943 onward, US forces in the Pacific began to launch progressively larger offensives, at progressively greater distances from their bases. Nevertheless, supplies flowed ever more smoothly toward the front. American logistics were sound, and the reforms of 1942–43 had largely succeeded. A few examples serve to make this point:

- Enormous operations thousands of miles from ports had become routine. The Marshals campaign, for instance, took place over 2,500 miles from its base at Hawaii, and many of its ships had come all the way from San Diego.[250] This operation involved twelve carriers, eight battleships and over 355 other vessels, in addition to 1,175 aircraft.[251] The invasion force's amphibious landing ships, which were useful in so many ways, turned out to have enough excess oil capacity to refuel all of the fleet's minesweepers, minelayers, submarine chasers and other small vessels during the voyage to the Marshals.[252] Therefore, the Navy did not have to assign oilers or destroyers to support the minor ships.
- In June 1944, in the invasion of Biak Island, the US Army managed to get tanks, artillery pieces, 12,000 troops and over 3,000 tons of supplies ashore in a single day.[253] This was fortunate for the Americans, since the Japanese turned out to have about 12,000 troops of their own on the island, as opposed to the 2,000 which US intelligence officers had expected.[254]
- In late spring of 1944, the US Navy sent a fleet of 634 ships to attack the Marianas.[255] This operation included 25 carriers, 14 battleships, 2,000 aircraft and 300,000 men.[256] The Navy supplied this entire operation from mobile service squadrons, often using recently captured islands as meeting-points and sheltered anchorages.[257] Due to heavy fighting, both ships and ground troops exhausted their ammunition reserves much faster than expected.[258] Nevertheless, the support services managed to ship bombs and shells as quickly as they were required. Both American and Japanese observers praised the naval logisticians and noted the great firepower which US forces brought to bear.[259] Admiral R.L. Conolly, in his final report on the campaign, was able to report that logistical support had been 'completely satisfactory' throughout the Marianas operation.[260]
- After the Marines recaptured Guam in July of 1944, American commanders decided to build major air and naval bases there. Army and Navy personnel completed this project in good time and without serious interruption.[261] One might compare this incident to Operation Bobcat, in which US forces experienced great difficulty in building a considerably smaller facility. American procedures had improved, and tasks of this nature had become routine.
- American naval forces fully realised the concept of 'mobile basing'. The

Navy's fleet of logistics vessels allowed the support squadrons to repair warships and stockpile supplies in relatively undeveloped ports. Therefore, when the fighting moved into new areas, the navy's bases could move with it. The USN demonstrated this quite dramatically in autumn 1944, when Service Squadron Ten moved its main shore facilities from Eniwetok to the more recently captured island of Ulithi.[262]
- The service squadrons achieved remarkable success at returning damaged ships to action. Service Squadron Ten, for instance, was able to claim that none of the ships which reached its facilities were ever lost.[263]
- On 20 October 1944, US forces invaded the Philippines with over four divisions plus one in reserve.[264] This campaign indicates the degree to which American amphibious logistics had improved. When the troops went ashore, some of the beaches proved inaccessible to LSTs.[265] Since the shore parties could not ferry supplies inland without the trucks loaded on those vessels, this disrupted the original logistics plan. Nevertheless, the quartermasters landed as many trucks as they could, constructed pontoon bridges to unload the rest, and did an admirable job despite the unexpected problem. US logisticians had become proficient enough to deal with adversity. Despite the inaccessible beaches, shore parties got 107,450 tons of supplies ashore on 20 October alone.[266] The quartermasters of the 7th Infantry Division deserve special commendation. Not only did they manage to get all their materiel ashore, but they had their supply dumps established and fully functional by the end of the day.[267]
- The fleet train and the development of amphibious transport ships freed the Navy from logistical requirements which might have otherwise forced the Marines to fight additional battles.[268] Since naval detachments could operate at great distances from their bases, they could bypass enemy-held islands which lay between them and their actual objectives. There were numerous cases in which the US Navy simply isolated Japanese-controlled islands and left the garrisons to starve or surrender. This policy saved untold amounts of time, materiel and human life. Indeed, the geographical logic of island combat had changed. Whereas amphibious strategists of an earlier generation had thought in terms of capturing bases for ships, the amphibious strategists of the Second World War thought largely in terms of capturing bases for aircraft. A new dimension of warfare had emerged, and a new problem of combat support had emerged along with it, but an old problem had faded away.
- Operation Iceberg, the invasion of Okinawa, involved eight divisions, five of which actually made combat landings on the first day.[269] As with the landings in the Philippines, there were setbacks, and as with the landings in the Philippines, the shore parties overcame them with efficiency and professionalism. Problems which might once have led to disaster created mere setbacks instead. The American forces which landed on Okinawa required

1,256,000 tons of supplies, but despite reefs, kamikaze attacks, bad weather and poor roads, shore parties managed to unload this materiel quickly enough to satisfy the needs of the combat forces.[270] In this invasion, the quartermasters had come prepared to overcome unforeseen problems. Within a day, they had cut channels through coral reefs, improved the roads which led away from the beaches and built pontoon causeways to facilitate unloading.[271]

To sum up, American logistical capabilities made it possible for the United States to dispatch 600-ship task forces and multi-division assault parties wherever commanders wished to deploy them. In cases where less well-equipped military organisations might have had to make difficult choices, the American commanders were able to pursue multiple options simultaneously. In 1943, to cite a classic example, Army officers, notably MacArthur, wished to press the attack against Japan through the Solomon Islands to New Guinea and the Philippines. Navy officers, led by Admiral King, wished to advance on Japan through the Gilberts and Marshals. There were sound arguments behind both plans, and due to the vast quantities of resources which American logistical services were able to make available, US forces were able to execute both of them at once.[272]

The development of US logistical procedures during the war was a process, not of radical change, but of correcting mistakes. American commanders began the war with sound ideas about logistics. The existence of doctrine for amphibious warfare and mobile base operations allowed US forces to take the offensive at a moment when the Japanese might have inflicted considerably more damage. Bora-Bora, Guadalcanal and other learning experiences alerted US forces to points at which their support system was in danger of breaking down, and the American armed services responded with adequate reforms. These improvements in US logistical procedures allowed American commanders to continue their offensive in a steady fashion, at a pace of their own choosing. Accidents continued to play a role in the war, but US forces learned to manage them. One cannot attribute the success of American operations in the Pacific to simple material superiority. A nation cannot mount campaigns of this scale unless it can produce great fleets and amphibious forces, but the fleets and forces themselves are not enough. Without sound planning, robust support services and efficient administration of resources, a nation cannot bring these other advantages to bear. That is the lesson which US forces learned in 1942, and that is the lesson which those forces applied in 1943–45.

In October 1942, when the Japanese made their great final effort to crush the American force on Guadalcanal, President Roosevelt urged the Joint Chiefs of Staff to commit all available resources to the fight. General Marshall had responded that there were already enough 'resources' in the area. The problem was 'to distribute and maintain them by transport in critical combat areas'.[273]

This was the problem which US logistical services overcame in later campaigns.

FINDINGS

To sum up the findings of this case study, let us consider the usual questions.

1. How have high-level commanders perceived the problem of logistics?
Admiral Spruance, writing about the campaigns in the Pacific, observed that 'a sound logistic plan is the foundation upon which a war operation should be based'. This sentiment is hardly unusual, but it demonstrates his awareness of the problem and shows where his priorities lay.[274] Spruance saw planning as the crucial factor, and viewed logistics as a foundation for military operations themselves.

Commanders at the highest levels saw military logistics as the factor which allowed them to bring the industrial capacity of the United States into play against Japan. They noted, in particular, that logistics involves more than merely providing large quantities of goods. General Marshall's comment to President Roosevelt regarding Guadalcanal, quoted above, expressed this point quite well. Even before the war, General Leonard T. Gerow had frequently reminded the Roosevelt administration that it would be unwise to assume that America could defeat its enemies simply by outproducing them.[275] 'Weapons must not only be produced but also brought effectively to bear against the enemy.'[276] This required transportation, support services and sound plans – 'the whole panoply of organized military power'.[277]

2. How have logistical factors helped or harmed the overall performance of armed forces?
American forces owe their early naval victories of this campaign to the carrier task forces and their oilers. These units carried out the first raids on enemy territory, forced Japanese commanders to take a defensive stance, and ultimately goaded the foe into self-destructive action. These same naval detachments overcame great distances to check the Japanese advance in the battle of the Coral Sea. Without them, the Japanese might have captured Port Moresby, American forces might have faced a more powerful opponent at Midway, and the first year of the war might have taken a very different course. As the war continued, the USN's growing fleet train allowed American strategists to deploy land and sea forces wherever they chose.

Likewise, American forces owe their relatively smooth advance through the Pacific islands to the peacetime studies of the US Marine Corps. The USMC innovations involved far more than logistics, but their logistical component was indispensable. Without, for instance, the development of the amphibious tractor, the Marines might have lost their battles on Guadalcanal and Tarawa. If American forces had had to develop their amphibious capabilities from scratch, the Pacific War would have taken far longer, and US troops would have suffered far more casualties.

The cautious doctrine of US submarine commanders and the poor performance of US torpedoes limited the early effects of undersea warfare. However, the long-range 'fleet' submarines unquestionably increased the speed with which American forces managed to inflict harm upon their foes. One should not ignore their effects. Logistics equals speed, and speed, with exceptions discussed in the next chapter, equals opportunity. Events throughout the war demonstrated these relationships. The US Navy's oilers made it possible for American forces to counterattack at sea within months of Pearl Harbor. At Bora-Bora and Guadalcanal, on the other hand, unsolved problems in the US logistical system retarded the progress of American operations. These delays presented enemy forces with chances to damage American units severely, and the fact that the Japanese failed to take advantage of these opportunities does not make the fact any less worrisome.

Overall, logistical factors enabled American commanders to take the offensive, to maintain pressure upon their opponents, and to derive the greatest possible advantage from the industrial might of the United States. In the realm of tactics, the US logistical system meant that troops in the Marianias could count on effectively unlimited support from naval gunnery. Even in campaigns such as Tarawa, where gunfire support left something to be desired, the problem was not lack of shells.[278] In the realm of strategy, the US logistical system meant that a nation which had shipyards capable of producing amphibious task forces of 600–800 ships could also get those task forces to objectives thousands of miles from their bases. Thus, logistics played its role as the 'arbiter of opportunity' throughout the war.

3. What factors have given countries logistical advantages?
Many things contributed to the logistical advantage which US forces enjoyed in the Pacific War. This study has mentioned the introduction of the fleet train, the decision to procure long-range submarines and the development of amphibious doctrine. Nevertheless, despite the diversity of these factors, one can draw three general lessons about the things which a nation must do in order to secure logistical advantages in war.

First, supplying war is a large-scale enterprise. Naval commanders talked about a mobile base in the 1920s, but it took hundreds of logistics ships to make the fleet train a reality. The Marines did not begin to solve the logistic problems associated with amphibious landings until they increased the number of amphibious tractors in an invasion force by more than a factor of three. In the Second World War, at any rate, there was no way to do logistics on the cheap. Some believe that information technology may change this principle, but the prudent have every reason to be wary of this claim. (For more on this issue, see Chapter 6.)

Second, different branches of the services must co-operate with one another, and all must work together to protect logistical operations. Numerous historians have criticised Admiral Frank Turner's decision to withdraw the aircraft carriers which had been protecting the Marines while they unloaded supplies at Guadalcanal.[279] In hindsight, one can find few tactical reasons to justify his action. Future strategists would be well advised to make sure that they do not put amphibious forces in a similar situation.

Third, as British squaddies would have it, planning and preparation prevents piss-poor performance. Supply operations in the Pacific invariably ran more smoothly when the logisticians had time to develop detailed plans and rehearse them under realistic conditions. The absence of preparation was a great handicap to the Marines at Guadalcanal. Likewise, planning and preparation that US forces devoted to their campaigns in the Gilberts and the Marshalls seem to have prevented similar mishaps there. These statements may seem obvious, but they directly contradict the findings of Van Creveld, and therefore, it is worth considering them in some detail.

One can summarise Van Creveld's argument as follows. In *Supplying War*, Van Creveld found that successful commanders have tended to treat logistics as an afterthought, even in such massive campaigns as the Germans' Barbarossa invasion of the Soviet Union.[280] Furthermore, on occasions when commanders did devote great efforts to logistical planning, their efforts appeared to be futile. Van Creveld cited the Allied invasion of Normandy as evidence of the latter point.[281]

The Pacific War is, at the very least, an exception to Van Creveld's rule. Furthermore, when one studies the American campaigns against Japan, one begins to see limits to the tenets of *Supplying War*. The type of campaigns Van Creveld selected for his book and the fashion in which he chose to analyse them had a great influence upon his discoveries. There are two key differences between the case studies in *Supplying War* and the island battles of the Pacific War.

First, as John Lynn and others have noted, Van Creveld's focus on land wars on the European continent made it relatively easy for him to find instances of improvisation.[282] Ships at sea and amphibious forces on jungle atolls have less room for flexibility in their logistical plans. The Marines on Guadalcanal were lucky enough to capture food and construction equipment from the Japanese, but this was a rare stroke of good fortune. On general principle, forces in the Pacific had to ship everything they needed, often including fresh water, from home ports thousands of miles away. Naval forces have dealt with this problem throughout history, and technologically advanced armies tend to face similar challenges whenever they deploy in underdeveloped parts of the world.

Van Creveld examines one instance in which commanders attempted to sustain a campaign under comparable circumstances; that of Rommel in the desert. This example, however, may be misleading, since Van Creveld himself concludes that Rommel's task was impossible.[283] Germany and its Italian ally simply did not have the wherewithal to supply the Afrika Korps by sealift. American forces, on the other hand, not only had the resources they needed, but learned to use them effectively. Therefore, for those who wish to understand the logistics of such operations, the American campaigns in the Pacific may be more instructive than those of Rommel in North Africa.

Second, when Van Creveld studies planning, he tends to emphasise the preparations which leaders make before a campaign has even begun. In the Normandy Campaign, for instance, commanders drew up their much-maligned logistical timetables well before the troops ever hit the beaches. Van Creveld's focus is understandable, and, indeed, usually quite appropriate. Preparation, by definition, is something which one does in advance. However, it is a well-known maxim of warfare that no plan survives first contact with the enemy.[284] Therefore, it seems only fair to give commanders credit for their ability to improve their planning skills after they have gained combat experience in the relevant theatre of operations.

If one studied only the Coral Sea and Guadalcanal, the Pacific Campaign would seem to bear out Van Creveld's hypothesis perfectly. Naval supply officers had simply not known how many logistics ships they would need to support the fleet. The best logistical ideas, such as Admiral Nimitz's decision to divide his fleet, were improvisations. The plans which existed often fell apart under fire. However, as the war went on, logistics planning became more effective, more detailed and more routine. Naval officers learned from the experience of transferring the fleet to Hawaii. Marine officers learned from Guadalcanal and Tarawa. After every operation, throughout the armed services, commanders put their discoveries to good use.

As US forces gained experience, the planning process became more effective. Commanders learned to take the vagaries of island warfare into account, and to prepare for all possible contingencies. This made it possible for them to undertake far larger operations with far more certainty of success. When US logistics broke down in the Solomons, the Japanese had a brief opportunity to wipe out the American division on Guadalcanal. Although American forces took sobering levels of casualties in later campaigns, they never again faced the risk of simple defeat.[285] Effective preparation allowed US commanders to cushion the blows which Clausewitz referred to as the friction in war.

4. What logistical problems are associated with particular styles of warfare, and how have commanders addressed them?
This study addresses many types of operations, each of which involved its own problems and solutions. In amphibious assaults, logistical innovations

often involved such seemingly minor details as the way in which stevedores positioned cargo within a ship. For commanders overseeing the entire war, major logistical improvements often involved organisational reform. For those who fought in unusual environments, technological developments frequently played a vital role. The LST was a great boon to amphibious troops, and the long-range submarine was a significant advantage to undersea forces.

The general lessons discussed under the third question may apply here as well. However, one must also note that there is no substitute for real knowledge of the specific situations involved. Issues which seem highly technical when considered individually fit together to make up the larger themes of the campaign. Therefore, to understand the Pacific War, or any other historical episode of similar scope, one must be intellectually agile. One must be prepared to delve deep into detail at some points and step back and consider the larger picture at others. To decide which approach to take at any given time, one must rely on one's own judgement.

This may not suit the current fashion in academic research, which calls upon the researcher to make sharp distinctions between different 'levels of analysis', but such is the nature of the subject matter.[286] Van Creveld, in his determination to perform a systematic study of logistics in well-defined types of warfare, systematically overlooked the real importance of logistics in a world where warfare continually defies our attempts at easy classification. The course of events and the statements of men with combat experience have shown that his findings are narrow. To avoid similar mistakes, one must take a more open-minded approach. One must allow the nature of the things one studies to shape one's methodology, and not the other way around.

CONCLUSION

The Japanese had hoped to take advantage of their momentary military superiority in order to put themselves in a position where the United States would find it prohibitively costly and time-consuming to defeat them. However, the combined logistical advantages of US forces allowed American commanders to counterattack early in the war. This put an early end to whatever tactical advantages the Japanese had managed to seize in their initial offensive. Then, as US industry began to produce war materiel in ever greater quantities, the logistical services of the US armed forces were able to get this equipment into battle with relatively little delay. Thus, the United States managed to defeat the Japanese strategy at every point. The link between logistical preparation and strategic initiative appears clear.

MILITARY LOGISTICS AND STRATEGIC PERFORMANCE

NOTES

1. John Lynn, *Feeding Mars: Logistics in Western Warfare from the Middle Ages to the Present* (Boulder, CO: Westview Press, 1993), p. 13.
2. Ibid., pp. 79–100, 109–136 and 217–49.
3. John Costello, *The Pacific War* (London: William Collins, 1981), p. 112.
4. Nobutaka Ike, (ed.) *Japan's Decision For War: Records of the 1941 Policy Conferences* (Stanford, CA: Stanford University Press, 1967), p. 247.
5. Ronald H. Spector, *Eagle Against the Sun: The American War With Japan* (New York: The Free Press, 1985), p. 44. At the level of military operations, there were certainly precedents for the Japanese strategy. Japan's leaders remembered the difficulties which the European navy of Imperial Russia had faced in its attempts to reach the Far Eastern theatre of operations during the Russo-Japanese War of 1904. That particular campaign had ended in the battle of Tsushima, in which the Japanese admiral Togo destroyed the Russian fleet. Although few could have expected the US Navy to perform as badly as the Tsar's fleet, the Japanese also expected to enjoy advantages they had not possessed in 1904. The island bases which they had taken from their opponents would belong to them. With the bases in their hands, Japan's leaders expected that they would be able to use their strategic depth in the Pacific to full advantage. They hoped that they would be able to spot any American fleet as soon as it reached the longitude of the Bonin Islands.

    As the US Navy proceeded westward, Japan's island holdings would allow the Japanese to bring the American fleet under air attack. Eventually, the Japanese commanders hoped to wear down the US Navy enough so that they could goad it into accepting battle on terms which favoured Japan. In the words of the 15 November proposal, 'At the appropriate time, we will endeavour by various means to lure the main fleet of the United States [near Japan] and destroy it.' (Nobutaka Ike, *Japan's Decision for War*, p. 248.)
6. Duncan S. Ballantine, *US Naval Logistics in the Second World War* (Princeton, NJ: Princeton University Press, 1949), p. 41.
7. Worrall Reed Carter, *Beans, Bullets, and Black Oil* (Washington, DC: US Government Printing Office, 1953), pp. 1–2.
8. The historian Herbert P. LePore, among others, has noted the 'pedestrian' nature of logistical innovation during the interwar period. He feels that this has led other researchers to overlook the importance of logistics in the campaigns which followed. Herbert P. LePore, 'Contribution to Victory: The Distribution and Supply of Ammunition and Ordnance in the Pacific Theatre of Operations', *Army History*, Issue No. 34 (Spring/Summer 1995), p. 31.
9. Spector, *Eagle Against the Sun*, p. 57; Ballantine, *US Naval Logistics* p. 33; For a thorough discussion of Plan Orange, see Edward S. Miller. *War Plan Orange: The US Strategy to Defeat Japan, 1897–1945* (Annapolis, MD: Naval Institute Press, 1991), passim.
10. Spector, *Eagle Against the Sun*, p. 56.
11. Spector, *Eagle Against the Sun*, p. 57; Ballantine, *US Naval Logistics*, p. 33. Note that Japan received the Carolines, Marshals and Marianas as mandates under the Treaty of Versailles in 1919. Thomas H. Buckley, *The United States and the Washington Conference: 1921–1922* (Knoxville, TN: University of Tennessee Press, 1970), p. 90.
12. Ballantine, *US Naval Logistics*, p. 34.
13. Ibid.
14. Spector, *Eagle Against the Sun*, p. 57.
15. See Carter, *Beans, Bullets and Black Oil*, p. 5.

16. Geofrey Marcus, *Quiberon Bay* (London: Hollis & Carter, 1960), p. 47.
17. Carter, *Beans, Bullets and Black Oil*, p. 1.
18. Ibid., pp. 1–2.
19. Ballantine, *US Naval Logistics*, p. 33.
20. Carter, *Beans, Bullets and Black Oil*, p. 2.
21. Ballantine, *US Naval Logistics*, p. 33.
22. Ibid.
23. Ibid., p. 35.
24. Carter, *Beans, Bullets and Black Oil*, p. 4.
25. Ibid.
26. Ibid.
27. Ibid., p. 5.
28. Ballantine, *US Naval Logistics*, p. 46.
29. Ibid., p. 36.
30. Ibid.
31. Ibid., p. 37.
32. Ibid., pp. 36–7.
33. Spruance, in Carter, *Beans, Bullets and Black Oil*, p. vii.
34. Norman Friedman, *US Submarines Through 1945: An Illustrated Design History* (Annapolis, MD: Naval Institute Press, 1995). p. 99.
35. Ibid., p. 165.
36. Ibid.
37. Ibid., p. 163.
38. Roger Chesneau (ed.) *Conway's All the World's Fighting Ships 1922–1946* (London: Conway Maritime Press, 1980), p. 141.
39. Spector, *Eagle Against the Sun*, p. 480.
40. Ibid.
41. Chesneau, *All the World's Fighting Ships*, p. 141.
42. Spector, *Eagle Against the Sun*, 483.
43. Ibid., p. 486.
44. Chesneau, *All the World's Fighting Ships*, p. 141.
45. Ibid.
46. Allan R. Millett, *Semper Fidelis: The History of the United States Marine Corps* (New York: The Free Press, 1991), p. 320.
47. Ibid.
48. Ibid., p. 321.
49. Ibid., pp. 321–2.
50. Millett, *Semper Fidelis*, p. 72.
51. Ibid., pp. 325–6.
52. Jeter A. Isely and Philip A. Crowl, *The US Marines and Amphibious War: Its Theory, and its Practice in the Pacific* (Princeton, NJ: Princeton University Press, 1951), pp. 68–9.
53. Ibid., p. 16.
54. Victor H. Krulak, *First to Fight: An Inside View of the US Marine Corps* (New York: Simon & Schuster, 1991), p. 95.
55. Isely and Crowl, *The US Marines and Amphibious War*, p. 43.
56. Ibid.
57. Ibid.
58. Ibid., p. 44.
59. John A. Lorelli, *To Foreign Shores: US Amphibious Operations in World War II* (Annapolis, MD: Naval Institute Press, 1995), p. 46.

60. Alfred Vagts, *Landing Operations: Strategy, Psychology, Tactics, Politics from Antiquity to 1945* (Harrisburg, PA: Military Service Publishing Company, 1952). p. 42.
61. Ibid.
62. Ibid.
63. Isely and Crowl, *The US Marines and Amphibious War*, p. 44.
64. Ibid.
65. Ibid.
66. Krulak, *First to Fight*, p. 96.
67. Ibid., p. 97.
68. Ibid., p. 98.
69. Ibid.
70. Ibid.
71. Ibid., p. 97.
72. Ibid.
73. Richard M. Leighton and Robert W. Coakley, *Global Logistics and Strategy 1940–1943* (Washington, DC: US Government Printing Office, 1955), pp. 682–3.
74. See, for instance, Terry C. Pierce, 'Voodoo Logistics Sink Triphibious Warfare,' *Proceedings of the US Naval Institute*, Vol. 122, No. 9 (September 1996), pp. 74–7.
75. Mark S. Watson, *Chief of Staff Prewar Plans and Preparations* (Washington, DC: US Government Printing Office, 1950), p. 97.
76. Ibid.
77. Ibid., pp. 97–8.
78. Ibid., p. 100.
79. Ibid.
80. Ibid., p. 101.
81. Ballantine, *US Naval Logistics*, p. 39.
82. Ibid., p. 96.
83. Carter, *Beans, Bullets and Black Oil*, p. 4.
84. Ballantine, *US Naval Logistics*, p. 96.
85. Carter, *Beans Bullets and Black Oil*, pp. 3–4.
86. Ibid., pp. 5–9.
87. Ballantine, *US Naval Logistics*, pp. 38–42.
88. Carter, *Beans, Bullets and Black Oil*, pp. 5–6.
89. Spector, *Eagle Against the Sun*, p. 148; Carter, *Beans, Bullets and Black Oil*, p. 11.
90. Spector, *Eagle Against the Sun*, p. 148.
91. Ibid., pp. 147–8.
92. Ibid., p. 148.
93. Ibid., p. 149.
94. Ibid.
95. Carter, *Beans, Bullets and Black Oil*, p. 17.
96. Ibid.
97. Ibid.
98. Ibid., pp. 17–18.
99. Ibid., pp. 19–20.
100. See Spector, *Eagle Against the Sun*, pp. 149–50.
101. Costello, *The Pacific War*, p. 245.
102. Spector, *Eagle Against the Sun*, p. 150.
103. Costello, *The Pacific War*, p. 245.
104. Ibid.
105. Ibid.
106. Ibid.

107. Ibid.
108. Ibid., p. 248.
109. Ibid., pp. 248–9.
110. Spector, *Eagle Against the Sun*, p. 158.
111. Ibid., pp. 158–9.
112. Ibid., p. 166
113. Carter, *Beans, Bullets and Black Oil*, p. 21.
114. Spector, *Eagle Against the Sun*, p. 158.
115. Ibid., p. 21.
116. Ibid., p. 11.
117. Ibid., p. 22.
118. Leighton and Coakley, *Global Logistics and Strategy 1940–1943*, p. 176.
119. Ibid.; Spector, *Eagle Against the Sun*, p. 185.
120. Leighton and Coakley, *Global Logistics and Strategy 1940–1943*, p. 179.
121. Ibid., p. 180.
122. Ibid.
123. Ibid.
124. Ibid., p. 181.
125. Ibid., p. 182.
126. Ibid.
127. Ballantine, *US Naval Logistics*, p. 68.
128. Ibid., p. 69.
129. Leighton and Coakley, *Global Logistics and Strategy 1940–1943*, p. 183.
130. Ibid., p. 184.
131. Ibid.
132. Ibid.
133. Ibid.
134. Ibid.
135. Ibid.
136. Ibid., p. 180; Ballantine, *US Naval Logistics*, p. 71.
137. Ballantine, *US Naval Logistics*, p. 71.
138. Ibid.; Leighton and Coakley, *Global Logistics and Strategy 1940–1943*, p. 185.
139. Ibid., p. 388.
140. Ibid.
141. Ibid.
142. Lorelli, *To Foreign Shores*, p. 38.
143. Spector, *Eagle Against the Sun*, p. 191.
144. Ibid.
145. Isely and Crowl, *The US Marines and Amphibious War*, p. 94.
146. Ibid., p. 119.
147. Lorelli, *To Foreign Shores*, p. 43.
148. Ibid., p. 45.
149. Ibid.
150. Ibid.
151. Ibid., pp. 45–6.
152. Ibid.
153. Ibid., p. 40.
154. Ibid., p. 48.
155. Ibid., p. 47.
156. Ibid.
157. Costello, *The Pacific War*, p. 323.

158. Lorelli, *To Foreign Shores*, p. 51.
159. Ibid.
160. Ibid., p. 52.
161. Ibid.
162. Isely and Crowl, *The US Marines and Amphibious War*, p. 131.
163. Ibid., p. 128.
164. Ibid., p. 127.
165. Ibid.
166. Lorelli, *To Foreign Shores*, p. 52.
167. Isely and Crowl, *The US Marines and Amphibious War*, p. 127.
168. Ibid.
169. Lorelli, *To Foreign Shores*, p. 54.
170. Isely and Crowl, *The US Marines and Amphibious War*, p. 126.
171. Lorelli, *To Foreign Shores*, p. 54.
172. Isely and Crowl, *The US Marines and Amphibious War*, p. 130.
173. Costello, *The Pacific War*, p. 326.
174. Isely and Crowl, *The US Marines and Amphibious War*, p. 128.
175. Costello, *The Pacific War*, p. 326.
176. Ibid.
177. Ibid.
178. Isely and Crowl, *The US Marines and Amphibious War*, p. 133.
179. Spector, *Eagle Against the Sun*, p. 195.
180. Pierce, *Voodoo Logistics*, p. 75.
181. Spector, *Eagle Against the Sun*, p. 197; Isely and Crowl, *The US Marines and Amphibious War*, p. 135; Pierce, *Voodoo Logistics*, p. 75.
182. Pierce, *Voodoo Logistics*, p. 75.
183. Isely and Crowl, *The US Marines and Amphibious War*, p. 133.
184. Spector, *Eagle Against the Sun*, p. 195.
185. Isely and Crowl, *The US Marines and Amphibious War*, p. 136.
186. Ibid., p. 135.
187. Ibid., p. 133.
188. Lorelli, *To Foreign Shores*, p. 55.
189. Pierce, *Voodoo Logistics*, p. 75.
190. Leighton and Coakley, *Global Logistics and Strategy 1940–1943*, p. 398.
191. Ibid.
192. Ibid.
193. Ibid., p. 399.
194. Pierce, *Voodoo Logistics*, p. 75.
195. Leighton and Coakley, *Global Logistics and Strategy 1940–1943*, p. 399.
196. Pierce, *Voodoo Logistics*, p. 75.
197. Ibid.
198. Ibid.
199. Ibid.
200. Ibid.
201. Isely and Crowl, *The US Marines and Amphibious Warfare*, p. 135.
202. Leighton and Coakley, *Global Logistics and Strategy 1940–1943*, p. 416.
203. Ibid., p. 711.
204. Ibid.
205. Ibid.
206. Ibid.
207. Ballantine, *US Naval Logistics*, p. 106.

208. Ibid., pp. 106–7.
209. Ibid., p. 107.
210. Ibid., pp. 107–8.
211. Ibid., p. 108.
212. Ibid.
213. Ibid., p. 154.
214. Ibid., p. 136.
215. Ibid., p. 184.
216. Ibid., *passim*.
217. Ibid., p. 108.
218. Ibid., p. 134.
219. Leighton and Coakley, *Global Logistics and Strategy 1940–1943*, p. 683.
220. Spector, *Eagle against the Sun*, p. 230.
221. Isely and Crowl, *The US Marines and Amphibious War*, p. 173.
222. Ibid., pp. 173–4.
223. Spector, *Eagle Against the Sun*, p. 230.
224. Isely and Crowl, *The US Marines and Amphibious War*, p. 173.
225. Ibid.
226. Ibid.
227. Lorelli, *To Foreign Shores*, p. 174.
228. Costello, *The Pacific War*, p. 435.
229. Lorelli, *To Foreign Shores*, p. 174.
230. Ibid.
231. Ibid.
232. Ibid.
233. Isely and Crowl, *The US Marines and Amphibious War*, p. 210.
234. Ibid., p. 208.
235. Lorelli, *To Foreign Shores*, p. 174.
236. Ibid., p. 197.
237. Ibid.
238. Ibid., p. 198.
239. Ibid., p. 197.
240. Ibid.
241. Ibid.
242. Ibid., p. 198.
243. Ibid., p. 202.
244. Ibid.
245. Ibid., p. 193.
246. Isely and Crowl, *The US Marines and Amphibious War*, p. 254; Lorelli, *To Foreign Shores*, p. 202.
247. Lorelli, *To Foreign Shores*, p. 202.
248. Ibid.
249. Ibid.
250. Carter, *Beans, Bullets and Black Oil*, p. 115.
251. Costello, *The Pacific War*, p. 450.
252. Carter, *Beans, Bullets and Black Oil*, p. 115.
253. Lorelli, *To Foreign Shores*, p. 212.
254. Ibid., p. 212.
255. Carter, *Beans, Bullets and Black Oil*, p. 137.
256. Ibid.
257. Ibid., pp. 138–41.

258. Ibid., pp. 151–8.
259. Ibid., pp. 154, 157.
260. Ibid., p. 162.
261. Ballantine, *US Naval Logistics*, p. 71; Carter, *Beans, Bullets and Black Oil*, p. 303.
262. Carter, *Beans, Bullets and Black Oil*, pp. 217–31.
263. Ibid., p. 294.
264. Lorelli, *To Foreign Shores*, p. 271.
265. Ibid., p. 273.
266. Ibid.
267. Ibid.
268. Isley and Crowl, *The US Marines and Amphibious War*, p. 174.
269. Lorelli, *To Foreign Shores*, p. 295.
270. Ibid., p. 301.
271. Ibid.
272. Leighton and Coakley, *Global Logistics and Strategy 1940–1943*, p. 415.
273. Ibid., p. 395.
274. Carter, *Beans, Bullets and Black Oil*, p. vii.
275. Leighton and Coakley, *Global Logistics and Strategy 1940–1943*, p. 127.
276. Ibid.
277. Ibid.
278. For an excellent account of the Tarawa landings, see Isely and Crowl, *The US Marines and Amphibious Warfare*, pp. 192–252.
279. Ibid., pp. 128–9.
280. Martin Van Creveld, *Supplying War* (Cambridge: Cambridge University Press, 1977), p. 236.
281. Ibid.
282. Lynn, *Feeding Mars*, p. 13.
283. Van Creveld, *Supplying War*, p. 201.
284. Attributed to Moltke the Elder. A precise translation of Moltke's words would be '[n]o plan of operations can look with any certainty beyond the first meeting with the major forces of the enemy'. Hajo Holborn, 'The Prusso-German School: Moltke and the Rise of the General Staff', in Peter Paret (ed.) *Makers of Modern Strategy from Machiavelli to the Nuclear Age* (Princeton, NJ: Princeton University Press, 1986), p. 289.
285. Pessimists might say that the Marines came perilously close to defeat at Tarawa. The point is arguable. In the Gilberts, however, one cannot draw such a clear connection between the risk of catastrophe and problems of logistics.
286. See, for instance, J. David Singer, 'International Conflict: Three Levels of Analysis,' *World Politics*, Vol. 12, No. 3 (April 1960), pp. 453–61.

4

Making Haste Slowly: Communist Logistics in Vietnam

The Vietnam War is notorious as a conflict in which the 'rules' of conventional warfare did not apply.[1] The rules about the importance of logistics, however, remained in full force. North Vietnam and its guerrilla allies won the war with a strategy which depended upon a sophisticated support system, involving over 10,000 miles of roadway and running across four countries.[2] This infrastructure, known as the Ho Chi Minh Trail, allowed the Hanoi regime to fight the war on terms of its choosing. When one investigates the logistics of communist forces in Vietnam, one sees that the arguments of this thesis remain valid in a wide variety of strategic, cultural and geographic environments.

GUERRILLAS AND THE LOGIC OF WARFARE

The example of Vietnam serves to clarify some of the finer points in this paper's theoretical argument. In the first chapter it was argued that logistical matters intersect with strategical matters at the point where opposing combatants attempt to control the tempo of a war. One must, however, take care to avoid simplistic interpretations of this argument. Some of the case studies in these pages imply that the side that acts faster has an advantage, and despite Sun Tzu's maxim that no commander had ever benefited from a protracted war, this is not always the case.[3]

Certainly, an enthusiast of logistics would find it convenient to claim that victory always goes to the swift. As noted previously, it is easy to see why an army which can equip itself rapidly will be able to launch operations relatively quickly as well. When one studies guerrilla operations, however, it becomes apparent that whereas speed can be vital in warfare, patience can be the key to victory as well. Therefore, one must beware of explaining the importance of logistics glibly. In order to understand the full importance of supply factors, one needs to return to the roots of the argument about speed, strategy and logistical preparation.

In a firefight, the first shot is often the only shot which counts. Nevertheless, when one discusses the war plans of entire armies, one should not assume that both sides wish to meet on the battlefield as rapidly as possible. This is only true when both sides believe that they have some reasonable chance of incapacitating the enemy armed forces through direct military action. When one side is handicapped in terms of numbers or technology, this may not be the case. Happily for those whose fortunes depend upon seemingly inferior forces, there are many indirect ways for armies to wear down their opponents.

In war, time is never neutral. When speed favours one side, its delay favours the other. If nothing else, those who find themselves at a disadvantage may try to postpone battle in the hope that their opponents will eventually make a mistake. Furthermore, one can attempt to make the social and material costs of military operations so high for one's opponents that they become willing to end the war. Weaker armies may avoid pitched battle in favour of hit-and-run attacks on vulnerable points, and there are entire philosophies of warfare based on this principle.[4] Furthermore, an army may not have to defeat enemy forces in order to advance its political programme. Irregular forces may control the civilians who live in their areas of operations through terror, and they may achieve prestige among the population through symbolic acts.

None of these principles is unique to guerrilla warfare. Ever since the campaigns of Fabius and Hannibal, it has been axiomatic that there are occasions in which the best way for a general to cripple his enemy is by refusing to fight him. Clausewitz addressed this point in some detail, and indeed, it was a watershed in the development of his fundamental argument. When Clausewitz sought a precise definition of war, he concluded:

> [The violence of war] is not of the kind that explodes in a single discharge, but is the effect of forces that do not always develop in exactly the same manner or to the same degree ... War is a pulsation of violence, variable in strength and therefore variable in the speed with which it explodes and discharges its energy. War moves on its goal with varying speeds; but always lasts long enough for influence to be exerted on the goal and for its own course to be changed in one way or another – long enough, in other words, to remain subject to the action of a superior intelligence.[5]

At the heart of this verbiage lies an important point. The goal in war is independent of war itself. To adopt a mechanical metaphor, warfare is not a force but a machine. One uses violence to exert 'influence' upon some outside body, which may be anything from a military unit to the population of a given province to the Western news media. Different types of target respond to violence in different ways over differing periods, and one does not always have to achieve military victory in the normal sense in order to accomplish one's goals. Furthermore, war is a competitive activity, and it is possible to win even while suffering great losses as long as one's opponent finds his own losses more difficult to bear. The critical factor in war is not speed, but timing, and logistics is as important to those who wish to draw out a war as to those who wish to launch a blitzkrieg.

Supplies and transportation networks cannot help commanders to choose the best moment to act, nor can they help commanders to pick the best objectives for their forces. Logistics can, however, increase the number of options which commanders have at their disposal. A robust supply system can, to adopt Clausewitz's formulation, increase the range of different 'goals' which an army can pursue. The importance of logistics manifests itself in two critical ways, in both conventional and unconventional warfare.

First, war involves many levels of operations, and even when delay is valuable at some of those levels, haste will be necessary at others. Just as forces on the strategic defensive must often adopt offensive measures at a tactical level (and vice versa), forces which have adopted an overall strategy of protracted war must conduct raids, ambushes, tactical withdrawals and even large-scale attacks with speed and agility. Guerrilla leaders, like all military commanders, prize the ability to put their plans into effect at short notice. Therefore, they need a logistical system capable of sustaining such offensives. As time passed, the Vietnamese Communists increasingly found it necessary to seize the tactical initiative in this fashion.

Second, an effective supply and reinforcement system allows military units to sustain their activities for extended periods, even in the face of heavy losses. Such a support system gives a commander greater control over the timing of both short operations and long ones. To summarise, logistics gives military units flexibility and staying power. Once again, one sees numerous examples of these points when one studies the Communist performance in Vietnam.

ROOTS OF A LONG WAR

In order to understand the way in which the Ho Chi Minh Trail supported the Communist strategy, one must understand the type of war which the Hanoi regime hoped to fight. The origins of the North Vietnamese way in warfare are entwined with the origins of the war itself. In the mid-1950s, Vietnam's Communists committed themselves to the total defeat of the South Vietnamese regime. Their attempts to seize power by non-violent means failed, and when they tried to conquer the South through violence, they found themselves compelled to fight the armed forces of the United States of America. In order to defeat their seemingly invincible enemy, the Vietnamese Communists adopted a strategy of protracted war.

The story of the Second Vietnam War begins where the story of the First Vietnam War ends. In 1954, the communist guerrilla forces known as the Viet

Minh, and led by Ho Chi Minh, defeated the French and freed Vietnam from colonial rule. However, in the peace negotiations which followed, the Viet Minh were unable to achieve complete control over their country. Under pressure from the Soviet Union and the People's Republic of China, the Communists accepted a compromise treaty which divided Vietnam into two states, separated by a demilitarised zone (DMZ) on the 17th parallel.

Although the Viet Minh received control over the northern Democratic Republic of Vietnam (DRV), with its capital in Hanoi, the native administration which the French had established during the colonial period continued to govern the southern Republic of Vietnam (RVN), with its capital in Saigon. According to the treaty, this partition would only last for two years. In 1956, there were supposed to be general elections in both halves of Vietnam. Then the North and South would become one nation again, under a democratically elected administration.

The Communists felt bitter about the compromise. They had won independence for their country through seven years of hard fighting, and they felt entitled to govern it. When Zhou Enlai, China's representative to the peace talks, endorsed the treaty, Pham Van Dong, the Viet Minh negotiator, muttered 'he has double-crossed us'.[6] In 1979, the North Vietnamese government issued a White Paper which accused China of forcing the Viet Minh to accept a negotiated settlement when they might have won a total victory on the battlefield.[7]

Despite their resentment, the North Vietnamese may have planned to abide by the agreement. Hanoi's official policy stated that peaceful political action was 'the only and correct strategy of struggle'. On the other hand, the private remarks of communist leaders indicate that the North Vietnamese had a more hard-headed view of the situation. In 1955, the Prime Minister of the DVN, Pham Van Dong, told a foreign observer 'you know as well as I do that there won't be elections'.[8]

Meanwhile, as the governments of North and South Vietnam took steps to protect themselves from what they perceived as internal enemies, the possibility of a peaceful reunification became increasingly remote. Under the direction of RVN Prime Minister Ngo Dinh Diem, South Vietnamese troops arrested 25,000 suspected communists – and killed 1,000, according to DVN estimates.[9] The Hanoi regime, for its part, killed many times this number of suspected 'landlords' in an attempt to wipe out the property-holding class.[10] The North Vietnamese could not afford to compromise with the South Vietnamese, and vice versa.

Therefore, it is not surprising that the North Vietnamese leaders prepared for war with the RVN. After the peace treaty, between 50,000 and 90,000 of the Viet Minh troops who had previously operated in South Vietnam went to the North, where they remained ready to fight again.[11] Meanwhile, the communist government ordered between 10,000 and 15,000 of its most loyal supporters to stay in South Vietnam and maintain their clandestine organisations there.[12] In the winter of 1955–56, the DVN sent a general named Van Tien Dung south to organise local communist sympathisers for guerrilla warfare.[13]

When 1956 came, neither the DVN nor the RVN took any steps to organise elections. That spring, the delegates who attended the Ninth Plenum of the Communist Party noted that, according to Marxist–Leninist theory, conflict between North and South Vietnam was inevitable:

> While we believe that it is possible to prevent war, we do not forget that as long as imperialism exists there will still be an economic basis for war ... While we acknowledge that some nations are capable of advancing to socialism via the path of peace, we must remember that, since the bourgeois class [in Vietnam] still possesses a strong military and police apparatus and resolutely uses weapons to suppress the revolutionary movement, a fierce armed struggle to win political power will be unavoidable, so the proletarian class must prepare in advance.[14]

In December 1956, the Communist Party Regional Committee responsible for South Vietnam officially recognised 'that revolution was the only correct way to lead the South Vietnamese people toward taking control over the administration'.[15] Nevertheless, the Hanoi regime remained cautious. The North Vietnamese leaders were particularly reluctant to take any action which might provoke a 'total war' with the United States.[16] Initially, the DVN Politburo hoped to win power through a policy of political activism in which Communist Party forces would fight only in 'armed self-defence'.[17]

The general uprising did not materialise, and the communist cadres in the South lobbied for a more aggressive role. Therefore, in 1957, the Communist leadership authorised southern cadres to attack the 'traitors' who played a role in supporting the South Vietnamese regime.[18] Communist guerrillas assassinated teachers and effective government officials but spared the more corrupt and unpopular authorities whose practices tended to discredit the Saigon regime.[19]

The level of fighting escalated as the RVN army (ARVN) attempted to destroy communist bases, and the Communist Party activists set ambushes for government troops. During this period, the Saigon government popularised the expression Viet Cong, a derogatory term meaning Vietnamese Communist, as a term for the guerrillas.[20] Meanwhile, in 1957, the North Vietnamese began to organise their forces into a modern, professional army officially known as the People's Army of Vietnam (PAVN), but generally referred to as the North Vietnamese Army (NVA).[21] In May of 1959, the Politburo announced that the time had come to 'push the armed struggle to the enemy'.[22] The following year, Hanoi officially organised the Viet Cong activists in the south into a guerrilla army known as the National Liberation Front (NLF) and commanded by PAVN officers.[23] In March of 1962, the Communist Party of the DVN established a Central Office of South Vietnam (COSVN) to serve as the supreme administrative body for the insurgency movement.[24]

Throughout the early 1960s, American military advisors played a modest but increasing role in ARVN's campaigns against the Viet Cong. In 1965, the United States deployed combat troops in Vietnam. This event crystallised the strategic issues of the Vietnam War. Until the US troops left the country, the North Vietnamese Army could not overrun the RVN, nor could NLF guerrillas establish permanent control of the South. Since the Vietnamese communists could not hope to defeat the US armed forces in a direct confrontation, they had to erode the American people's will to continue the fight.

The Vietnamese Communists believed that they could outlast their enemies in a long war of attrition. Indeed, this concept was basic to their system of military thought. Vietnamese history and folklore features innumerable accounts of outnumbered, overmatched patriots who defeated foreign invaders by fighting on in contests which lasted for decades, or even for centuries. In the nine centuries between 39 AD and 938 AD, for instance, successive generations of rebels fought to liberate Vietnam from the Chinese. The Hanoi regime encouraged its followers to take inspiration from these historical episodes. A North Vietnamese book entitled *Our Military Tradition*, to name one example, celebrates the 'incessant' struggle of the Vietnamese people 'in great battles that took place one century after another'.[25]

Ho Chi Minh applied these ideas to the struggle against America and the Republic of Vietnam in 1959, when he wrote: 'Time is the condition to be won to defeat the enemy. In military affairs time is of prime importance. Time ranks first among the three factors necessary for victory, coming before terrain and support of the people. Only with time can we defeat the enemy.'[26] He reiterated this theme in 1966, a little over a year from the time when US combat troops first officially went into action. In July, Ho told a conference of the Communist Party that the Vietnamese people would defeat the Americans because of their willingness to fight for as long as necessary.[27] The war might last for 20 years, Ho admitted, and Hanoi and Haiphong might be destroyed, but the people would never be afraid of the United States because nothing was more valuable to them than independence and freedom.[28] When Ho Chi Minh died in 1969, his will exhorted the Vietnamese people not to lose patience with the long campaign.[29]

The other North Vietnamese leaders adhered to a similar philosophy. Pham Van Dong, for instance, said 'It is impossible for Westerners to understand the force of the people's will to resist, and to continue to resist. The struggle of the people exceeds the imagination.'[30] In March of 1966, Le Duc Tho, then an influential member of the Politburo, wrote a letter to PAVN General Hoang Van Thai in which he affirmed that the ongoing war would be a protracted struggle, which the communist forces would have to win bit by bit.[31]

The North Vietnamese leaders took care to disseminate these strategic ideas throughout their armed forces. When new recruits joined the VC (Viet Cong) or NVA, their instructors taught them the slogan that 'revolution is not a short-term business'.[32] When Communist commanders gave speeches, they often exhorted the troops to remember that if they did not win the war, their sons would, and that if their sons did not, their grandsons would.[33] Some VC and NVA troops felt bitter about the sacrifices their leaders expected them to make. One private, captured in 1966, stated: 'The new recruits who weren't married heard President Ho declare that we would go on fighting for another five, ten, or even twenty years, from this generation to the next, lost confidence because how could their children continue the fight if they didn't even have time to get married.'[34]

Nevertheless, the typical Communist soldier seemed to accept the necessity of a long war with a spirit of resignation. One captured NVA sergeant summed up the general mood when he said, 'As for me, I thought I would be sacrificing myself for the people.'[35]

Just as the Communist leaders believed that their forces could carry on the fight for decades, they felt confident that their opponents could not. The North Vietnamese leaders believed that internal factors would eventually force the United States out of the war. In good Marxist tradition, Communist Party officials maintained their faith in what they called the 'objective reality' of 'contradictions' within the American and South Vietnamese regimes, which would eventually cause their enemies to fold.[36] General Vo Nguyen Giap, the commander of the North Vietnamese armed forces, stated the principle more succinctly when he said that the United States people 'lacked the patience' for protracted war.[37]

Once again, Communist leaders made an effort to communicate these concepts to their troops. One historian notes:

> [W]hile the NVA trainee received much information on the barbarism of the American soldier, he was also told that the non-military people of the United States were supportive of the Revolution, and that they were opposed to the conflict and wanted US troops withdrawn from the war zone. Cadre and ranking officers bragged about 'winning the war on the streets of New York and the campuses of New England'.[38]

Thus, the concept of protracted warfare became the backbone of Hanoi's strategy. The North Vietnamese leaders' decision to wage a long war against the United States determined the type of logistical problems their forces would face. Since Communist commanders could not defeat their opponents in open battle, they could not secure their supply routes through the direct use of force. Nevertheless, they had to provide their troops with the necessities of combat for an extended period of time.

MILITARY LOGISTICS AND STRATEGIC PERFORMANCE
NOT BY GUERRILLAS ALONE

One cannot win a boxing match by passively absorbing punches. Ho Chi Minh and his followers did not merely intend to outdo their enemies in endurance; they intended to force their enemies out of the war. Although they felt that time was naturally on their side, they also hoped to inflict greater and greater amounts of damage upon their opponents each year, so that the American and South Vietnamese governments would find themselves in an increasingly untenable political situation. Therefore, the North Vietnamese went beyond the classic principles of guerrilla warfare and developed a hybrid style of fighting which mixed traditional methods of insurgency with operations by entire battalions, regiments and divisions. This forced them to find ways of supplying larger, organised units, and thus added a new dimension to their logistical challenge.

The writings of Mao Zedong, the leader of the Communist movement in China, provided a starting point for North Vietnamese strategy. There were numerous parallels between Mao's victorious campaign against the Chinese nationalists and Ho Chi Minh's campaign against the Saigon regime. Both struggles pitted Marxist–Leninist revolutionaries against the forces of a western-backed, nominally nationalist, semi-authoritarian and moderately corrupt government. Both struggles took place in primarily rural Asian countries, where the insurgents had the ability to conceal themselves in difficult terrain. Giap acknowledged a debt to Chinese concepts of strategy, although he emphasised that he and his comrades had adapted them to the circumstances of Vietnam: 'The Party has correctly and ably applied the military line of Marxist–Leninist theory and Mao Zedong's thought to the concrete conditions of Vietnam in scoring outstanding successes in the movement for national liberation ...'[39]

Mao's prescription for guerrilla warfare called for insurgents to overcome their enemies in three phases.[40] The first is known as Withdrawal, because at this stage of the conflict, the insurgents must withdraw from the ordinary political life of their country and take refuge in hidden sanctuaries in order to survive. During the Withdrawal phase, guerrilla action consists largely of assassinations, symbolic attacks and hit-and-run raids against relatively vulnerable targets. The operational goals of guerrillas at this stage are to capture weapons, rally political supporters to their cause, frighten political opponents into silence and compel government forces to take them seriously. Insurgents may also organise a clandestine government and attempt to impose its rulings upon the populace through extortion and propaganda.

When a Maoist insurgency enters its second phase, known as Equilibrium, the guerrillas step up the level of violence considerably, and begin to form organised military units. On propitious occasions, insurgents in this phase may deliberately engage enemy military units, in order to demonstrate their ability to challenge the armed forces of the government. This prepares the way for the third phase, known as General Counteroffensive, in which insurgent units attempt to break the government armed forces in a more conventional military campaign.

Mao's ideas were compatible with older Vietnamese notions of resistance to invaders. The Vietnamese did, however, place greater emphasis on political persuasion, and they also expected the final phase of guerrilla warfare to culminate in *khoi nghai*, the general revolt of the populace.[41] Le Duan summed up Vietnam's traditional strategy as follows:

> The goal must be achieved … in the Vietnamese way, that is by partial insurrections, the formation of revolutionary bases, launching guerrilla warfare and then culminating in a general insurrection, mainly through the use of political forces combined with armed forces to seize power for the people.[42]

General Giap acknowledged that Mao's principles had guided the Viet Minh to victory over the French.[43] The North Vietnamese commander described this doctrine as the appropriate way to fight an 'overwhelmingly superior' enemy.[44] Nevertheless, when the Vietnamese Communists confronted America and the RVN, they did not wish to start the entire three-stage process over again. North Vietnamese leaders noted that a return to a strategy of withdrawal would devastate the morale of the guerrilla forces in the South.[45]

Indeed, the North Vietnamese leaders could not be sure that the NLF would be able to carry on a war by themselves. In late 1963, a North Vietnamese colonel named Bui Tin had infiltrated South Vietnam and inspected the forces there.[46] Bui Tin found that the guerrillas were poorly organised for the coming campaigns.[47] The government forces were stronger than Northern propaganda implied, and many of the NLF's troops had deserted to help their families in the rice fields.[48] Bui Tin did not think that it would be possible to train the guerrillas for a more intensive level of warfare.[49] Instead, he suggested that Hanoi would have to send units of the PAVN into the South. 'We had to move from the guerrilla phase into conventional war. Otherwise, our future would have been bleak.'[50]

David R. Palmer, an American major-general who, during an earlier stage of his career, served as an advisor to the RVN National Military Academy, developed this argument in greater depth:

> Another revealing observation was that Viet Cong guerrillas, despite better weapons and higher morale and the advantage of the initiative, had been singularly unsuccessful in defeating a demoralised and disoriented South Vietnamese army. They had more or less fought each other to a stand-off. If the Viet Cong at their peak could not overpower the ARVN at its weakest, insurgency leaders indeed had some cause for concern.

Moreover, the great effort had boomeranged. The cumulative effect of means such as kidnapping, assassination, terrorism and impressment was to move the end farther from reach. The insurgents had lost, perhaps forever, their aura of being the army of the people. All in all, Hanoi could not view with optimism the future of its army in the South.[51]

When Palmer examined the state of ARVN forces and DVN society, he found even more reasons for the Communists to question Mao's prescription for pure guerrilla warfare.

> Definitely discouraging when gauged in Hanoi was the sputtering but improving army of South Vietnam. Even though thousands of soldiers deserted ARVN units yearly, peasant youths were deserting just as fast from conscripted service in the Viet Cong. More significantly, South Vietnamese officers did not quit, while communist cadre quite frequently did so. More and better equipment, improved training, the experience of years of combat against insurgents, and a deepening hatred of the Viet Cong were a few of the factors making the ARVN a more potent force. That it would continue to improve was the sole prediction a practical General Giap could make.
>
> The last group to whom communists could hopefully look was the populace – the bulwark of previous successes, the 'sea' which provided sustenance to the guerrilla 'fish'. Unhappily, as Ho Chi Minh saw it, even the previously dependable peasants revealed disturbing indications of turning against the insurgents ... After ten years and thousands of terrorist executions, hardly a family in all the South had been left untouched by this communist tactic. The reservoir of resentment welled over in 1964. Large numbers of refugees from Viet Cong-dominated regions streamed into safer areas. Voting with their feet, those peasants emphatically rejected the insurgents. In that year also, a previously rare phenomenon began to occur more and more often: the people began voluntarily supplying the government with information of Viet Cong activities and locations. This movement of his people away from his cherished cause could well have been the bitterest pill for Ho to swallow.
>
> As the pendulum swings, the Republic of South Vietnam was no longer at the bottom of its arc. Neither was it at the top, but the movement up had begun – the low point was past. To the leaders in Hanoi the omens spelled a clear message ... Giap's maximum effort to win in 1964 with orthodox revolutionary warfare had fizzled. Somehow, Hanoi felt, the pendulum had to be stopped short.[52]

Furthermore, the Communist leaders understood that if they allowed the US intervention to curtail their actions, they would be allowing their enemies to control the tempo of the war. A Communist Party member named Hoang Tung explored these ideas in a document entitled *Historic Encounter*, which noted that if the NLF and PAVN reverted to the first phase of guerrilla warfare, they would have to wait for an indefinite period of time before they got the opportunity to escalate the conflict again.[53] Although the Communists were prepared to fight for decades and possibly even generations, they were not prepared to surrender the strategic initiative in this manner. A spokesman for the DVN Politburo, Truong Chinh, summed up the Party's thinking as follows:

> On the one hand, we must thoroughly understand the guideline for a protracted struggle, but on the other we must also seize the opportunities to win victories in a not too long period of time … There is no contradiction in the concept of a protracted war and the concept of taking advantage of opportunities to gain victories in a short time.[54]

Truong Chinh's logic was sound. The idea of protracted war is based on the principle that, over the course of time, the weak may wear down the strong. There is nothing in this concept to discourage the weak from taking all available measures to accelerate the process. Indeed, as a practical matter, they often must. The Lord, it is said, helps those who help themselves, and the gods of war seem to have much the same philosophy.

These ideas had deep roots in the everyday wisdom of the Vietnamese people. Vietnamese culture places great emphasis on the concept of *thoi co*, the moment of opportunity, and Communist Party leaders frequently referred to this notion in their discussions of military strategy.[55] It is a mistake to act before this moment arrives, but it is also a mistake to let *thoi co* slip by. If the North Vietnamese leaders wished to exploit such opportune moments when they arose, they had to deploy forces capable of doing so. Therefore, they could not rely on small, isolated bands of guerrillas.

For reasons such as these, the Hanoi regime sent regular units of the PAVN to support the revolution in the South. This intervention began in the summer of 1964, and when the American combat troops arrived in 1965, the North Vietnamese only stepped up their operations.[56] Le Duan, among others, explained the reasoning behind this bold approach. Although he admitted that any attempt to escalate a conflict which involved the United States carried the risk of disaster, he quoted Napoleon Bonaparte: 'Let's act and see.'[57] The Vietnamese Communist Party confirmed its support for Le Duan's position at its Eleventh Plenum, which met in March of 1965, shortly after the US Air Force began to bomb targets in the North. The Eleventh Plenum issued a resolution which read, in part:

> Our basic mission is to positively restrain and defeat the enemy in the 'special war' in the South, endeavour to take advantage of opportunities, concentrate the forces of the entire nation to win a decisive victory in

the South ... using all of our strength to attack the enemy in the South, defending the North, and fulfilling the task of national liberation throughout the nation.[58]

Le Duan initially hoped that a Communist offensive would touch off a *khoi nghai* and topple the Saigon regime. The rebels could then form a nominally 'neutralist' government in South Vietnam, but the NLF would remain in control from behind the scenes.[59] The new regime would negotiate the withdrawal of US forces, and then the Communists would openly take power. As Palmer noted, the Communist cause had lost much of its popularity in South Vietnam, and perhaps for this reason, the *khoi nghai* failed to materialise.[60] However, the Party's decision to send army units southward provided foundations for the military strategy which PAVN commanders used to defeat the United States.

Over the following years, General Nguyen Chi Thanh, the commander of the revolutionary forces in the South, pursued an increasingly aggressive campaign. Thanh did not believe that the United States had either the manpower or the political will to accomplish its varied aims in Vietnam, and therefore, he intended to stretch his enemy's resources as thinly as possible.[61] Therefore, Thanh harassed US and ARVN forces (to be known, occasionally, as the Allies) without pause, and launched entire regiments into attacks on enemy forces in areas he judged vulnerable.[62] He hoped to place unbearable strain on ARVN and win continual propaganda victories in the Western media.[63] He also hoped to make American commanders disperse their units into defensive positions, in order to keep the US forces from staging decisive offensives of their own.[64]

Thanh's strategy was prodigiously expensive, both in terms of materiel and in terms of lives. In order to support Thanh's forces, the North Vietnamese nation had to adopt a policy of 'all for the front lines', which mobilised the entire population to produce goods for the army.[65] North Vietnamese officials have stated that even they do not know how many of their troops died in the war, but estimates run as high as 851,000.[66] Other PAVN officers criticised Thanh's indifference to risk and loss, but even his most persistent rivals agreed that Communist forces needed to press their enemies relentlessly.[67] Indeed, Thanh's most senior critic, General Giap, was the man who eventually ordered the NLF guerrillas to launch their most ambitious and costly operation of the war, the Tet Offensive of 1968.[68]

Year after year, Party officials reaffirmed their support for the principle of aggressive action. The Twelfth Plenum of the Communist Party, which met in December of 1965, issued resolutions in support of offensive operations, and in 1966, Politburo member Le Duc Tho urged PAVN generals to 'take the initiative on the entire battlefield'.[69] In April 1967, the Party issued Resolution Number 13, which called for 'decisive victory in South Vietnam in the shortest possible time'.[70] Although there were always individuals who called for a more traditional Maoist approach, the North Vietnamese political and military establishment remained united behind a strategy which mixed the concept of protracted war with a refusal to abandon the strategic initiative.

One should note that in addition to the ideas of Maoist insurgency, strategic initiative and protracted warfare, there was a fourth intellectual component to North Vietnam's strategy. The Vietnamese Communists placed enormous emphasis on the concept of *dau tranh*, an expression which many English-speaking authors translate as 'struggle'. 'Crusade' might be a more accurate term, because *dau tranh* signifies a military and psychological campaign to inspire the entire population of a country with certain political beliefs. Those who engage in *dau tranh* seek to exact total commitment from every individual. This thesis will address Vietnamese concepts of political warfare only where they have consequences for the supply and movement of NLF and PAVN forces. However, those who wish to understand the war plans of the Vietnamese Communists in more depth should pay close attention to this concept. The book *PAVN*, by Douglas Pike, provides a useful introduction to *dau tranh* in theory and practice.[71]

Having examined the principles which guided North Vietnamese strategy, one may ask how the Communist leaders put their ideas into practice. As noted above, the Communists had to support their units over the course of many years, despite the fact that they could not rely on conventional methods to protect their lines of communication. Furthermore, if they wished to hold the initiative, the North Vietnamese not only had to deploy large military units, they had to sustain them in the field despite severe losses. Since their operations did not take place along a well-defined front line, they could not focus their logistical efforts on getting supplies to a single point. To pursue their chosen strategy, the Communists had to develop a logistical infrastructure which would allow them to move a steady stream of troops and materiel deep into hostile territory, even in the face of US firepower.

THE ROUTES SOUTH

In 1957, the North Vietnamese began to develop a system of trails which allowed them to send troops and supplies to the Communist guerrillas in the south.[72] Some of the routes went straight across the demilitarised zone between the two halves of Vietnam while others went through the neighbouring country of Laos, but since the government of Laos was hostile to Communism at that time, both routes were dangerous. For the following four years, the network remained little more than a series of jungle tracks, and the total number of people who travelled along it numbered in the hundreds.[73] Then, in 1959, a combination of two events allowed the route to develop into the massive logistical system known as the Ho Chi Minh Trail. First, the DVN government officially decided to initiate 'special war' in the south, and second, communist insurgents in Laos captured a strip of territory which bordered the two Vietnams, thus making it available to their comrades in the DVN.[74]

The North Vietnamese promptly organised large, formal institutions to manage their logistical operations. In May 1959, the PAVN General Directorate of Rear Services (GDRS) created a military unit known as the 559th Transportation Group (TG) to oversee movements through Laos and Cambodia into South Vietnam.[75] The GDRS also formed a second Transportation Group, the 500th, to co-ordinate movements within the DVN.[76] TG officers developed a variety of institutions and procedures which allowed them to fulfil their role in Hanoi's strategy.

At the height of its strength, the 559th TG included over 50,000 soldiers and 100,000 civilian personnel.[77] It operated between 11 and 15 units known as *binh trams*, (BTs) or 'military stations', which maintained depots and sanctuaries along the trail.[78] *Binh trams* were large, well-armed units, each of which included entire battalions devoted to signals, engineering, food-provision, truck-transportation, communications/liaison, combat medicine, route security, transportation control and air defence.[79] By the end of the war, most BTs had at least two battalions of each type.[80] The air defence battalions were equipped with SA-2 missiles, in addition to guns of various calibres.[81]

The BTs maintained way stations at regular intervals along the routes south. PAVN commanders placed these installations between 12 and 20 km apart, depending on local terrain, so that troops and supply convoys on their way south could stop at one each night.[82] Some of these points, known as commo-liaison stations, existed primarily to control traffic, maintain campsites, provide sources of water, and return stragglers to their units. Others, known as interstations, provided troops with food, medical care and other necessities as well. The BTs concealed their way stations beneath jungle foliage and positioned them well away from the civilian populace.[83]

Although all the soldiers who infiltrated South Vietnam via the Ho Chi Minh Trail used commo-liaison facilities each night, many never actually saw these installations. Troops camped at sites roughly 30 to 60 minutes walking distance from the way station itself.[84] Most way stations maintained two or more remote bivouac sites, so that groups of infiltrators bound for different destinations could spend the night at the same way station without ever meeting each other. These measures minimised the amount of information which deserters and prisoners could give the enemy. Furthermore, by spreading their bivouacs and installations over a large area, the North Vietnamese reduced the amount of damage which the US Air Force could do in a single bombing attack.

For the same reasons, North Vietnamese commanders took measures to disperse and disguise combat formations as they moved down the Ho Chi

Minh Trail. Soldiers seldom travelled with their ordinary units. Instead, their commanders split them into arbitrary groups which typically included 40–50 troops, but could be as small as five or as large as 500.[85] Whenever possible, troops left their heavy equipment behind and re-equipped themselves from depots near the areas of operations.[86] In some circumstances, however, the NVA made exceptions to these procedures and marched entire units down the trail with all their gear.[87]

The 559th TG practised a variety of other security measures as well. NVA authorities issued each infiltrator an identification number, which allowed authorities to keep track of him throughout the journey south. The Communists deliberately varied the number system in order to confuse US intelligence officers.[88] Initially, regulations required PAVN soldiers to surrender all personal possessions and exchange their uniforms for the black pyjamas of the NLF, so that there would be no evidence to prove that they came from the North.[89] Communist officers abolished this practice in 1964, however, on the assumption that their enemies already knew that NVA regular forces were involved in the war.[90]

North Vietnamese army units used every available form of transportation to move troops and equipment along the trail. The typical infiltrator travelled by foot, but the PAVN used trucks whenever the local infrastructure and the level of enemy air activity allowed.[91] Bicyclists, foot porters, oxcart caravans, and even pack elephants carried supplies.[92] Communist troops used streams and rivers to bypass areas in which rough terrain or enemy intervention rendered the land routes impassable.[93] The North Vietnamese had a fleet of over 67 steel-hulled trawlers, with which they made over 42 known attempts to sneak materiel into South Vietnam by sea.[94] Between 1968 and 1971, as PAVN troops began to use motor vehicles extensively, the North Vietnamese laid two pipelines through Laos into South Vietnam, which were capable of carrying roughly 10,000 gallons of fuel per day.[95]

The North Vietnamese continually developed their road network. In the two years between 1964 and 1966, Communist forces expanded their main corridor through Laos from a network of poorly maintained footpaths to a system of parallel roads which could support motor traffic along seven separate highways.[96] These roads were not paved, and many of them tended to become impassable during periods of heavy rain.[97] From 1966 to 1968, however, PAVN labourers scraped out drainage systems which corrected this problem.[98] During the same period, Communist forces built five new roads through the jungle, known as Routes 236, 2302, 237, 917 and 238.[99] Construction and improvement continued at a similar pace in the later years of the war.[100]

To build and maintain these roads, PAVN engineers conscripted over 75,000 labourers from Laos and the two halves of Vietnam.[101] A Communist organisation known as 'Vanguard Youths' provided, by North Vietnamese estimates, 'tens of thousands' of teenage girls for the road-building effort.[102] (The DVN preferred to use females for construction work so that young men could serve in combat units.) These labourers worked with hoes, shovels and wheelbarrows, despite the constant threat of aerial bombardment. Most work took place during the dry season, which lasted from March to June.[103] The Soviet Union provided the DVN with a few bulldozers and mechanical earth graders, but the North Vietnamese built the Ho Chi Minh Trail almost entirely by hand.[104]

To move supplies within the RVN itself, the North Vietnamese resorted to smuggling. Communist commanders planned and organised even these clandestine activities with a high degree of precision. The US Combined Intelligence Center described a typical operation of this nature as follows:

> Supplies are moved down this river [the Mekong] by the members of the T-30 Waterways Company. There are six members belonging to this unit. These members own and operate 35-foot motorised sampans. The members receive $VN 5,000 from the VC for the maintenance on their boats, $VN 5,000 for the gasoline for the trip, and $VN 5,000 for other expenses which might arise during the trip. These 35-foot sampans have double bottoms. On the top layer of the sampan, the regular cargo is placed, such as pigs, chickens and foodstuffs. On the lower layer of the sampan, the contraband is placed. These boats are capable of transporting small amounts of large calibre ammunition, small arms and medical supplies. These members also receive the legal documentation necessary to transport the cargo that is on the first layer of the sampan. Also, the operator of the sampan often sells some of his goods along the route to keep his cover as a travelling merchant.[105]

A journey along the Ho Chi Minh Trail was dangerous and time-consuming. PAVN troops required a minimum of 19 days to complete the trip from their starting point at the North Vietnamese city of Vinh to the combat zones in the Republic of Vietnam.[106] Troops bound for the extreme south could take as many as 90 days to reach their destinations.[107] Furthermore, of the troops which set out on the Ho Chi Minh Trail, from 15 per cent to 17 per cent succumbed to malaria or became casualties of US air and artillery attacks along the way.[108]

The following account, while apocryphal, helps to put the hardships of the typical PAVN infiltrator into human terms:

> After a brief visit home, [Private] Nguyen reported to his unit and was issued with a backpack along with four 82-mm mortar rounds. Along with an extra uniform, a bag of rice and a canteen of water, Nguyen's load was now over a hundred pounds. Nguyen, who weighed only a few more pounds than his pack, squared his shoulders, and with country,

village and family in his thoughts, headed south to help liberate his cousins from the coils of capitalism and oppression by the Americans.

The first few days of Nguyen's journey were uneventful except for the raw sores that developed from the rubbing of the pack straps on his shoulders. Along with his unit, Nguyen shuttled between river boats, trucks and an occasional foot march as he covered the first two hundred miles. Late one evening, as Nguyen's squad was getting off of a Russian-made truck, his sergeant told him that they were nearing the Laotian border just north of the DMZ. From there onward, they would move on foot.

Their timing was not so good. It was the middle of the monsoon season and the daily rains kept Nguyen soaked. As the days passed and the journey progressed, Nguyen began to weaken. Twice, he had to stay behind to recover from bouts of malaria before joining new units. Another time, Nguyen wandered lost in the jungle for two days after a B-52 strike had killed the rest of his squad and dazed the young private. Bites and stings from mosquitoes, ants and scorpions became almost as routine as picking fat, blood-sucking leeches off his body.

At a way station in Cambodia, Nguyen learned that his destination was Long An province near Saigon. Nguyen, who now weighed less than his pack due to short rations, malaria attacks and the early stages of beri-beri, wondered how he was going to make it on feet that were blistered and becoming infected.

That afternoon things got worse, American jets screamed out of the sky dropping bombs and napalm. Nguyen's best friend, who had been walking with him for the last two weeks, was burnt alive. Nguyen's lungs were seared by the hot-burning napalm, but he was able to crawl to safety in a water-filled bomb crater.

Things did not get any better the next day. Shortly after one of the guides had told Nguyen's group that they had crossed the border into South Vietnam, helicopter gunships spotted the column. Rockets and bullets cut the jungle and another couple of Nguyen's friends to pieces. That night, huge artillery shells exploded around Nguyen's foxhole. It was little comfort when a cadre told him that the American gunners did not know that they were there but were merely shooting 'Harassing and Interdictory' (H&I) fires [sic].

With a malarial fever of over 103 degrees, little food, two more air attacks and an artillery barrage to his credit, Nguyen reported to his new unit, which at the time was attacking a small government outpost. Minutes after arrival, Nguyen unloaded his heavy pack and handed his four mortar rounds to his new squad leader. Much to Nguyen's surprise, the four rounds were fired one after the other in less than a minute. Then the squad leader turned to him an with a smile said, 'Good job, Nguyen. Now go back and get four more.'[109]

To dwell on the factual inaccuracies in this account would be to overlook the larger truths which it expressed. Unlike Nguyen, actual infiltrators rarely knew where they were until they reached the combat zone itself.[110] Furthermore, with the exception of guides, officers and cadres, troops who marched down the Ho Chi Minh Trail did not march back again.[111] Unless a soldier was wounded, he remained in the South for the duration of the war. However, all the dangers and miseries which Nguyen encountered were real, and real PAVN soldiers risked all of them.[112]

The sergeant's final comment, 'now go back and get four more', also has the ring of allegorical truth, if not factual veracity. North Vietnamese commanders were willing to expend human life and energy as extravagantly as necessary in order to achieve even the smallest incremental gains. They justified their readiness to sacrifice lives by referring to the historical traditions of their country, the aspirations of its citizens, the putatively scientific theories of Marxist thinkers and the words of living heroes such as Ho Chi Minh. One should not assume that the North Vietnamese commanders invoked tradition and principle as mere window dressing, in an attempt to manipulate their followers. These ideas were more than rhetoric for the Vietnamese people.

Ordinary North Vietnamese troops shared the spirit of sacrifice. The diaries and letters of real infiltrators who followed in the footsteps of the fictitious Private Nguyen express faith in the Party and hope for the day of reunification.[113] PAVN soldiers wrote of fear, misery, small bitternesses and deep personal angst, but they understood their role in the war, and they accepted it as much as infantry soldiers anywhere accept their fate. Tradition, social conformity and political ideology played a tangible role in making the North Vietnamese logistical system what it was.

MOBILISATION IN THE SHADOWS

The Ho Chi Minh Trail was only part of the Communist logistical system. PLF and PAVN forces obtained over three-quarters of their logistical support from the civilians of South Vietnam.[114] COSVN established a well-organised system of taxation, commerce, forced labour, local transportation networks and clandestine industries to provide for the needs of Communist fighters.[115] The southern logistical organisations not only increased the total volume of supplies which VC/NVA troops had available to them, they made it possible for Communist units to fight on at times when Allied forces had disrupted their usual lines of communication. Therefore, Communist commanders could count on reliable and relatively abundant support under a wide variety of combat conditions.

In regions where the VC and NVA had influence, the Communists integrated the entire population into their logistical system. Communist commanders conscripted peasants as unpaid labourers in whatever numbers they desired, whenever it suited their purposes. In emergencies, the guerrillas were known to impress thousands of people at a time to build fortifications and dig tunnel networks.[116] At other times, the Communists exacted their labour tribute in a more regular fashion. In Binh Ba village, for instance, VC cadres imposed the following regime:

> Everyone in the village had to do three months' labour a year. All young men had to do labour in battlefields, carrying wounded and ammunition; 7–20 day missions. Men under 45 and single females transported rice and goods, but not in battle. Men over 45 worked on the destruction of roads.[117]

Civilians dug graves and carried dead soldiers from the battlefield.[118] This service had great psychological importance to the Vietnamese, who, like people from most parts of the world, attach great cultural significance to the treatment of the dead. Indeed, NLF commanders feared that the peasants would turn against them in general revulsion if they failed to give their fallen soldiers proper funerals.[119] Furthermore, by removing casualties from the battlefield, the VC made it difficult for Allied intelligence officers to assess the results of an engagement.

South Vietnamese civilians manufactured clothing for NLF and PAVN soldiers. The typical VC division had 20 to 30 sewing machines, which it distributed among peasant families.[120] Communist regulations required these families to produce four uniforms per day, although actual output averaged about two and a half.[121] The NLF and PAVN paid these peasants from 2 to 35 piastres for each suit of clothes.[122]

As for other equipment, a VC organisation known as Rear Services Group 83 maintained a network of agents and front companies which could buy almost anything but weapons and ammunition from civilian markets.[123] Table 1 shows the goods that Group 83 procured from commercial sources between October 1965 and April 1966.

The VC participated in the black market as well, and established control over it wherever possible. Criminal rings in the Saigon area manufactured false identification papers for Communist operatives.[124] In Tay Ninh province, near Cambodia, the VC organised a daily bazaar at which over 300 black-marketeers at a time would gather to sell a wide variety of goods for inflated prices.[125] In order to protect this market from government agents, NLF agents changed its location each day and notified the merchants through a variety of secret means.[126]

To raise money for these purchases, the NLF imposed taxes on regions under its control. Whenever possible, the Communists went a step further and forced South Vietnamese farmers to sell their produce and livestock on VC-operated markets.[127] The NLF kept part or all of the profits from such

Table 1: Group 83 Commercial Procurement

Material	Quantity
Gasoline	33,200 litres
Lubricant Oil	3,040 litres
Paraffin	232 cans (20 litres each)
Asphalt	123 cans
Cloth	46,200 metres
Canvas	800 metres
Diesel Oil	20,760 litres
Grease	150 kilograms
Parachute Cord	37,572 metres
Recording Tapes	20
Plastic Material	44,444 metres
Dry Battery, PRC 10	2,443
Dry Battery, PRC 6	70
Dry Battery, Regular	3,910
Flashlights	112
Electric Wire	35,880 metres
Tin	31,267 sheets
Pick mattocks	860
Machetes	1,181
Refrigerator	1
Typewriters	2

Note: Individual units of the VC and NVA also obtained food and equipment directly from peasant villages, both by purchase and by force. The above information is to be found in Holliday and Gurfield, *Viet Cong Logistics*, pp. 19–20 and 44.

transactions for its own purposes. This practice not only allowed the Communists to raise revenue, it gave them control over the food supply in rural areas.[128] In this fashion, the guerrillas rendered the civilian population dependent upon their goodwill.

Communist forces transported men and materiel throughout South Vietnam along a network of footpaths, waterways and segments of the RVN national road system.[129] When expedient, the VC and NVA used sampans, oxcarts, trucks and even captured armoured personnel carriers to transport their supplies.[130] Nevertheless, throughout the war, the Communist forces moved the overwhelming majority of their supplies on the backs of peasant conscripts.[131] The Viet Cong established a system of bivouac areas for porters on their way to different parts of South Vietnam, just as the 559th Transportation Group established campsites along the Ho Chi Minh Trail.[132]

Not only did this transportation network allow VC and NVA troops to operate in every corner of South Vietnam, it reinforced the other Communist logistical systems. For instance, the trails within the RVN provided alternatives to some of the routes through Laos and Cambodia.[133] When Allied forces blocked portions of the Ho Chi Minh Trail, the Communists could often move their supplies through South Vietnam itself. The fact that the Viet Cong and NVA kept supplies moving through the transportation system at all time made it difficult for their enemies to deprive them of supplies. Even when US/ARVN forces destroyed PLF/PAVN depots, the Communists could rely on having fresh supplies 'in the pipeline', moving between the bases of the transportation system.[134]

Civilians also provided military units with the equivalent of clandestine depot facilities. The typical NLF regiment kept 30 days' worth of rice on hand at all times, with one-third of the supply located with the troops and two-thirds distributed among peasant families for safekeeping.[135] Individual soldiers generally carried enough rations for seven days on their persons.[136] Not only did these practices allow Communist troops to maintain large stockpiles without the need for storage facilities, but they made it difficult for American and ARVN units to distinguish enemy supply depots from civilian granaries.

Through their use of civilian resources and their willingness to make do with minimal levels of support, the Communists freed trained soldiers for duty on the battlefield. One typical VC division, for instance, employed only 391 full-time soldiers in its transportation battalion but relied on 1,200 civilian conscripts to carry its supplies.[137] Civilians, in other words, more than tripled the size of this division's transportation establishment. Of the 12,360 soldiers in this division, 9,716 (79 per cent) served in combat units, with only 2,644 (21 per cent) in support roles.[138] One notes that, in the US Army, these percentages were reversed. In the summer of 1967, over 80 per cent of the American troops in South Vietnam served in non-combat units.[139]

MUNITIONS SUPPLY

Viet Cong and NVA forces in South Vietnam imported 95 per cent of their ammunition and nearly all of their weapons from the North.[140] If the Ho Chi Minh Trail had served no other purpose, this fact alone would have made it vital to the Communist war effort. Nevertheless, the PLF and PAVN did not allow themselves to become totally dependent on any one source of supply. Communist troops used a variety of techniques to make sure that they would be able to survive interruptions to their supply lines.

In order to ensure that they would always have plenty of ammunition, VC and NVA units attempted to maintain a stockpile of enough shells and bullets for one to three months of fighting at all times.[141] On the march, Communist troops carried one-third of their ammunition with their units and concealed the rest in tunnels, villages, jungle caches and a variety of more imaginative hiding-places.[142] Many units, for instance, placed munitions in waterproof cases and hid them in rivers and drainage ditches near their areas of operations.[143] When VC and NVA troops went into battle, they carried one day's worth of ammunition in their packs, and even in combat, Communist soldiers attempted to save 50 rounds apiece to cover their withdrawal.[144] After an engagement, PLF/PAVN troops typically needed two to six days to resupply themselves from their hidden depots.[145]

The Communists also maintained secret ordnance factories throughout South Vietnam. After a firefight, civilian labourers and guerrilla troops would scavenge for spent cartridges and unexploded munitions from the battlefield. The NLF then sent these items to workshops where conscripted labourers worked under VC and NVA specialists to recover the explosives from dud shells.[146] The workers then reassembled these materials into makeshift grenades, booby traps and mortar rounds. Ordnance workers also reloaded spent cartridges, in order to provide Communist forces with fresh ammunition.

The following passage describes the output and personnel requirements of typical ordnance factories:

> One very small workshop was located in a villager's house. It's job was to fabricate antipersonnel mines and muskets, without machines and using only three workers. About 30 mines and 3 muskets were produced every month from gunpowder and sheet iron supplied by the village committee. Another workshop had about 40 workers and each month produced some 200 mines and bangalore torpedoes [a sausage-shaped demolition device, placed by hand and normally used to clear paths through minefields and barbed wire], the latter weighing about 1.5 kg each. A province workshop with 80 workers and 20 guards had a foundry with a monthly output of about 500 mortar shells ... A worksite in Long An province employing 20 men manufactured 2,000 rifle rounds per day as well as unknown quantities of grenades and mines.[147]

The village ordnance factories could not sustain large-scale operations. These facilities did, however, help PLF/PAVN units make their stockpiles last as long as possible. Furthermore, the arms workshops allowed small, irregular units to operate indefinitely, even without outside support. Therefore, they extended the reach of Communist violence into areas which the normal supply routes did not reach, and helped to prevent the Allied forces from completely pacifying any part of the country. The next section will discuss the Viet Cong irregular forces in more detail.

THE AUXILIARY ARMY

COSVN organised numerous militia organisations which, among other things, helped the Communists use their limited supplies of food and armaments in the most economical manner possible. This auxiliary army was capable of carrying out a wide variety of military functions with minimal amounts of supply. The militia forces ranged from the full-time fighters of the Local (Provincial) Forces, who fought in company-sized units and lived in jungle camps to the 'farmers by day and soldiers by night', who lived among the civilian population and operated in clandestine three-man cells.[148] No matter which type of unit they belonged to, the auxiliaries tended to have less training, less education and less commitment to Marxist ideology than the fully fledged members of the PLF.

One should not confuse the auxiliary organisations with the PLF Main Force. Although authors often refer to both kinds of fighters as 'Viet Cong', the different types of guerrillas received different levels of support and played different roles in the Communist war plan. The logistical apparatus described in other parts of this chapter existed primarily for the benefit of the Main Force and the NVA. NVA and Main Force units used their relatively lavish quantities of supplies to sustain a mobile campaign against the armed forces of South Vietnam and the United States. Militia organisations, on the other hand, were ill-prepared to engage Allied troops in pitched battle, and seldom attempted to do so.

For the Communist high command, the auxiliary units were extraordinarily inexpensive to maintain. Since militia troops seldom moved far from their home villages, they placed few burdens on the Viet Cong transportation network. When supplies of equipment were plentiful, the Communist high command would issue each auxiliary soldier a rifle and perhaps 50 bullets.[149] Often, however, there were not enough firearms to go around, and then the militia troops had to do without. US analysts determined that, in one typical district of South Vietnam, only one out of every five auxiliary soldiers actually carried a gun.[150] The rest of the troops had to make do with three grenades apiece.[151]

When the militia soldiers needed fresh ammunition, they usually had to capture it from the enemy or manufacture it themselves in the improvised munitions factories described earlier. Local workshops could not provide the auxiliary troops with all the munitions they needed, but they did allow the guerrillas to continue the fight at all times. Based on their studies of Dinh Tuong province, US analysts estimated that the improvised arms industry could provide the Provincial Forces (and, presumably, the more localised militia organisations as well) with 25 per cent of their normal ammunition requirements.[152] The same study concluded that, even if Allied forces managed to find and destroy the munitions workshops, VC technicians would have been able to establish new ones in a matter of months.[153]

A few of the better-equipped auxiliary units possessed heavy weapons, but even they had to get by with sparing rations of ammunition. One Provincial Force detachment, for instance, had an 81mm mortar. Viet Cong commanders authorised this unit to maintain a stockpile of 20 shells, but did not integrate it into their transportation network.[154] When the militia fighters used up their ammunition, they had to send a detachment on a month-long journey through mountainous terrain in order to get more shells from the nearest PLF depot.[155]

Since auxiliary soldiers required little support, the Communists were able to field great numbers of them. Historians and military analysts do not know how big the Communist militia organisations actually were, but the following figures provide a rough estimate.[156] When the Viet Cong took control of a township, they would usually organise between 25 and 36 of the inhabitants into a village militia.[157] In a typical district of several dozen villages, the Communists would also impress between 200 and 1,000 people to form the local Provincial Forces.[158]

According to the US Army Order of Battle Summary, COSVN controlled 52,236 militia troops in the spring of 1967.[159] Authors who base their work on North Vietnamese sources suggest that the number was actually well over 150,000.[160] By way of comparison, the Order of Battle Summary states that the Communists fielded a total of 70,355 NVA/VC Main Force troops during the same period, while the North Vietnamese estimates imply that the regular troops numbered over 100,000.[161] No matter which set of figures one chooses to accept, one should note that, speaking roughly, the militia organisations allowed the Communists to double the size of their armed forces.[162]

The militia units could not have carried out Hanoi's strategy of winning 'victory in a not too long period of time'.[163] Nevertheless, they played a key part in the Communist war effort. Auxiliary troops planted mines, spread propaganda, gathered intelligence, assassinated individual enemies, arrested VC/NVA defectors, stood guard at construction sites, protected VC/NVA supply convoys and, perhaps most importantly of all, served as a shadow police force to enforce Communist decrees among the people of South Vietnam.[164] Militia forces routinely kept townships of 2,000 to 15,000 civilians under Communist control.[165] By taking over these functions, the auxiliaries distracted ARVN and the US Army, freed the VC/NVA Main Forces to concentrate on combat operations, and ensured that the civilian population would continue to provide for the needs of Communist forces.

A STEADY DOSE OF WAR

The trails through Laos and the Viet Cong infrastructure in the South allowed Communist commanders to control the intensity of the war. Therefore, the Communists were able to maintain continual pressure upon their enemies, despite enormous losses of their own. At the level of grand strategy, the Communist logistical system allowed the North Vietnamese leaders to channel all the resources of their nation into the war. At the operational level of combat, the supply network allowed the PLF and PAVN to attack in whatever numbers they considered expedient, at times and places of their own choosing. Therefore, in spite of repeated defeats upon the battlefield, the Communists made steady progress toward victory.

Thanks to their logistical system, the Viet Cong and NVA were able to time their attacks to coincide with moments of American and South Vietnamese weakness. In the spring of 1965, for instance, Giap and Thanh temporarily found themselves in a position where they could mass troops for large-scale battles more effectively than their opponents. The American experience here serves as a case study in the importance in itself of supply factors. Throughout the early 1960s, American military planners had urged the US government to build a logistical complex in the RVN, but the authorities in Washington had not acted on this suggestion, and when American policymakers decided to send large combat forces to South Vietnam, there were not enough ports, airfields or storage facilities in the country to receive the new military units. Due to this logistical shortfall, the United States was unable to carry out its build-up until the summer.[166]

The Ho Chi Minh Trail, on the other hand, was already capable of sustaining large troop movements. Therefore, Giap rushed PAVN units into South Vietnam to take advantage of the time which remained before American reinforcements could arrive. The summer monsoon increased the odds in favour of the Communists, because muddy ground affected US and ARVN trucks more severely than VC and NVA foot porters.[167] Troops of the PAVN marched into South Vietnam in much greater numbers than US intelligence analysts had thought possible and, in conjunction with the PLF, won a series of sharp victories.[168] By May, the Communist forces were destroying ARVN units at a rate of about a battalion per week, and the Viet Cong were capturing new district capitals every six or seven days.[169]

In June, ARVN troops stiffened their resistance, and as the summer progressed, American troops arrived in greater numbers.[170] Nevertheless, despite the overwhelming superiority of the US military apparatus on paper, the logistical advantages of the Viet Cong and NVA allowed Communist commanders to achieve numerical advantages on the battlefield until the autumn.[171] Nobody knows how close the Communists came to victory, but the PLF and PAVN might easily have overrun substantial portions of the RVN, destroyed major Allied military units or even captured the belt of territory which ran from Pleiku to Qui Nhon, thus cutting South Vietnam in two.[172] The government of the RVN had just undergone a military coup, and any one of these defeats might have been enough to shock the unstable regime into surrender. As events turned out, the US commander, General William Westmoreland organised a successful defence of the South and went on to defeat the North Vietnamese invaders in the battle of Ia Drang, but Communist forces had seized the strategic initiative in a dramatic way, and they continued to hold it for the rest of the war.

Until his death in July 1967, General Thanh engaged US and ARVN forces in more and more battles, which led to greater and greater numbers of casualties on both sides.[173] These attacks not only killed Allied soldiers, they tied down ever-increasing numbers of Allied troops in defensive operations. The frontiers of South Vietnam were over 900 miles long, and the Ho Chi Minh Trail network allowed the NVA to cross these borders at virtually any point.[174] Furthermore, PLF guerrillas and PAVN infiltrators could stage operations throughout the interior of the countryside. As the PLF and PAVN launched larger and larger attacks, the Allies could no longer afford to let down their guard anywhere.

Westmoreland describes the situation as follows:

> In World War I close to 6 million Allied troops were needed to man the 455 miles of the Western Front. In World War II, 4.5 million Allied troops were needed to man a 570-mile Western Front. In Korea, close to a million United Nations troops were needed to man a 123-mile front across the waist of the Korean Peninsula. To have defended the land frontiers of South Vietnam in similar density would have required many millions of troops, plus others to carry on the fight against the insurgency, numbers that it would have been absurd to contemplate.[175]

For this reason, General Westmoreland adopted a strategy which American journalists called the 'big-unit war'.[176] US and ARVN forces did not even attempt to establish an impenetrable defensive line along the RVN borders, or to maintain a presence in all areas at all times. Instead, they attempted to find and destroy large groups of enemy soldiers. This allowed the PLF and PAVN to disperse when they wished to avoid combat and concentrate their forces at times when they wished to draw their enemies into battle.[177] Meanwhile, the Viet Cong auxiliary army continued to impose Communist rule upon significant portions of the countryside with relatively little opposition.

There were exceptions to this pattern. ARVN attempted to pacify rural areas, the US Marines deployed units known as Combined Action Platoons to protect villages from Viet Cong intimidation and the US Army carried out frequent 'sweep' operations to clear designated areas of Communist guerrillas, to name but three examples.[178] Furthermore, the RVN government attempted to match the Communist auxiliary units by building up its own militia organisations, known as the Regional Forces and the Popular Forces.[179]

These measures, however, failed to counter the Hanoi regime's strategy. Allied troops scored countless successes against VC militia and VC Main Force troops alike, but they never managed to implement a consistent, comprehensive programme to root out Communist influence in the countryside. Westmoreland explains one reason why this was so:

[T]he very existence of large enemy units made it essential that American troops be prepared on short notice to drop what they were doing and move against a developing big-unit threat. When the troops moved away from the population, the guerrillas obviously gained a chance to recoup their losses, but I never had the luxury of enough troops to maintain an American, Allied or ARVN presence everywhere all the time.[180]

As for the Regional and Popular forces, the Saigon regime was unable to arm or equip them quickly enough to change the course of the war.[181]

Despite Westmoreland's attempts to economise on manpower, the aggressive Communist strategy forced the American commander to request reinforcements, in his own words, 'any number of times'.[182] Table 2 shows the rate at which VC/NVA operations drew Allied forces into the war.

These troop deployments not only involved financial expenditures, political controversy and hardships for the soldiers involved, they imposed indirect costs upon the Allied military position throughout the world. Some, for instance, suggested that the Communist regime in North Korea might take advantage of the fact that Allied troops were occupied in Vietnam to invade its southern neighbour. American intelligence analysts saw no evidence that the North Koreans were assembling forces for such an attack, but US commanders still found it prudent to prepare for the possibility.[183]

In 1967, Giap observed that, despite the Allied build-up, US and ARVN troops were still stretched 'as taut as a bowstring' from the Mekong Delta to the DMZ.[184] Meanwhile, the Vietnam war had become unpopular among influential segments of the American population, and new troop commitments had become politically controversial. *Time, Life, The New York Times* and other influential American publications began to publish editorials which questioned the American involvement in Vietnam.[185] For the first time,

Table 2: Allied Troop Levels in Vietnam, 1964–68

	Australia	Republic of Korea	Republic of Vietnam	Thailand	United States
1964	200	200	514,000	–	23,310
1965	1,560	20,620	643,000	20	184,310
1966	4,530	25,570	735,900	240	385,300
1967	6,820	47,830	798,800	2,200	485,600
1968	7,660	50,000	820,000	6,000	536,000

Note: New Zealand and the Philippines also committed troops to the Vietnam war, which reached maximum strengths of 550 and 1,580 respectively. The Republic of China sent 30 advisors to the RVN, and Spain sent ten. The above information is to be found in S. Stanton, *Vietnam Order of Battle* (Washington, DC: US News Books, 1981), p. 333.

public-opinion polls had begun to indicate that a small majority of the American people opposed the war.[186]

Secretary of Defence Robert McNamara, Senator William Fulbright and other influential members of the US government articulated concerns about the wisdom of the Vietnam War as well.[187] These doubts in Washington, DC, had immediate consequences on the battlefield. When Westmoreland stated that he needed a minimum of 80,500 new troops in 1967, US President Lyndon Johnson refused to send him more than 55,500.[188] The Communist forces had forced the Johnson Administration to acknowledge that there were limits to what the American polity was willing and able to do. North Vietnam's strategy of protracted war had begun to produce the results which Giap and Ho Chi Minh had hoped for.

To an outside observer, it might have appeared that the Viet Cong and NVA had exhausted themselves as well as their enemies. Each time the Communists had attacked in strength, the Allied forces had decimated them. In 1965, Allied troops had utterly defeated a PAVN invasion of South Vietnam at Ia Drang and in 1968, US troops staged a 'Dien Bien Phu in reverse' against the North Vietnamese troops which attacked them at Khe Sanh, to name a pair of examples.[189] Meanwhile, Communist ideology had begun to lose its appeal in the South. In 1967, American social scientists produced a number of statistics which implied that the insurgency movement was dying out.[190]

The Communists, however, were able to reconstitute their forces and strike again with more force than ever. As 1967 drew to a close, the PLF and PAVN began the series of attacks known as the Tet Offensive. Despite all their previous casualties, the Communist forces sent over 80,000 fresh troops into battle.[191] It was the Communist logistical system which made this comeback possible. The VC and NVA could recover from losses because they had the logistical ability to deploy as many troops as they could raise and equip.

Although Communist guerrillas had trouble obtaining weapons during the early years of the war, aid from the Soviet Union and the People's Republic of China quickly made arms shortages a thing of the past for them.[192] By the early 1960s, PAVN troops enjoyed an abundance of weaponry.[193] Even guerrillas in South Vietnam were remarkably well armed. In 1965, US intelligence officers conducted a survey of Viet Cong soldiers in Allied prison camps and discovered that only 6 per cent of the Main Force veterans complained of difficulties in getting the weapons and ammunition they needed to carry out their missions.[194] Even when the American interrogators questioned captured veterans of the VC auxiliary organisations, they found that only 26 per cent of the prisoners reported shortages of arms.[195]

Therefore, by the mid-1960s, the only effective limit to the size of the North Vietnamese Army was the size of the North Vietnamese population. Thanks to their logistical system, the Communists were able to translate their human potential directly into fighting power. The Ho Chi Minh Trail allowed the

North Vietnamese leaders to dispatch troops and materiel to the combat zone at any rate they desired. Certainly, convoys and troop columns suffered attrition along the way, but this did not lead to shortages at the front. As noted above, PLF Main Force and PAVN units practically never ran out of ammunition. Likewise, the PAVN commanders were able to send troops south as quickly as they could train them.

The PAVN maintained 52 training units, each of which could process 500 recruits in a three-month training cycle, for a total of 2,000 recruits per year.[196] Some of these units served in administrative roles rather than as active training formations, but it seems reasonable to estimate that the PAVN was able to train at least 80,000 combat troops per annum.[197] Since roughly 100,000 physically fit young men reached draft age in the DVN every year, one may conclude that the North Vietnamese achieved something close to the total mobilisation of their populace.[198]

As a grisly aside, one may note that, despite their level of mobilisation, the Communist forces often lost soldiers faster than they could train new ones.[199] During these manpower shortfalls, the North Vietnamese often shortened the training period or required instructors to handle larger groups of students in order to get fresh troops into combat faster.[200] The DVN also recruited women and recalled retired soldiers to service in order to expand its armed forces.[201] Meanwhile, COSVN continually conscripted new Viet Cong soldiers from the areas of South Vietnam which fell under its control.

The following figures show how steadily the Communists poured troops and equipment into the war. In 1966 and 1967, NVA soldiers infiltrated the RVN at a rate of 5,000 to 10,000 per month.[202] By introducing new troops into the South at this pace, the PAVN commanders were able to increase the strength of their forces in the war zone from 65,000 to 70,000, casualties, battlefield defeats and aerial bombardment notwithstanding.[203] Communist forces suffered tremendous casualties during the Tet Offensive, but the NVA tripled the rate at which it sent new soldiers south during this period.[204] Therefore, the PAVN managed to maintain troop levels of roughly 100,000 men in the South throughout the winter of 1968, and even to launch a second offensive later that year.[205] From July to October, the PAVN reduced its monthly rate of infiltration to the range of 5,000 to 10,000 again, and NVA troop levels stabilised between 70,000 and 80,000.[206]

In other words, despite the losses which it suffered during the intense fighting of 1968, the NVA found it possible to increase its total strength by approximately 10,000 men, and to sustain its new force levels on a permanent basis. In addition to these reinforcements, the Hanoi regime also sent individual troops to maintain the strength of PLF guerrilla units, so that, by 1968, one out of every three VC-Main-Force soldiers was from North Vietnam.[207] Even the village and province militia units often accepted North Vietnamese replacements.[208] Analysts at the US armed forces Combined

Intelligence Center concluded that the PAVN's monthly rate of infiltration into the RVN was 'directly responsive' to Communist manpower requirements.[209]

The Communist system of stockpiles and redundant transportation routes allowed VC and NVA troops to feed and equip themselves even when Allied forces managed to cut off their normal sources of supply. PLF and PAVN forces devoted considerable effort to prepositioning food in areas where COSVN expected logistical difficulties.[210] Therefore, American attempts to deprive guerrillas of sustenance seldom had much effect. Researchers at the RAND Corporation noted:

> Viet Cong reaction to the GVN [Government of South Vietnam] food-denial program depends on local factors. The former Assistant Chief of Staff of Operations, Front, 5th Division, operating in Long Khanh and Phuoc Tuy provinces, said that rice stocks could be replenished within 10 days following their seizure, depending on the availability of transportation and the quantity seized. For example, in May–June 1966 a GVN/US force seized a 30-day rice supply for the 5th Division near the Tuc Trung rubber plantation in Long Kanh. The rice was replaced in five days with no apparent degradation of combat effectiveness.[211]

The North Vietnamese also used their logistical system to maintain the vitality of their political apparatus in the South. The cadres who agitated and organised for the Communist cause travelled back and forth between North and South Vietnam as their duties required.[212] Therefore, Party officials in the DVN could summon the cadres for training and indoctrination whenever necessary. This undoubtedly helped the Communist Party of North Vietnam keep control over its supporters in the RVN. The training and indoctrination sessions also may have helped the civilian arm of the Viet Cong sustain itself during the late 1960s, when it began to suffer from corruption and apathy.[213]

Furthermore, the Hanoi regime used the Ho Chi Minh Trail to evacuate the children of prominent Communist sympathisers from South Vietnam to the DVN. One captured PAVN soldier told US interrogators that the DVN took roughly 200 minors north every year, but this figure may have been only a fraction of the total.[214] The evacuation policy served the triple purpose of protecting the children of well-known Marxist–Leninists from anti-communist reprisals, giving the Party additional leverage over the children's parents and making it possible for the Hanoi regime to indoctrinate the youths as future political activists.[215] When the children reached their teens, the North Vietnamese sent them back south as cadres to stiffen the ideological fibre of the Viet Cong.[216]

COMMUNIST LOGISTICS IN VIETNAM

THE FINAL OFFENSIVES

By the late 1960s, the people and policy-makers of the United States had indeed concluded that they had to end the Vietnam War one way or another. At the same time, the Communist leadership committed itself to massive offensives which involved both guerrilla and conventional attacks. The first and most famous operation of this nature was the Tet Offensive of 1968, and many commentators identify it as the turning point of the war. North Vietnam's logistical system brought the Communist forces to this point, and North Vietnam's logistical system allowed them to exploit it.

A full historical study of the Tet Offensive and its consequences lies beyond the scope of this work.[217] One can sum up the significance of this battle as follows. When the North Vietnamese commanders launched this campaign, they hoped to inspire the long-awaited *khoi nghai* throughout the RVN. If this had taken place, the South Vietnamese people would have risen as one to overthrow their government, and the United States would have found itself without a friendly regime to support.

The people of South Vietnam, however, responded to the Communist appeal with general apathy and occasional hostility. Meanwhile, Allied armed forces devastated the PLF/PAVN attackers in a well-planned and well-executed counteroffensive. In terms of casualties and in terms of their original political objectives, the VC and NVA suffered a potentially fatal defeat. From that point onward, it was difficult for anyone to maintain that Communist ideology enjoyed much popular support in the RVN. The PAVN suffered severe casualties, and the PLF suffered such crippling losses that it never recovered.

Tet was, however, a decisive victory for the North Vietnamese. At a moment when the makers of policy and opinion in the United States were prepared to turn against the war, the Tet Offensive made up their minds. The shock of the Communist attacks combined with the brutality of the fighting turned substantial numbers of influential Americans against the war. Tet happened to take place in an American election year, and this magnified its effect upon the US government. Richard Nixon, the new American President, was hardly a pacifist, but he committed himself to creating a situation in which he could withdraw US forces from Vietnam, not with victory, but with 'honor'.

Giap, among other North Vietnamese commanders, admitted that he never expected Tet to produce the type of results it achieved.[218] Nevertheless, when one reviews the general concepts which shaped North Vietnamese strategy, one sees that Giap and his comrades always intended that something like Tet should occur. Tet fitted into the larger pattern of Communist strategy, in which VC and NVA forces attempted to wear down the will of their enemies. During the 1968 election, Giap noted, quite accurately, that the patience of the US government had worn thin.[219]

As the 1970s began, the intensity of the fighting and the number of casualties escalated to new levels for both sides. Just as the PLF/PAVN logistical system allowed the Communists to stage Tet after the losses of the mid-1960s, it allowed them to stage new offensives after the losses of Tet.[220] In 1972, regular units of the North Vietnamese Army invaded the RVN across the DMZ (Demilitarised Zone). ARVN repelled this invasion and inflicted great losses upon Communist forces, aided by substantial support from the US Navy and Air Force. The next year, however, the United States withdrew the last of its combat forces from the RVN.

In 1975, the Hanoi regime staged a second attack upon the South. On that occasion, the United States declined to intervene, and the North Vietnamese Army overran the Republic of Vietnam. The staff of the US embassy fled the country by helicopter, and for the supporters of the Saigon regime who failed to escape, the consequences were dire. The Communists sentenced hundreds of thousands of South Vietnamese to indefinite periods of 're-education' in camps set up for the purpose.[221] Students of logistics will note that the North Vietnamese relied on the Ho Chi Minh Trail, which had come to involve paved highways and multiple fuel pipelines, to support their final invasion.[222]

Logistics is about movement as well as materiel, and not only did the Ho Chi Minh Trail allow the North Vietnamese to supply their forces in this final campaign, it gave them an advantage in combat mobility as well. As the American colonel Harry S. Summers explained:

> South Vietnam is shaped like a bow, with the coastal transportation network available to South Vietnamese forces following the bow itself. Representing the bow-string was the relatively straight Ho Chi Minh Trail. As a result North Vietnamese forces could move anywhere in South Vietnam faster than could their South Vietnamese counterparts, an advantage that proved crucial in North Vietnam's decisive 1975 blitzkrieg.[223]

FINDINGS

We may now raise the standard questions for this study.

1. How have high-level commanders perceived the problem of logistics?
To many American military analysts, particularly those who, with the benefit of hindsight, wish that their country had pursued a more aggressive course of action, the relationship between the Ho Chi Minh Trail and Communist strategy is painfully obvious. The author Norman B. Hannah, who held a position in the US State Department during the 1960s, identified the Communist supply lines through Laos as 'the key to failure' for the US armed forces in Vietnam. Colonel Harry S. Summers, in the preface to Hannah's book, wrote:

American military commanders knew that isolating the battlefield – cutting the Viet Cong off from their sources of external supply – was essential if the war was to be won. To do that required cutting North Vietnamese lines of supply and communication both at sea and on the ground. With Operation Market Time the US and South Vietnamese Navies established successful barriers to seaborne infiltration of men, supplies and material. But the ground infiltration route – the so-called Ho Chi Minh trail – was never effectively interdicted.

Begun in May 1959 long before America became directly involved in the war, the Ho Chi Minh trail was North Vietnam's key to victory. It was their equivalent of the sea-bridge between the United States and Europe which made Allied victory possible in World War II.[224]

Summers and Hannah identify the mountainous region of Vietnam and Laos around the 17th parallel of latitude as a bottleneck where American forces might have closed the Ho Chi Minh Trail. They feel that the US Army could have won the war, or, at least, radically altered its outcome by moving troops into Laos and blocking the Communist lines of communication. Summers developed these ideas further in his well-received book *On Strategy: A Critical Analysis of the Vietnam War*. Colonel Charles F. Brower IV, General Bruce Palmer Jr and General Westmoreland himself have publicly advanced similar arguments.[225]

The Communists themselves apparently concluded that the importance of their logistical network was self-evident. Communist Party leaders debated the role which guerrillas, conventional forces and political measures designed to bring about a general uprising should play in the war, but the records show no evidence that they argued about whether or not to maintain the trail network which supported all three. North Vietnamese commanders did, however, recognise their logistical system as the factor which allowed their forces to launch operations with confidence. In October 1974, when the North Vietnamese general Tran Van Tra attempted to persuade higher officials in the Hanoi regime to support his plans for a final invasion of South Vietnam, one of his key arguments was the fact that the Ho Chi Minh Trail had grown large enough to support such an effort.[226] The North Vietnamese leaders eventually accepted a version of Tra's plan.

In a book entitled *The Ho Chi Minh Trail*, published for a general audience by Hanoi's Red River press in 1985, an anonymous author describes the strategic logic of the Communist supply network succinctly:

> One could not let one's compatriots in the South fight the American invader alone and with bare hands. Messages, weapons, food and men had to pass at all costs. The enemy, the French and the Americans, occupied also Laos and Kampuchea, the three Indochinese countries making up a strategic entity, and the three peoples a unique fighting

MILITARY LOGISTICS AND STRATEGIC PERFORMANCE

front. From one country to another, communications had also to be safeguarded and strengthened at all costs.

A sole way remained: 'The Long Cordillera'.[227]

What this text mentions in passing serves to confirm three important points about the role of the Ho Chi Minh Trail in Communist strategy. First, and least surprising, the authors of this text take it for granted that the VC and NVA could not have fought a modern war without the Trail.[228] Second, the authors acknowledge that the geographical region which they call 'the long cordillera' was critical to their supply network. This was the same area which Hannah, Summers and others identified as the key chokepoint in the Ho Chi Minh Trail and the Vietnamese source seems to support their interpretation.

Third, the North Vietnamese authors see Laos, Kampuchea and Vietnam as 'a single strategic entity'. Again, this supports the opinions of numerous American commanders. The Communists saw the war as a part of a larger struggle, in which national boundaries were of secondary importance. Through good luck and good diplomacy, they managed to achieve more freedom of action in Laos and Cambodia than their opponents, and that is what made the Ho Chi Minh Trail possible, along with all the strategic advantages it brought the Communist forces.

2. How have logistical factors helped or harmed the strategic performance of armed forces?
The Ho Chi Minh Trail was the womb from which the Communist fighting forces were born. Even in the years immediately following the partition, before the network which became known as the Trail had been established, Marxist–Leninist activists sought sanctuary for their movement in the North and then passed covertly across the border to spread their political ideas in the RVN. The Ho Chi Minh Trail made it possible for the North Vietnamese to revive the faltering southern insurgency in the early 1960s, and to deploy PAVN troops in the South. Year after year, the North Vietnamese used their logistical network to replace combat losses, regroup disintegrating organisations and return from seeming defeats to launch new offensives. Without the Ho Chi Minh Trail, the Communists could not have fought a protracted war, nor could they have executed their strategy of winning 'in a not too long period of time'.

The Ho Chi Minh Trail also gave Communist forces enough speed and tactical mobility to take advantage of momentary opportunities on the battlefield. One must, however, note that there is a difference between possessing such capabilities and using them successfully. VC and NVA forces often fared poorly in combat, for reasons which had little to do with logistics. The Communist offensive in the spring and summer of 1965, for instance, was bold and timely, but it ended in the American victory at Ia Drang. Nevertheless, it is more advantageous for armed forces to have the capability to carry out a given operation than for them not to have that capability, even if other factors make that operation extremely dangerous or difficult. Desperate gambles can succeed as well as fail, audacious manoeuvres can catch the enemy unprepared, new tactics can make the impossible possible, and, even when one does not actually wish to take a given action, it can be useful to let one's opponents think that one might.

3. What factors have given particular forces advantages in logistics?
A variety of human and geographical factors allowed the Communist forces to assemble their logistical system. Although the mountainous jungle terrain of the 'long cordillera' made it difficult for the Communists to build roads, it also offered them cover and concealment. Furthermore, as Westmoreland noted, the shape of South Vietnam and its long borders with Laos and Cambodia made it effectively impossible for Allied troops to block all the points where VC/NVA infiltrators could enter the country. Summers was also correct when he noted that the bow-like shape of the RVN gave troops on the Ho Chi Minh Trail a mobility advantage over their opponents.

The North Vietnamese claimed that their people's culture, history and national pride allowed them to perform feats which were beyond the capacity of Westerners. Communist leaders also emphasised the principles of Marxism, Leninism and Maoism which stated, in a putatively scientific and irrefutable fashion, that the capitalist societies were doomed to turn in upon themselves while socialist movements harnessed the enthusiasm of the people on behalf of their cause. Certainly, the people of North and South Vietnam endured incredible suffering to build the Communist logistical network and keep supplies moving through it. Certainly, many of the Communist leaders' most successful ideas had a basis in Vietnamese tradition. Their country's history undoubtedly served as a source of inspiration to them, and the fact that their plans fitted nicely into the Vietnamese cultural heritage undoubtedly helped them communicate those ideas to colleagues and subordinates.

One must note, however, that for most of the people who supported Hanoi's war effort, Communist ideas were not only compelling but compulsory. Communism does not seem to have been particularly popular, at least in the South. Despite the hopes of the North Vietnamese commanders, a general uprising never took place, and over 150,000 Viet Cong guerrillas defected to the government side between the years 1963 and 1969 alone.[229] (Note, however, that only 1,700 NVA regulars changed sides.) The VC and NVA, did however, create institutions to control, indoctrinate and make use of the civilian population, even within the RVN.

Therefore, the Communists were able to suppress rivals, spread their own ideas and demand submission from political agnostics. Furthermore, most importantly of all, they were able to put people from all these categories to work on projects which supported the movement as a whole. Ideology and national tradition provided a foundation for the Communist insurgency, but the reason these factors played such a significant role in the war is that the Communists managed to use them as the basis for effective organisations. Since the NLF/PAVN supply network relied heavily upon civilian labour, the institutions which provided that labour were particularly important to Communist logistical efforts.

The Cold War also worked in North Vietnam's favour. In both the West and the East, people perceived the Vietnam war as part of a global struggle between the Communist nations and the Western democracies.[230] Therefore, the leaders of the USSR and the Peoples' Republic of China were willing to arm the VC and NVA. Without aid from those two countries, the North Vietnamese might have built the Ho Chi Minh Trail, but they would have had little to send down it.

Details regarding arms transfers between the superpowers and North Vietnam remain scarce and controversial. Chinese sources, however, claim that Beijing sent the North Vietnamese 240,000 guns, 2,730 pieces of artillery, 15 planes, 28 naval vessels and 175 million rounds of ammunition between 1955 and 1963.[231] The Chinese claim to have sent Hanoi 90,000 rifles and machine guns in 1962 alone.[232] For another perspective on the degree to which the North Vietnamese benefited from outside aid, one might consult Table 3, which uses US Defense Intelligence Agency statistics for the year 1966.

The single most important factor working in the Communists' favour, however, was the international political situation which allowed VC and NVA convoys to pass through Laos and Cambodia at will while restricting the actions of US and RVN forces there. As long as the Allies respected the neutrality of these countries, they could neither stop the North Vietnamese from sending convoys south nor could they prevent their enemies from infiltrating men and materiel into the RVN. Although US aircraft and artillery

Table 3: Composition of Viet Cong Weapons (In %)

	Chinese	Soviet	US	French	Home-made/Other
VC Main Force	51	7	24	13	5
Irregular Forces	3	0	38	32	15
NVA	80	18	0	0	2

Note: This information is to be found in J. Van Dyke, *North Vietnam's Strategy for Survival* (Palo Alto, CA: Pacific Books, 1972), p. 222.
These figures are approximate and do not add up to 100%.

units attempted to block the Ho Chi Minh Trail with intense bombardment, this effort ultimately proved futile. US troops entered Cambodia briefly in 1970 and the ARVN staged an unsuccessful invasion of Laos the following year, but from the point of view of those who wanted to stop the Communist movement by cutting off the Ho Chi Minh Trail, these efforts were much too little, much too late.[233]

The diplomacy of the Vietnam War lies beyond the scope of this study, as do the military problems which the United States Army might have faced if it had chosen to invade Laos. One should note, however, that it would have been hard for the Allies to move into the neutral countries earlier, and that such a move would not necessarily have won the war for them.[234] To gain an idea of the difficulty of invading Laos, one might note that, in 1968, General Westmoreland estimated that he would need 206,000 additional American troops to conduct such an operation.[235]

Furthermore, since the Communists had both Laos and Cambodia open to them, the Allies would have had to invade both countries in order to cut off the Communist supply routes entirely. Otherwise, the USSR and China could have continued to support the VC and NVA by sea, through the port of Sihanoukville in Cambodia. This would have presented the Communist forces with enormous difficulties, but it would not necessarily have stopped their war effort. If the VC and NVA had been willing to adopt a less aggressive strategy, they could have made do with reduced quantities of ammunition and reinforcements.[236] Therefore, the Allies would have still had to counter the insurgency movement, a problem which neither US nor South Vietnamese forces ever fully solved.

An invasion of Laos and Cambodia would have raised severe political problems as well, both in southeast Asia and within the United States. The RAND Corporation noted that, if Allied forces had entered the so-called 'long cordillera', the Laotian government would almost certainly have collapsed, unless the United States chose to support it with military force.[237] Under these circumstances, the PAVN would almost certainly have seized the northern part of Laos. Similar scenarios would have been equally plausible in Cambodia.

In other words, the United States could well have found itself fighting three Vietnam-type wars instead of one. The US body politic would have been reluctant to support prolonged operations in Laos and Cambodia in any event, particularly in the later years of the war. One might note that even when American forces staged their relatively limited invasion of Cambodia in 1970, the public and media outcry led the US Congress to pass the Cooper-Church amendment, which prohibited US ground forces from entering the neutral countries.[238] For these reasons and others, the VC and NVA logistical network remained secure.

4. *What logistical problems are associated with particular styles of warfare, and how have commanders addressed them?*
As one follows the history of the Vietnam War, one sees how different levels of combat require correspondingly different levels of logistical support. The more aggressively VC and NVA commanders wished to challenge the armed forces of their opponents, the more men and materiel they required. Their lack of a modern air force and dependence on guerrilla tactics, however, handicapped all of their logistical efforts. Communist supply convoys were always vulnerable to air and artillery bombardment, and Communist units were always at risk of being cut off.

The VC and NVA coped with these problems through their remarkable ability to adapt to changing conditions. Even regular units of the PAVN could resort to classic guerrilla hit-and-run tactics when they lacked the means to carry out more organised operations. The NLF guerrillas, for their part, varied in capabilities, but the Main Force units, at least, were quite prepared to launch large, well-organised attacks when the opportunity presented itself. Many factors contributed to the flexibility of the VC/NVA forces, but the key factors seem to have been the compliance of the soldiers and the effective organisational techniques of the Communist leadership.

Communist forces also diversified their logistical networks as much as possible. Speaking broadly, the entire VC/NVA contingent in the combat zone had two independent lines of communication; one being the branch of the Ho Chi Minh Trail which led directly through Laos and the other being the branch which descended into Cambodia and curved back to approach the RVN from the south. Individual PLF/PAVN units typically had three, four or more complimentary sources of supply, which included stockpiles, land routes, river routes, ocean routes, clandestine factories, the black market and Communist-controlled villages. Some of these sources were more useful than others, and units which found themselves forced to depend on locally available supplies for long periods of time typically had to curtail their operations. Nevertheless, the fact that Communist troops had multiple types of logistical capabilities minimised the chances that their enemies would manage to cut off all their many sources of support simultaneously.

The Communists suffered terrible losses from US aircraft. Nevertheless, they found ways to maintain their supply routes even under attack from American firepower. Again, the secret of VC/NVA success lies, not in one revolutionary technique, but in a variety of mutually complementary efforts. The Communist efforts to survive US bombardment warrant study, especially by those who believe that sensors, precision-guided munitions and computer networks will soon usher in a Revolution in Military Affairs (RMA). A summary of key methods the VC and NVA used to keep their logistical network operative in the face of American bombardment follows.

Camouflage and Security Measures. The North Vietnamese used camouflage extensively, with considerable success.[239] Furthermore, as noted earlier in the text, the Communists took elaborate and effective measures to keep enemy intelligence analysts from figuring out which of their units were on the Trail or where those units might be going.

Make Hay While the Sun Shines. The popular concepts of graduated escalation and limited war led US forces to halt or restrict their bombing campaign on 16 occasions. Communist forces took full advantage of these interludes to move supplies.[240]

Repair. As the US Air Force destroyed roads, railways, bridges and docks, the Communists laboured to fix them. US intelligence agencies estimate that, by 1967, 97,000 North Vietnamese worked constantly at this job, while another 370,000 to 500,000 devoted at least several days each month to repair.[241] This figure does not include civilians in the RVN, who had been conscripted to work on trails in the South.

Hidden Bridges. Since bridges were a prime target for air attack, the North Vietnamese developed pontoon bridges made from bamboo which were hard to bomb and easy to repair.[242] In some cases, the Communists built portable bridges which they could conceal in the forest by day in order to keep American reconnaissance planes from finding them. The North Vietnamese also hid bridges by submerging them a foot or so beneath the water. Trucks could cross these artificial fords but aerial observers could not see them.

Bomb and Sensor Disposal. US forces attempted to disrupt Communist repair efforts by dropping time-fused bombs which remained in the target zone for minutes, hours or days before exploding. They also seeded the Ho Chi Minh Trail with sound-sensitive sensors known as 'black boxes' designed to detect enemy troops and pinpoint them for air attack. In response, Communist forces trained large numbers of their troops to find and disarm such devices.[243]

Remote Base Areas. The Communists built base camps in mountains, dense jungles and other inaccessible terrain so that, even when air attacks disrupted their operations, enemy ground troops could not move in to exploit that disruption. Therefore, after a bombing raid, the VC and NVA were often able to return and rebuild their bases. The best-known example of a VC remote-base area was the infamous Iron Triangle between the Saigon and Tinh rivers.[244]

Air Defences. In addition to their assortment of improvised techniques, Communist forces deployed modern air defences, along with an air force of approximately 150 fighters.[245] One can find a more comprehensive account of

Communist techniques for surviving air and artillery attack in such sources as Jon M. Van Dyke's *North Vietnam's Strategy For Survival*, Donald J. Mrozek's *Air Power and the Ground War in Vietnam* and James W. Gibson's *The Perfect War: Technowar in Vietnam*.[246]

CONCLUSION

Every historical event is unique, but the Vietnam War involved a particularly large number of singular cultural, ideological, geographical, political and tactical circumstances. Without the proximity of Laos and Cambodia, without the struggle between the Communist countries and the West or without the Chinese and Vietnamese concepts of guerrilla warfare, it would have been an entirely different war. Nevertheless, when one examines the process by which the Communists won their victory, one finds that their experience shares a common theme with the campaigns of other victorious armies in this study. The factor which allowed them to unite the various circumstances of their particular historical situation into a coherent and victorious strategy was their mastery of logistics.

Future wars may not resemble that in Vietnam in detail. They will have cultural, political, technological and geographical peculiarities of their own. Nevertheless, if combatants hope to exploit their circumstances in a systematic way, they will need the material means to do so. Likewise, if one wishes to understand what they are doing, one does well to begin by looking at their logistical capabilities.

NOTES

[The author is grateful to Colonel Gregory Banner of the US Army for his invaluable help in researching this chapter. The author acknowledges a debt to Colonel Banner's master's thesis in his analysis of the prospects for an Allied invasion of Laos, published as Gregory Banner, The War for the Ho Chi Minh Trail (Fort Leavenworth, KS: thesis presented to the US Army Command and General Staff College, 1993).]

1. For contrasting points of view about the degree to which America's experience in Vietnam resembled a conventional war, compare Harry G. Summers Jr, *On Strategy: A Critical Analysis of the Vietnam War* (New York: Dell Publishing, 1984), *passim* and Andrew F. Krepinevich Jr, *The Army and Vietnam* (Baltimore, MD: Johns Hopkins University Press, 1986), *passim*. Summers portrays the Vietnam War as a relatively simple clash between organised armies while Krepinevich emphasises its distinctive nature as an insurgency.
2. *The Ho Chi Minh Trail* (Hanoi: Red River Foreign Language Publishing House, 1985), p. 21.
3. Tao Hanzhang, *Sun Tzu's Art of War: The Modern Chinese Interpretation*, trans. Yuan Shibing (New York: Sterling Publishing, 1987), p. 97.

4. Brian Bond, *Liddell Hart: A Study of His Military Thought* (London: Cassell, 1977).
5. Carl von Clausewitz, *On War*, ed. and trans. Michael Howard and Peter Paret (Princeton, NJ: Princeton University Press, 1976), p. 87
6. Stanley Karnow, *Vietnam – A History: The First Complete Account of Vietnam at War* (New York: Penguin Books, 1984), p. 204.
7. William J. Duiker, *The Communist Road to Power in Vietnam* (Boulder, CO: Westview Press, 1981), p. 171.
8. Ibid., p. 183.
9. Ibid., p. 184.
10. Karnow, *Vietnam – A History*, p. 225.
11. Duiker, *The Communist Road to Power*, p. 183.
12. Ibid.
13. Ibid., p. 187.
14. Ibid., p. 188.
15. Ibid., p. 191.
16. Ibid., p. 219.
17. Ibid., p. 191.
18. Carlyle A. Thayer, *War By Other Means: National Liberation and Revolution in Viet-Nam 1954–60* (Boston, MA: Allen & Unwin, 1989), p. 142.
19. Duiker, *The Communist Road to Power*, p. 192.
20. Ibid., p. 197.
21. Douglas Pike, *PAVN: People's Army of Vietnam* (New York: Da Capo Press, 1986), p. 41.
22. Thayer, *War By Other Means*, p. 185.
23. Ibid., p. 188.
24. L.P. Holliday and R.M. Gurfield, *Viet Cong Logistics* (Santa Monica, CA: RAND, 1968), p. 4.
25. Pike, *PAVN*, p. 12.
26. Ibid., p. 219.
27. Peter Macdonald, *Giap: The Victor in Vietnam* (London: Warner, 1993), p. 200.
28. Ibid.
29. Michael Lee Lanning and Dan Cragg, *Inside the VC and the NVA: The Real Story of North Vietnam's Armed Forces* (New York: Ivy Books, 1992), p. 201.
30. Macdonald, *Giap*, p. 197.
31. Duiker, *The Communist Road to Power*, p. 268.
32. Lanning and Cragg, *Inside the VC*, p. 201.
33. Ibid., p. 201.
34. Ibid., p. 202.
35. Ibid.
36. Gabriel Kolko, *Anatomy of a War: Vietnam, the United States and the Modern Historical Experience* (New York: The New Press, 1985), p. 138.
37. Duiker, *The Communist Road to Power*, p. 286.
38. Lanning and Cragg, *Inside the VC*, p. 82.
39. Pike, *PAVN*, p. 51.
40. A summary of Mao's prescriptions appears in Duiker, *The Communist Road to Power*, pp. 134–7. For Mao's original work, see Mao Tse-Tung: *Selected Military Writings of Mao Tse-Tung* (Peking: Foreign Languages Press, 1968); *Problems of War and Strategy* (Peking: Foreign Languages Press, 1954), *passim*. For a sampling of Lin Piao's work, which is also important to an understanding of the Communist way of war in the 1960s, see Samuel Griffith, *Peking and People's Wars* (London: Pall Mall Press, 1966), *passim*.
41. Lanning and Cragg, *Inside the VC*, p. 199.

42. Duiker, *The Communist Road to Power*, p. 206.
43. Lanning and Cragg, *Inside the VC*, p. 199.
44. Ibid.
45. Duiker, *The Communist Road to Power*, p. 260.
46. Karnow, *Vietnam – A History*, p. 331.
47. Ibid., p. 332.
48. Ibid.
49. Ibid.
50. Ibid.
51. Bruce Palmer Jr, *The Twenty-Five Year War: America's Military Role in Vietnam* (Lexington, MA: University Press of Lexington, 1984), p. 85.
52. Ibid., p. 87–8.
53. Duiker, *The Communist Road to Power*, p. 408, n. 12.
54. Palmer, *The Twenty-Five Year War*, p. 81.
55. Pike, *PAVN*, p. 18.
56. Palmer, *The Twenty-Five Year War*, p. 85.
57. Duiker, *The Communist Road to Power*, p. 262.
58. Ibid.
59. Ibid., pp. 261–2.
60. The Communists made a significant attempt to touch off a general revolt when they launched the Tet Offensive of 1968, but even then, the civilian population did not rise up as they had hoped.
61. Duiker, *The Communist Road to Power*, p. 273.
62. Ibid.
63. Ibid.
64. Ibid.
65. Ibid., p. 273.
66. Lanning and Cragg, *Inside the VC*, p. 22.
67. Duiker, *The Communist Road to Power*, p. 275.
68. Palmer, *The Twenty-Five Year War*, pp. 211-19.
69. Duiker, *The Communist Road to Power*, pp. 267-8.
70. Palmer, *The Twenty-Five Year War*, p. 210.
71. Pike, *PAVN*, passim.
72. Edgar O. Ballance, 'The Ho Chi Minh Trail', *The Army Quarterly & Defence Journal* (April 1967), p. 105.
73. Ibid.
74. Thayer, *War By Other Means*, p. 185; Ballance, 'The Ho Chi Minh Trail,' pp. 105-6.
75. *VC/NVA Logistics Study* (Military Assistance Command, Vietnam, Combined Intelligence Center Vietnam, 1971), p. 2.
76. Lanning and Cragg, *Inside the VC*, p. 141.
77. Ibid., p. 84.
78. *VC/NVA Logistics Study*, p. 4; *North Vietnam Personnel Infiltration into the Republic of Vietnam* (Military Assistance Command, Vietnam: Office of the Assistant Chief of Staff – J-2, 16 December 1970), p. 29; Lanning and Cragg, *Inside the VC*, p. 84.
79. *VC/NVA Logistics Study*, p. 4; Lanning and Cragg, *Inside the VC*, p. 84.
80. Lanning and Cragg, *Inside the VC*, p. 84.
81. Ibid.
82. *North Vietnam Personnel Infiltration*, p. 52.
83. *VC/NVA Logistics Study*, pp. 5–6.
84. Ibid., p. 5.
85. Lanning and Cragg, *Inside the VC*, p. 84.

86. Ibid., p. 86.
87. Ibid.
88. *North Vietnam Personnel Infiltration*, p. 18.
89. Lanning and Cragg, *Inside the VC*, 83.
90. Ibid.
91. Ballance, 'The Ho Chi Minh Trail', p. 108.
92. 'Laos: More Troublesome Trail', *Time* (December 17, 1965), pp. 28–9.
93. *Supply Lines through Laos and Cambodia into South Vietnam* (Vietnam: Military Assistance Command Vietnam, Office of the Assistant Chief of Staff – J-2, 28 February, 1969), p. 1.
94. *VC/NVA Logistics Study*, unnumbered page in appendix.
95. *VC/NVA Logistics Study*, p. C-1; *The Ho Chi Minh Trail*, p. 18.
96. William E. DePuy, 'Vietnam: What We Might Have Done and Why We Didn't Do It', *Army* (February 1986), p. 24; *VC/NVA Logistics Study*, p. 29.
97. *VC/NVA Logistics Study*, p. 29.
98. Ibid.
99. Ibid.
100. DePuy, 'Vietnam: What We Might Have Done', p. 24; *VC/NVA Logistics Study*, p. 30–1
101. Kenneth O. Gilmore, 'Along the Infamous Ho Chi Minh Trail', *Reader's Digest* (October 1970), p. 165.
102. *The Ho Chi Minh Trail*, p. 15.
103. *North Vietnam Personnel Infiltration*, p. 60; *Supply Lines through Laos and Cambodia*, p. 29.
104. Gilmore, 'Along the Infamous Ho Chi Min Trail', p. 166; *The Ho Chi Minh Trail*, p. 15.
105. *Supply Lines through Laos and Cambodia*, p. 21.
106. *North Vietnam Personnel Infiltration*, p. 52.
107. Ibid.
108. Ibid., p. 67.
109. Lanning and Cragg, *Inside the VC*, pp. 74–6.
110. Ibid., p. 76.
111. Ibid.
112. One sees evidence of this in the diaries of NVA infiltrators. Ibid., pp. 2–15.
113. Ibid.
114. Holliday and Gurfield, *Viet Cong Logistics*, p. 1.
115. Ibid., p. 4.
116. Ibid., p. 8.
117. Ibid.
118. Ibid., p. 61.
119. Ibid., p. 62.
120. Ibid., p. 60.
121. Ibid.
122. Ibid.
123. Ibid., p. 19.
124. Ibid., p. 20.
125. Ibid.
126. Ibid.
127. Ibid., p. 30.
128. Ibid.
129. Ibid., pp. 47–56.
130. Ibid., p. 48.

131. Ibid.
132. Ibid.
133. Ibid., p. 91.
134. Ibid., p. 90.
135. Ibid., p. 13.
136. Ibid.
137. This unit was known as the Sao Vang division. Ibid., pp. 12–23.
138. Ibid.
139. Duiker, *The Communist Road to Power*, p. 286.
140. *VC/NVA Logistics Study*, p. 26; Lanning and Cragg, *Inside the VC*, p. 152.
141. Holliday and Gurfield, *Viet Cong Logistics*, p. 90.
142. Ibid., p. 46.
143. Ibid.
144. Ibid., pp. 45-6.
145. Ibid., p. 46.
146. Ibid., p. 42.
147. Ibid., p. 44.
148. Lanning and Cragg, *Inside the VC*, pp. 93-4.
149. Holliday and Gurfield, *Viet Cong Logistics*, p. 16.
150. Ibid., p. 17.
151. Ibid.
152. Ibid., p. 90.
153. Ibid.
154. Ibid., p. 45.
155. Ibid.
156. Lanning and Cragg, *Inside the VC*, p. 94.
157. Holliday and Gurfield, *Viet Cong Logistics*, p. 17.
158. Ibid.
159. Lanning and Cragg, *Inside the VC*, p. 313.
160. Duiker, *The Communist Road to Power*, p. 285.
161. Lanning and Cragg, *Inside the VC*, p. 313; Duiker, *The Communist Road to Power*, p. 285.
162. One partial explanation for the discrepancy may be that the US Army did not count either part-time guerrillas or support troops, whereas the North Vietnamese authorities included both in their total. Lanning and Cragg, *Inside the VC*, p. 309; Duiker, *The Communist Road to Power*, p. 410, n. 44.
163. Palmer, *The Twenty-Five Year War*, p. 81.
164. Holliday and Gurfield, *Viet Cong Logistics*, p. 16; Lanning and Cragg, *Inside the VC*, pp. 93–4.
165. These figures for the population of typical Vietnamese villages come from Holliday and Gurfield, *Viet Cong Logistics*, p. 70.
166. Palmer, *The Twenty-Five Year War*, p. 107.
167. Ibid.
168. Ibid., p. 105.
169. Ibid.
170. Ibid., p. 106.
171. Ibid., p. 107.
172. Ibid., pp. 107–16.
173. Duiker, *The Communist Road to Power*, p. 288.
174. William C. Westmoreland, *A Soldier Reports* (New York: Da Capo Press, 1980), p. 147.

175. Ibid.
176. Ibid., p. 146.
177. Palmer, *The Twenty-Five Year War*, p. 152.
178. Westmoreland, *A Soldier Reports*, p. 166.
179. Ibid., p. 147.
180. Ibid.
181. Ibid.
182. Ibid., p. 142.
183. 'How To Win the War In Vietnam: Admiral Sharp's Prescription', *US News and World Report* (2 October 1967), p. 22.
184. Duiker, *The Communist Road to Power*, p. 286.
185. Karnow, *Vietnam – A History*, pp. 487–8.
186. Ibid., p. 488.
187. Ibid., pp. 485–6.
188. Duiker, *The Communist Road to Power*, pp. 285–6.
189. Palmer, *The Twenty-Five Year War*, p. 177; Westmoreland, *A Soldier Reports*, p. 347.
190. Duiker, *The Communist Road to Power*, p. 287.
191. Ibid., p. 292.
192. Lanning and Cragg, *Inside the VC*, p. 137.
193. Ibid., p. 128.
194. Ibid.
195. Ibid.
196. *North Vietnam Personnel Infiltration*, p. 91; Lanning and Cragg, *Inside the VC*, p. 15.
197. Ibid., p. 89.
198. Ibid., p. 5.
199. Palmer, *The Twenty-Five Year War*, p. 209.
200. *North Vietnam Personnel Infiltration*, p. 15.
201. Ibid., p. 5.
202. Ibid., p. 60.
203. Ibid., p. 61. Astute readers may sense a discrepancy between these statistics, which come from a report by the US Armed Forces Combined Intelligence Center and the earlier statistics on VC/NVA strength, which came from the Military Advisory Command, Vietnam (MACV) Order of Battle Summary. The Order of Battle Summary reported that there were a total of 70,355 troops of the NVA and VC Main Force in South Vietnam during early 1967. (Lanning and Cragg, *Inside the VC*, p. 313.) The Combined Intelligence Center data implies that, during the same period, the Communist forces in South Vietnam fielded 65,000 troops from the NVA alone. (*North Vietnam Personnel Infiltration*, p. 61.) Since the VC Main Force almost certainly fielded more than 5,355 troops during that period, one must treat both sources with a degree of scepticism. The information in these reports is sufficient to illustrate broad points about the nature of the Communist logistical system, but the precise figures are almost certainly wrong.
204. Ibid., p. 60.
205. Ibid., pp. 60–1.
206. Ibid., p. 61.
207. Lanning and Cragg, *Inside the VC*, p. 52.
208. *North Vietnam Personnel Infiltration*, p. 3.
209. Ibid., p. 60.
210. Holliday and Gurfield, *Viet Cong Logistics*, p. 40.
211. Ibid.

212. *North Vietnam Personnel Infiltration*, p. 82.
213. Duiker, *The Communist Road to Power*, p. 287.
214. *North Vietnam Personnel Infiltration*, p. 83.
215. Ibid.
216. Ibid.
217. For more details, and for information to back up the summary which appears in the following paragraphs, see Palmer, *The Twenty-Five Year War*, pp. 255–67.
218. Macdonald, *Giap*, pp. 260 and 268–9.
219. Duiker, *The Communist Road to Power*, p. 286.
220. *North Vietnam Personnel Infiltration*, pp. 58–60.
221. Duiker, *The Communist Road to Power*, p. 363.
222. Norman B. Hannah, *The Key to Failure: Laos and the Vietnam War* (New York: Madison Books, 1987), p. xiii.
223. Ibid.
224. Ibid., pp. xii–xiii.
225. Summers, *On Strategy, passim*; Bruce Palmer Jr, *The Twenty-Five Year War, passim*; Charles F. Brower, *Strategic Reassessment in Vietnam: The Westmoreland 'Alternate Strategy' of 1967–1968* (Newport, RI: Naval War College, 1990), *passim*; Westmoreland, *A Soldier Reports*, pp. 350–62. Thanks to Colonel Gregory Banner, whose master's thesis provided a foundation for this brief literature review. Banner, *The War for the Ho Chi Minh Trail*, p. 1.
226. Karnow, *Vietnam – A History*, p. 663.
227. *The Ho Chi Minh Trail*, p. 8. 'Cordillera' means a mountain chain or ridge.
228. This was, of course, a politically prudent opinion for a North Vietnamese writer in the 1980s. The Hanoi regime often attempted to take credit for the Communist victory, at the expense of South Vietnamese guerrillas and political activists. (Duiker, *The Communist Road to Power*, p. 349) Nevertheless, even when analysed from an objective point of view, the importance of the Ho Chi Minh Trail exceeds the requirements of propaganda. The authors' assertions are politic, but they are also true.
229. Lanning and Cragg, *Inside the VC*, p. 50.
230. The following sources elaborate on the idea that Vietnam was merely part of a broader conflict. Rood writes from a Western point of view, while Xiaoming explores the Communist perspective. Harold W. Rood, *Kingdoms of the Blind* (Durham, NC: Carolina Academic Press, 1980), p. 283; Xiaoming Zhang, 'The Vietnam War, 1964–1969: A Chinese Perspective', *Journal of Military History*, Vol. 60, No. 4 (October 1996), pp. 731–62.
231. Xiaoming Zhang, 'The Vietnam War', pp. 735–6.
232. Ibid., p. 736.
233. Karnow, *Vietnam – A History*, pp. 629-30.
234. Banner, *The War for the Ho Chi Minh Trail, passim*.
235. Westmoreland, *A Soldier Reports*, p. 358.
236. Banner, *The War for the Ho Chi Minh Trail*, pp. 101–2.
237. Ibid., p. 107.
238. Ibid., pp. 98–9.
239. Van Dyke, *North Vietnam's Strategy*, p. 53.
240. Ibid., p. 54.
241. Ibid., p. 44.
242. Ibid., p. 48.
243. Ibid., pp. 40–9.
244. Donald J. Mrozek, *Air Power and the Ground War in Vietnam* (London: Pergamon–Brasseys, 1989), p. 140.

245. Van Dyke, *North Vietnam's Strategy*, pp. 59–65.
246. Van Dyke, *North Vietnam's Strategy, passim*; Mrozek, *Air Power, passim*; James William Gibson, *The Perfect War: Technowar in Vietnam* (Boston, MA: The Atlantic Monthly Press, 1986), *passim*.

5

The Cold War

From the end of the Second World War in 1945 to the collapse of the Soviet Union and its satellite regimes in the early 1990s, the assorted nations of NATO and the Warsaw Treaty Organisation (WTO) prepared for a third world war to determine the fate of Europe. This was a conflict which neither side could afford to fight on its opponent's terms. There were sharp contrasts between NATO and the Warsaw Pact in types of national resources, types of armed forces and philosophies of warfare. In a war, the side which managed to make the war follow a course which emphasised its own strengths would have been likely to win.

The power of modern weapons, particularly nuclear weapons, made leaders on both sides eager to win any war quickly, without a long and destructive struggle. The Soviet Union could not afford to absorb the full force of Western firepower, while NATO strategists, for their part, were loath to accept a prolonged ground campaign in the German heartland. Therefore, war planners in both the West and the East heeded Sun Tzu's maxim that 'what is of supreme importance in war is to attack the enemy's strategy'. For both NATO and the Warsaw Pact, 'attacking the enemy's strategy' frequently turned out to mean attacking the enemy's logistical system.[1]

The history of Cold War strategy on NATO's Central Front illustrates the links between logistics, national resources and the art of strategy. This chapter traces those connections, focusing on the period from the early 1980s to the fall of the Berlin Wall in 1989. First, it looks at the logistical problems which NATO forces faced and then it goes on to show how Pact strategists planned to exploit them. The next two sections reverse this perspective by examining Communist logistical difficulties and looking at how NATO developed a doctrine designed to take full advantage of such factors.

THE WESTERN PREDICAMENT: STANDING TALL WITH FLAT FEET

In order to understand the logistical system which supported NATO strategy, one must understand the types of forces which NATO fielded and how Western commanders hoped to use them. The Western countries based their defense posture on the principle that 'the military forces of NATO could compensate for their numerical inferiority relative to the forces of the Warsaw Pact by their qualitative superiority'.[2] Western armies aspired to field more technologically advanced equipment, along with more highly trained soldiers to operate it. Furthermore, NATO planners hoped that a democratic political culture, Western levels of education and more flexible styles of command would help their forces seize the initiative on the battlefield.[3] The Arab–Israeli wars seemed to demonstrate both the success of Western weapons designs and the validity of the idea that quality can defeat quantity.[4] Studies of Soviet tactical performance during the Second World War offered the West further encouragement.[5]

Western countries certainly enjoyed advantages in wealth and education which should have given them the potential to field superior troops and machines. In discussions of these subjects, numbers may be grossly misleading, but for purposes of this study a few comparative statistics make the point. In 1979, only 9 per cent of Soviet citizens had some form of higher education, whereas in the United States almost 15 per cent of the population had a full four years of college.[6] Nearly half the students in Soviet college programmes were studying part time, through correspondence courses.[7] The total gross national product of the Warsaw Pact in 1980 came to an estimated 752 billion US dollars, as opposed to 5,098 billion US dollars for NATO.[8] When one considers economic capacity in terms of gross national product per capita, one finds figures of US$2,005 and US$8,909, respectively.[9]

How did this potential translate into actuality? Suffice it to say that the vision of the Cold War as a contest between NATO quality and Pact quantity demands caveats on both counts. The Warsaw Treaty Organisation (WTO) possessed a clear numerical advantage in tanks, but not in troops or aircraft. On the other hand, though NATO did deploy more advanced equipment, the Soviet Union and its allies practised a style of warfare which made many Western technical refinements unnecessary.

Table 4 indicates the numerical balance between NATO and the Warsaw Pact, as it existed 'on paper'.[10]

Charts such as Table 4 cannot predict the strength of forces which would have actually engaged one another on the Central Front. That figure would have depended on the intensity of fighting on other fronts, the course of the naval war, the amount of time available for mobilisation, the extent to which the Soviet Union dared to withdraw units from its Chinese border and numerous other factors, all of which lie within the realm of the unknown. These data do, however, indicate the relative size of the opposing armed forces. In the field of tanks, the Eastern nations always maintained a substantial quantitative lead but, even before the NATO conventional build-up of the 1980s, the Pact possessed only a marginal advantage in aircraft.

Table 4: The NATO/Warsaw Pact Military Balance

	1981	1988	% Change
Army Manpower			
Warsaw Pact	2,613,000	2,829,000	+10.8
NATO	2,712,758	2,750,934	+10.1
Ratio (Pact/NATO)	0.96:1	1.02:1	–
Tanks			
Warsaw Pact	70,420	67,600	+4.0
NATO	26,028	30,684	+1.8
Ratio (Pact/NATO)	2.70:1	2.20:1	–
Tactical Combat Aircraft			
Warsaw Pact	7,541	7,182	–5.0
NATO	6,845	8,268	+12.1
Ratio (Pact/NATO)	1.10:1	0.87:1	–

Notes: 1. The NATO figures include Greek, Italian and Turkish forces. These units were unlikely to play a direct role on the Central Front, but their presence elsewhere would presumably have limited the USSR's freedom to concentrate all of its assets upon Germany. However, these nations fielded personnel-intensive armies, and therefore, they skew the statistics on Army Manpower. Without the southern tier nations, NATO's 1981 manpower was 1,837,758, for a Pact/NATO ratio of 1.43:1. In 1988, the figure became 1,778,934, for a ratio of 1.59:1.

2. Just as comparisons of total manpower can be misleading, numerical comparisons of air forces can miss important points as well. As Table 4 shows, NATO and the Warsaw Pact fielded similar numbers of aircraft overall. However, when one compares the number which each side had ready for action on the Central Front, another picture emerges. In 1984, Air Marshal Sir Patrick Hine of the RAF estimated that, in an air battle over Germany, the Warsaw Pact air forces would have outnumbered NATO by 2.3:1.

3. Spain became a NATO member in 1982. In order to maintain the continuity of the table, especially in the third column, the figures above do not include Spanish forces. It is highly unlikely that Spain would have played a role in the battle for Northern Germany in any event. However, for those who enjoy such statistics, the addition of Spain brought NATO's army manpower to 2,980,934, its tank strength to 31,527 and its number of tactical aircraft to 7,392.

Turning from quantity to quality, the West secured a clear technological advantage in the air. As a rule of thumb, NATO air forces fielded new-generation avionics, munitions and targeting systems ten years before their Pact counterparts.[11] Soviet aircraft tended to have lower wing loadings and higher thrust-to-weight ratios, but due to NATO flight control systems, this did not always translate into superior response characteristics.[12] Cautious observers, however, observed that the struggle for air supremacy is more than a contest of aircraft against aircraft. WTO ground units had highly-developed anti-aircraft establishments, which would have reduced their need for fighter protection and the Pact might have reduced NATO's capabilities through missile attacks on airfields.[13]

NATO also achieved technological superiority in armoured vehicles, but the combination of Soviet doctrine and German terrain might well have rendered these advantages insignificant. Many Soviet tanks carried their fuel in external tanks, which was unquestionably a drawback.[14] By the mid-1980s, NATO tanks fielded laser gunsights, fire control computers, high-precision guns and composite armour and superior night-vision equipment.[15] During the same period, over 70 per cent of WTO tanks lacked such systems.[16] However, high-technology targeting systems are most valuable at long ranges, and in the close terrain which dominates roughly 83 per cent of the German border country, NATO's gunnery advantages would have been negligible.[17] Armour protection might have played a larger role, and Russian tanks tended to have an advantage in this department. The Pact disadvantage in night vision was often overstated, and furthermore, the significance of this factor would have depended entirely on whether or not NATO managed to seize the initiative and stage decisive engagements at night.[18]

Since NATO and the Warsaw Pact never fought, one can only speculate about the relative quality of their troops. The Communists themselves seemed to fear that the brutal living conditions which they imposed upon their troops would endanger morale.[19] Western observers often criticised Warsaw Pact training for its lack of live-fire exercises, its reliance on simulators as apposed to field practice and the stylised nature of its training drills.[20] Again, the Pact employed a different philosophy of warfare. The Communists did not believe that ordinary troops were capable of reaching generally high levels of combat proficiency, and therefore, they focused training exercises on teaching soldiers to perform a few specialised tasks well.[21] Ken Brower of the British Royal Military Academy's Soviet Studies Research Center noted that due to the way in which both nations selected their soldiers and rotated troops between assignments, neither the United States nor the USSR managed to achieve much social cohesion within military units.[22] Therefore, in Brower's opinion, both sides seemed vulnerable to catastrophic breakdowns under fire.

When academic observers examined the quality and quantity of forces which opposed each other on the Central Front, they often decided that a successful Communist invasion of the West would have been close to impossible.[23] However, commanders at the highest levels of NATO's military structure came publicly and emphatically to the opposite conclusion. In 1986, for instance, Bernard Rogers, the commander of the Supreme Allied Command,

Europe, stated 'If attacked conventionally today, NATO would be forced ... to decide whether it should escalate to the non-strategic nuclear level. (The alternative would be to accept defeat.)'[24] Despite the fact that the Communists never attempted an attack, one ought to consider the factors which led Rogers and others to such pessimistic conclusions.

The danger NATO faced was that the forces it possessed in theory might not have materialised in fact. Prudent observers warned that NATO might lack the political resolve to mount a timely Defense.[25] The fact that five different countries held sections of the front and that each of those nations had individual responsibility for making the decision to mobilise meant that failures of co-ordination would have been probable.[26] Furthermore, the logistical obstacles to mobilisation might have been greater than the political ones. Except for the Seventh Army, all NATO forces required some degree of reinforcement simply to enter combat.[27] In several cases, entire corps needed to be deployed in their sectors.[28]

NATO mobilisation also required extensive movement across the Atlantic Ocean. Leaving aside the long-term problem of putting American industrial strength at the service of the Western Alliance, over five of the divisions which the United States assigned to the initial Defense of Germany were stationed at peacetime bases in the continental United States.[29] In the event of war, these units would have had to cross the Atlantic Ocean to join the battle. The US Army frequently rehearsed this operation under the codename REFORGER (REturn of FORces to GERmany). Although the REFORGER divisions kept much of their heavy equipment prepositioned in Europe in the so-called POMCUS (Pre-positioned Overseas Material Configured to Unit Sets) facilities, their deployment would have required a massive air and sealift, and that process would certainly have been difficult, time-consuming and fraught with accidents. In Operation Desert Shield, 30 per cent of the US Ready Reserve merchant fleet experienced delays in mobilisation of ten days or more.[30] Furthermore, one must note that Desert Shield took place in the complete absence of enemy interference. During a general war in Europe, the Warsaw Pact submarine fleets and air forces would almost certainly have interfered with NATO shipping, and WTO special forces would almost certainly have committed sabotage against Western European ports.

The full story of Western logistical shortfalls remains classified.[31] However, numerous military and political officials commented on the shortfalls in the West's preparations. In 1977, US senators Samuel Nunn and Dewey F. Bartlett described NATO stockpiles as 'nothing less than a disgrace'.[32] In 1982, Bernard Rogers observed that, although his forces had a significant shortfall in manpower, there would be little point in raising more troops because there was no equipment to support them.[33] Two years later, the British Atlantic Committee declared that stockpiles constituted the West's most salient problem on land and lay 'at the heart of all NATO's inferiority'.[34] Although

NATO plans required enough ammunition to engage Pact troops for a month of high-intensity combat, official reports estimated that the actual stockpiles would have run out in seven days.[35]

In 1984, the US Department of Defense presented a report to the Appropriations Committee of the House of Representatives which included numerous details on the shortfalls of American logistics. The fact that the Communists rated the US Army units alongside those of the Bundeswehr as the most capable forces in Europe indicates that, at least in their estimation, other members of the alliance suffered from similar problems or worse.[36] According to official reports, American stockpiles contained enough supplies for ten days of combat.[37] However, when units experienced shortages in any given resource, they routinely counted some similar item in lieu of the missing commodity, thereby rendering such estimates both unreliable and highly optimistic.[38] The House Appropriations Committee report concluded simply that 'the army has lost control of its equipment inventories'.[39] Missiles, chaff, anti-tank shells, infantry anti-tank weapons and electrical equipment were known to be in particularly short supply, and some units possessed only half their official allotments of such basic commodities as rifles and small-arms ammunition.[40]

Furthermore, US forces would have faced some difficulty in distributing the materiel they actually possessed, since substantial numbers of units had only a fraction of the trucks, ammunition trailers and tracked cargo vehicles which appeared in their tables of organisation.[41] The fact that 60 per cent of all combat support forces were part of the Army Reserve meant that commanders would require time to call them up and process them into their units, and even after this procedure was complete, the support organisation had only 74 per cent of its authorised equipment.[42] Air Force supply officers estimated that they needed to have six spare engines in the logistical pipeline in order to ensure even an 80 per cent chance that one would be available in the theatre of action.[43]

For the logistical support which they did possess, US units relied heavily on foreign and civilian forces. In a major European war, American forces would have relied on allied support for half their ground transport and nearly half the ships in their cargo fleet.[44] The US Air Force estimated that, without civilian technicians, the number of aircraft capable of flying on any given day would decline from 65 per cent to 20 per cent.[45] Naval units also employed civilian contractual engineering technical personnel (Sets) and the commander of one aircraft carrier expressed his dependence on them with the statement 'without my Sets, I don't sail at all'.[46] This dependence on outside assistance can only have increased the administrative and political difficulties of organising Western supply, along with the opportunities for enemy special operations.

The West also suffered from a shortage of bases. This problem was most acute for air forces, which are tied to their airstrips and support facilities. In

1978, there were only 18 NATO airbases in Germany, and the use of civilian facilities would have brought that total to no more than 100.[47] Aircraft congested into such small numbers of facilities risk becoming mere targets.[48] During the same year, US forces had only 79 warehouses for storing pre-positioned materiel in Germany.[49] Not only was this number inadequate for the amount of equipment which American units required, but most of the storage facilities were in southern Germany, hundreds of miles from the likely battlefields. To quote from the 1980 report on US military posture: 'All services have insufficient ammunition stocks to meet wartime requirements. In addition, lack of adequate forward storage facilities restricts efforts to preposition, creates malpositioned inventories and places an additional burden on strategic lift assets.'[50]

One must also remember that the West's actual wartime logistical problems would have been more difficult than peacetime estimates suggest, not less. Even if NATO's stockpiles did contain enough ammunition for seven days of combat, the demand for munitions would have been far heavier in some areas than others. The units which found themselves in the path of the main enemy attack would have run out of ammunition rapidly, and their survival would have depended on their ability to draw supplies from other sectors of the war zone. As NATO reserves moved to the front, Communist attacks disrupted communications and Western commanders tried to cope with their other transportation handicaps, fatal shortages at critical places would have been inevitable. Furthermore, accidents, refugee movements and other extra-military factors would have disrupted the movement of troops and materiel. In 1980, logisticians received a graphic foretaste of what might have occurred when the addition of refugees and other civilian activity to a wargame known as Nifty Nugget caused a hypothetical operation to transport 400,000 troops from the United States to Europe to bog down.[51]

NATO's problems were not insoluble, and during the 1980s, the Western nations made efforts to correct them.[52] However, supply requirements are expensive, unglamorous and often undervalued by the military itself. Furthermore, the need for logistical support is eternal, and does not fluctuate with public support for defence spending. In an alliance of countries which wish to protect a democratic, non-militaristic society over an indefinite period of time, it seems inevitable that logistics will suffer. The danger that NATO units would engage their enemies as undersupplied fragments of their paper selves was real.

THE NATURE OF SOVIET OPERATIONS

One can now examine the type of attack which NATO's enemies planned to launch, its probable effects upon NATO logistics, and the overall consequences for NATO's ability to wage war. During the following discussion, readers should note that the member nations of the Warsaw Pact, unlike NATO, employed standard tactics and standard doctrine throughout the alliance.[53] Therefore, statements concerning Soviet military practice apply to the armed forces of Czechoslovakia, Poland and the German Democratic Republic, as well as to any other WTO forces.

Deception, surprise, massive firepower, descent upon unexpected points, destruction of Western assets deep behind NATO lines and overwhelmingly rapid rates of advance were the hallmarks of Soviet doctrine.[54] Orthodox Communist strategists believed that all the social, conceptual and technological trends of the modern era pointed in this direction. They based their beliefs on a variety of factors, which included Lenin's revolutionary exhortations, the experiences of the Red Army in the Second World War and the possibility that WTO morale might disintegrate in a long war.[55] The most influential element in their thinking, however, was the steady increase in the firepower of modern weapons, which seemed to have reached its culminating point with the development of nuclear explosives.[56]

To Russian military thinkers, the potency of late twentieth-century munitions made their updated variant of blitzkrieg both possible and necessary. On the one hand, the existence of modern weapons allows attackers to pulverise enemy defensive positions more rapidly, and on the other hand, it forces them to strike quickly, before their opponents manage to pulverise them.

In the words of the Soviet military writer Sidorenko:

> Nuclear strikes can destroy the strongest centers and strong points in the enemy defense, his reserves, means of mass destruction, and other important objectives, can form breaches in the enemy defense, and thereby can create favorable conditions for overcoming it swiftly by the attacking troops and developing the attack to great depth. Under these conditions, the primary mission of the attacking [units] will become the rapid exploitation of nuclear strikes, completion of the smashing of surviving enemy forces, and the seizure of specific positions, areas and objectives. With the employment of nuclear weapons, the decisiveness and scope of the offensive are increased, the times for the attainment of its goals are reduced, and the significance of surprise and the time factor increases even more.[57]

Although the author of this paragraph was particularly interested in the issue of nuclear war, Russian strategists came to similar conclusions when they studied precision-guided munitions and other developments in late twentieth-century armament.[58]

NATO's logistical system was peculiarly vulnerable to rapid attacks of the sort which the Soviet Union intended to mount, and Warsaw Pact strategists intended to take advantage of this fact. Russian writers emphasised the importance of destroying and capturing enemy arms and materiel.[59] The curriculum at the Voroshilov Military Academy identified the vulnerability of NATO depots and the length of transatlantic lines of communication as two key advantages which the Warsaw Pact would exploit in combat.[60] The Communists were also well aware that NATO's lack of airbases was a weakness, and they planned to destroy Western airfields early in any war.[61]

Furthermore, Warsaw Pact thrusts into Western territory would have struck directly against NATO's logistical weak points. If the Communists managed to achieve anything remotely approaching the 40–60 km per day rate of advance which their plans called for, Western units would have found themselves in combat long before they could move their reserve forces to the front, long before they could organise a wartime maintenance system and long before they could correct the deficiencies in their transportation network.[62] When American units arrived to take charge of their prepositioned POMCUS supplies, they might have found those stockpiles destroyed or in the hands of the enemy.

To quote from the Voroshilov curriculum, such an attack would have the effect of 'Depriving the enemy of the opportunity to deploy his groupings of forces on lines earlier prepared, destroying his forces in border areas and ensuring the penetration of attacks ... to great depths.'[63]

The fall of the Berlin Wall in 1989 and the subsequent disintegration of the USSR may tempt modern readers to dismiss the possibility that the Warsaw Pact could have conducted such an offensive. However, it would be a mistake to confuse the WTO war machine of the Soviet era with the remnants of those forces which form the Russian army of the late 1990s. The material size of the Pact armies are a matter of record and whether or not the Communists harboured implacably aggressive designs against the West, their military contingency plans indicate that their commanders considered themselves capable of carrying out vast offensive operations.[64] If the war in Chechnya casts doubt upon the current capabilities of the Russian armed forces, one must remember that morale and institutional skill can fluctuate sharply over the course of a few years. The apparent decline in Russian performance between 1985 and 1996 is only a little more dramatic than the improvement in Communist proficiency between 1941 and 1945. A comparison of German operational confidence in 1930 and 1940 might also serve to emphasise the difference a decade can make.

Whatever the technological deficiencies of the Eastern Bloc's armed forces, Soviet military thinkers possessed a keen sense of strategy. One Western analyst summed up the quality of strategic thought in the Soviet Union with the statement '[a]t the theater or operational level, the Warsaw Pact is clearly superior to NATO', and numerous other studies suggested similar conclusions.[65] The military potential of the Warsaw Pact depended largely upon its ability to put its strategic ideas into practice. When one examines Soviet military thought, one sees that the Soviet way of war demanded heroic feats of movement from units at every level.

Those who wish to understand Soviet strategy would do well to begin by considering the concept of *udar*, or shock.[66] The Communists intended to smash opposing forces so rapidly that their enemies would never get the chance to bring their actual strength to bear.[67] This was a strategy of mass, since it rested on the direct application of overwhelming combat power, but it was not a strategy of frontal attack nor was it a strategy of attrition. The Communists hoped to achieve shock, not through masses of troops, but through a mass of firepower.

M.V. Frunze wrote that fire constitutes the main force in modern battle.[68] Indeed, due to the effects of artillery, airpower and most especially nuclear weapons, the Communists saw large gatherings of men and equipment as a liability. Marshal Sokolovsky wrote that concentration of troops is 'fraught with grave consequences'. Furthermore, he added, 'there is no longer a need for it. The most important thing now is not the direction of the main blow but the areas of maximum effort.'[69] Therefore, the Communists undertook the task of physically dispersing their military units while concentrating the effects of their weapons.

Even at the level of tactical routine, Warsaw Pact doctrine placed unusual demands on the ability of commanders to co-ordinate the actions of dispersed units. Rather than employing all their frontline battalions together, Soviet regimental commanders typically sent their forces into combat in a series of two or three echelons.[70] Divisional commanders deployed regiments in multiple echelons as well.[71] Soviet leaders designed this system, not only to minimise their troops' vulnerability to area–effect weapons, but to cover flanks, provide a source of uncommitted units to repel counterattacks, encircle enemy units, widen holes in the enemy line, replace exhausted units and hammer weakened enemy positions with fresh troops.[72]

Furthermore, at the level of true strategy – the level at which commanders make plans which lead to the overall defeat of the enemy – the Communists placed great emphasis on the movement of large units. Although Western authors tended to study Communist plans to break through NATO lines, the Communists themselves were far more interested in setting up 'encounter battles', in which opposing forces would meet on the march and go into combat without receiving the opportunity to make extensive preparations.[73] Encounter battles are most likely to take place in contests of manoeuvre, where the defenders find themselves forced to fight at unexpected points, and the side which loses the strategic initiative suffers a severe disadvantage. Soviet strategists hoped to unhinge enemy defences and establish a fluid situation throughout the theatre of war, thereby creating opportunities to overwhelm isolated foes, encircle larger concentrations of opposing units and crush the enemy in detail.

The Communists intended to co-ordinate the action of their divisions, armies and fronts in the same fashion that chess players combine the moves of different pieces.[74] Warsaw Pact commanders hoped to use one sort of attack in one location in conjunction with another sort of attack in another to achieve maximum overall results, allowing NATO units no time to recover and no time to regroup.[75] Lecturers at the Voroshilov military academy described the principle as follows:

> The essence of the need to unify the efforts of all Services of the Armed Forces lies in the fact that the achievement of the final aim of strategic action is only possible through co-ordinated action of operational formations and large units of all Services of the Armed Forces. However, this principle does not mean that all types of military forces and means play equal roles in war. Each element plays a specific role and occupies a certain position by virtue of its combat capabilities and methods of conducting strategic actions.[76]

Given the importance which the Communists placed on large-scale manoeuvre, nobody should be surprised to learn that they placed equal emphasis on speed. According to the curriculum of one Russian military academy, 'delay is similar to death'.[77] V. Ye. Savkin explained the value of speed concisely and effectively in *Basic Principles of Operational Art and Tactics*:

> High rates of attack permit neutralising of many strong aspects of modern defence ... With high rates of advance and effective neutralisation of the enemy by fire, the attacker suffers fewer losses in personnel and equipment. With an increase in rates of attack a further decrease in losses occurs. Rapid penetration into the enemy's deep rear areas where his long-range means of nuclear attack are based and forces these means to change position under threat of capture, which will not allow the enemy to deliver massive retaliatory nuclear strikes. With high tempos of attack, the enemy is deprived of the time needed for occupying launch positions and preparing for launch.[78]

Another key element of Soviet military thought was surprise, and the problem of catching the enemy off guard at a strategic level led the Warsaw Pact to rely heavily upon deception. 'The enemy should be deceived about the purpose and time of friendly forces' readiness for deployment.'[79] This principle only increased the number of large-scale marches which the Communists would have had to carry out in the course of a war. Barring a particularly convenient political crisis, the need for secrecy would probably have forced would-be Soviet attackers to keep their prewar mobilisation to a minimum.

Although the USSR and its allies seemed to have positioned 80 divisions for a war in Europe, they kept 18 of those divisions in the Soviet Union itself and 15 more in Poland.[80] Due to satellite reconnaissance and Western signals interception techniques, it would have been extremely difficult for the Warsaw Pact to move these units into place for an invasion of West Germany without attracting Western attention and giving NATO a chance to mobilise its own forces in response. Therefore, it seems likely that many Soviet divisions would have had to make their march to the battlefield after the fighting had begun.

Naturally, Soviet plans changed over time. A study of innovation in Warsaw Pact military thought serves to demonstrate both the creativity of Eastern Bloc strategists and the enduring elements of the USSR's military predicament. Russian commanders could develop new ideas, adapt to new technologies and grapple with unaccustomed forms of war, but they could not change the nature of their military instrument without Herculean effort. The rise of Imperial Japan stands to remind us that one should never fall into the trap of underestimating another peoples' capacity to achieve feats of science and technology. However, the idea that the USSR could have retooled its society, industry, scientific institutions and military culture to dispense with mass armies and fight Western-style technological warfare seems inconceivable.

When the development of anti-tank guided missiles threatened the armour-heavy Warsaw Pact units, the Communists responded by dramatically increasing the amount of artillery in their units, in the hope that they could destroy missile sites by fire.[81] When Afghan rebels proved their ability to hold up columns of troops in mountain passes, Soviet military thinkers set up special research institutes to study warfare in close terrain.[82] These centres developed tactics in which helicopters would seize the high ground, so that large armoured units could carry out their customarily rapid advance.[83] Over the course of the 1970s and early 1980s, the Communists increased the potential speed of their forces by (in theory) equipping all of their artillery units with armoured, self-propelled guns.[84] The Russian marshal Nicolai Ogarkov pioneered the ideas which evolved into what Western strategists have dubbed the 'Revolution in Military Affairs'.[85] However, the Communists responded to changes in the conduct of warfare, not by changing their military concepts entirely, but by finding ways to make their strategy of manoeuvre by massive units more vigorous than ever.

The development of Warsaw Pact doctrine in the early 1980s serves to illustrate this point. In 1981, the Soviet general Krupchenko summed up the significance of technological advances as follows:

> Modern conditions have introduced new factors into the equation of how to develop success ... There are far greater opportunities nowadays than in the past, especially on account of the great depths to which rockets, long-range artillery, aircraft and desants [strikes by amphibious, airborne or airmobile troops behind enemy lines] can be used. Even so,

examples from the last war have not lost their relevance in theory or in practice. Rather, they encourage ideas and suggest solutions to the modern problem of how to get major forces in the offensive deep into the operational depths of the enemy, so as to achieve decisive aims at high speed.[86]

Krupchenko was discussing the subject of the Operational Manoeuvre Group (OMG), a concept which quickly became a staple of Eastern Bloc strategic thought. Operational manoeuvre groups were to consist of division-level detachments which would bypass front-line defences and drive deep into the enemy rear. Major Wojcieh Michalak of the Polish army explained the purpose of these groups.

> These troops are intended mainly for destroying groupings of nuclear missiles, command posts, radio-electronic warfare and AA defence weapons. They are also used *inter alia*, to prevent the withdrawal of enemy troops; to hinder the advance of his reserves from the depth; to paralyse his system of logistics; to capture major important areas and objectives and to hold these till the approach of the main forces.[87]

The OMG concept had enormous strategic potential, and Western observers did not discount the idea that it might cause NATO defences to collapse. However, one must also note that it raises the problem of keeping large units on the move to a new level.

THE SOVIET PREDICAMENT: TOO, TOO SOLID FLESH

One may now turn and examine the Warsaw Pact's ability to sustain its own forces. Needless to say, the Communists did not reveal the details of their logistical preparations. However, according to the best estimates available in the West, the Warsaw Pact possessed enough materiel to carry out its military plans. The Western expert David Isby stated that the Soviet Union deployed enough stores in East Germany alone to supply its forces on the Central Front with 16 days' worth of fuel and 37 days' worth of ammunition.[88] Since Soviet doctrine called on the Red Army to conclude a war with NATO in 15–21 days, these levels of supply seem quite reasonable.[89]

The Communists possessed far larger reserves of supplies within the USSR itself. Official regulations required the Red Army to maintain enough stockpiles to sustain combat operations until Soviet industry could expand to meet the needs of the war effort. Analysis of Soviet writings indicated that the logisticians had fulfilled this requirement.[90] Russian commanders wrote optimistically about their levels of supply. If one accepts Second World War rates of industrial mobilisation as a model, this meant that the USSR possessed enough reserve stockpiles for 90 days of hard fighting.[91]

Moving from stockpiles to transportation, the Soviet army fielded an ample fleet of vehicles. A Soviet motor-rifle division had enough organic transport to carry supplies for three to six days' worth of combat.[92] Furthermore, higher levels of the Soviet command structure had large transportation units at their disposal. According to Red Army doctrine, army and front commanders took responsibility for sending supplies forward, so that divisions could maximise their mobility by minimising their logistical tail.[93] The transportation units in an army could carry a day's worth of supplies for four to six divisions in combat, and the units organic to a front could supply another 18–25 division-days.[94] If the Communists had pressed civilian vehicles into service, they might have increased these figures by as much as a half, and military exercises frequently involved tests of the system for mobilising non-military transport.[95]

In addition to vehicular transport, the Red Army employed pipelines to keep its units supplied with POL. Each army possessed two automated pipe-laying systems. The PMT 100 pipelayer, which was a typical device of its kind, constructed pipelines at a rate of 2–3 km per hour.[96] When in service, a PMT-100 pipeline provided 2,000 tons of fuel per day, which was enough for roughly three and a half divisions on the attack.[97]

Using the Group of Soviet Forces, Germany (GSFG) as a model, the average full-strength Soviet army consisted of 4.6 divisions, plus an assortment of non-divisional units. The Communists stationed front-level headquarters and support units in the German Democratic Republic, and therefore, although tables of organisation did not specify any standard size for a front, it seems reasonable to treat the GSFG as a typical front-level organisation.[98] By these standards, a front contained five armies made up of some 23 divisions. According to these estimates, the Warsaw Pact had enough transportation capacity to carry five to eight days' worth of supplies for each division in a front at any given moment, even without using civilian resources.

Warsaw Pact units, like NATO units, undoubtedly possessed more assets on paper than in reality. However, the expansion of Red Army motor pools which took place in the late 1970s indicates Moscow's resolve to keep logistical units as close to full strength as possible.[99] The challenge of Soviet logistics was not lack of materiel. British Army field manuals concluded that the Communists 'do not have a problem with either stock levels or with the provision of transport to move supplies'.[100]

There were, however, gaps between Soviet strategic concepts and Soviet logistical capabilities, and no simple reform of the WTO supply system could have provided a remedy. The handicap of the Warsaw Pact was the sheer size of its armies. Operations on the scale which the Soviet commanders had planned would have stretched the road and rail capacity of Central and Eastern Europe to the limits. Indeed, even if one disregards the question of infrastructure, Soviet units would have found space itself in short supply on the German battlefield.

The British Army studied the routes which the USSR might use to deploy materiel to the German border from points east and came up with the following conclusions. On each 150–200-km sector of the front, the Warsaw Pact would have a maximum of four to six improved roads, three paved roads and one to two major railroads.[101] When one considers the fact that Soviet doctrine called on each individual division to use as many as four separate roads while on the march, one sees how scarce roads would have become.[102] Furthermore, the roads which did exist were likely to break down under the strain of supporting Warsaw Pact divisions. The units which participated in the 1968 Soviet invasion of Czechoslovakia frequently ran into delays when the steel treads of their tanks churned up the soft macadam pavement, and similar roads were common throughout the USSR.[103]

The dispersion of Warsaw Pact formations compounded this problem of space. According to doctrine, a Soviet division on the march was supposed to occupy an area 70 km long by 20–40 km wide.[104] When a division concentrated for an attack, it would assume a frontage of 4–6 km, but it would still extend to a depth of 30 km.[105] Warsaw Pact units theoretically required another 200–350 km of depth to deploy the headquarters and depots of army-level and front-level formations.[106]

Given the fact that the border region between the two Germanies was roughly 725 km long, a Warsaw Pact attack force of 47–80 divisions would have certainly had to compromise its official pattern of deployment.[107] The Luneberg Heath, the Harz Mountains and other areas of rough terrain on the inter-German border would have complicated deployment yet further, as would Germany's numerous cities. One should also note that, if Pact units deployed according to their official doctrine, an army-level unit with its divisions fighting on the border with the Federal Republic of Germany in Hof could easily have had rear elements stretching as far east as Poland. When one notes that during the 1968 invasion of Czechoslovakia, Soviet units became involved in traffic jams which often grew to be as much as a mile long, one sees that road congestion would have inevitably held up the movement of both supplies and combat units in a Warsaw Pact attack on the Federal Republic of Germany.[108]

The Warsaw Pact would certainly have found ways to surmount such difficulties. To quote the Soviet expert C.N. Donnelly, 'getting a quart out of a pint pot has long been a Soviet custom'.[109] The Red Army planned, for instance, to account for some of its logistical needs through plunder. Pact quartermaster units carried facilities to butcher locally acquired animals and each division had a fleet of trucks equipped with pumps to collect gasoline from the area.[110] Successful foraging would not only have saved road space by reducing the need for convoys, it would have allowed units to advance even when their supplies failed to arrive. Furthermore, the Communists would undoubtedly have employed rail transport, improvised new formations and relied on a whole host of other expedients to overcome the problems of space.

However, the more the Communists relied on ad hoc measures, the more difficulty they would have had in realising their strategy of manoeuvre. All the expedients listed above would rob the advance of the swiftness which Soviet doctrine considered so vital. In rail movements, for instance, the process of loading and unloading trains takes as much as half the time required for the journey itself.[111] Furthermore, since some units would undoubtedly find more forage and more opportunity for innovation than others, such practices would disrupt the uniformity of the Warsaw Pact advance. Unless Soviet commanders were content to reduce the speed of the offensive to the speed of the unluckiest units, they would have risked a situation in which their divisions arrived piecemeal upon the battlefield. Indeed, failures of communication and co-ordination might well have put the Pact attackers in such a situation whether they were willing to accept it or not.

THE WEST RESPONDS: TARGETING MOVEMENT

These questions of space and movement did not escape notice in the West. In the late 1970s, a number of Western military analysts drew attention to this issue, and to ways in which NATO might exploit it. To cite but one example, Soviet expert Charles Dick observed that NATO might counter the Soviet Union's formidable artillery forces by taking advantage of the fact that the Pact's ammunition load carriers 'will be very easily checked by a good obstacle plan, and should make lucrative targets for long-range artillery or air attack'.[112] Soviet logistical problems were not merely a brake on Warsaw Pact operations, they provided NATO with opportunities to create friction for their opponents.

These tactical opportunities to interfere with Soviet supply and movement dovetailed with a larger movement in Western operational doctrine. In the period 1979–80, NATO strategists developed the concept known as follow-on forces attack, or FOFA.[113] In 1982, at a speech to the Los Angeles World Affairs Council, General Bernard Rogers unveiled this idea in public with the following statement.

> In operational terms, we need the capability to hold the lead divisions of a major Warsaw Pact conventional attack while we conduct an effective interdiction and destruction campaign with conventional means against its follow-on forces, thereby neutralizing them before their weight can be brought to bear at the front lines. Such capabilities will also provide us the opportunity to carry out counterattacks to reverse the flow of battle.[114]

In this fashion, NATO commanders hoped to gain the operational depth they needed to fend off a WTO offensive while preserving the principle of 'forward defence' in West Germany.[115] Thus, FOFA helped to allay the concerns of Germans who feared that their homeland would bear the entire brunt of a third world war, and thereby strengthened the political unity of the alliance.

As the concept of FOFA took hold in NATO, the United States army developed an independent but highly compatible philosophy of operations known as the AirLand Battle.[116] Although NATO never formally adopted this concept, it had great influence on Western military thought, especially in the United States. The AirLand idea went through several stages of evolution, and it is an error to assume that all of them prescribed the same measures, or that they dealt exclusively with the problem of war in Europe. However, at every stage of its development, the AirLand battle emphasised the need for US forces to seize the initiative upon the battlefield by striking deep into enemy territory to keep units of the opposing army from reaching the battlefield. To quote from an article which Donn A. Starry, the commander of the US Army Training and Doctrine Command published shortly after introducing the first official pamphlet on AirLand:

> The defense must, therefore, begin well forward and proceed aggressively from there to destroy enemy attack echelons and at the same time to slow, disrupt, break up, disperse or destroy follow-on echelons in order to quickly seize initiative and go on the offensive.[117]

The mainstream interpretation of FOFA and AirLand, as expressed by Rogers, Starry and others in the paragraphs above, emphasises attacks on enemy combat units as they moved to the front. Other writers argued that Soviet supply convoys and depots might have proved to be more lucrative targets.[118] 'The destruction of one army-level POL distribution point would probably halt the equivalent of a division in a matter of days and interdiction of rail lines and pipelines would have a major impact on rates of advance.'[119] Whichever option battlefield commanders had chosen, one may observe that NATO had adopted a policy of attacking enemy supply and movement, and therefore, one of attacking enemy logistics.

Ideas such as FOFA and AirLand Battle are easier to conceive than to implement. However, in the early 1980s, a variety of technological developments made these concepts feasible for the first time. In 1979, Keith Dunn of the US Army War College noted:

> With the current accuracy of PGMs [precision-guided munitions] and the prospect that in the 1980s both tactical and strategic US Air Force planes will be equipped to carry highly accurate cruise missiles, the transshipment points [of the Warsaw Pact rail network] will become lucrative targets at very little cost to NATO. With long-range cruise missiles, NATO-US planes would not have to penetrate Warsaw Pact airspace but could still engage and destroy targets deep within Warsaw Pact territory.[120]

General Bernard Rogers explained the technological basis of FOFA at length in a 1983 article in *Military Technology*. To attack movement behind the front lines, one requires the ability to detect and identify enemy units deep within their own territory, and hence, Rogers called for advanced radar imaging systems such as the TR-1 and its successor the PAVE MOVER, which evolved into the J-STARS system of Desert Storm fame.[121] Homing munitions such as the AVKO SKEET, the SADARM (Sense and Destroy Armor) and the WAAM (Wide Area Anti-Armor Munition), allowed aircraft and artillery units to engage columns of vehicles beyond the range of direct sight with a high degree of confidence that their attacks would destroy a significant number of targets.[122] The global positioning system (GPS) gave NATO commanders the ability to place their deep attacks on target and co-ordinate them for maximum effect.[123]

The logistics of employing mass armies in Central Europe made the Soviet system of deploying its forces peculiarly vulnerable. With FOFA and AirLand, NATO's doctrine evolved to take advantage of that vulnerability. At the operational level, these doctrines turned the struggle over initiative into a struggle over movement. At the level of grand strategy, this transformation allowed the West to make the best possible use of its economic, social and technological advantages.

FINDINGS

We may now raise the standard questions for this study.

1. How have high-level commanders perceived the problem of logistics?
In both Russia and the West, commanders recognised that logistics are integral to military affairs. Furthermore, unlike Van Creveld, who found the connection between logistical infrastructure and war-making ability ephemeral and difficult to discern, they saw this relationship as obvious and fundamental. Not only did Russian commanders intend to attack Western supply dumps and communications infrastructure, they saw these attacks as part of a programme which would lead to the general collapse of NATO's forces. Likewise, the Western strategists who conceived of FOFA and AirLand Battle were not merely hoping to inflict attrition upon Warsaw Pact forces, they were hoping to disrupt the entire system by which their enemies made war.

Neither NATO strategists nor their counterparts in the Warsaw Pact treated logistics as something separate from the rest of the military art. The Russians developed their doctrine of deep battle in response to a wide variety of factors, of which the vulnerability of NATO logistics was only one. Likewise, although the military thinkers who developed FOFA and AirLand Battle hoped to disrupt the movement of Warsaw Pact units to the front, their ultimate goal was to disarticulate opposing forces and defeat their individual units in detail. In both cases, strategists focused on supplies and communications, not simply because these things are important for their own sake, but because they are the underpinnings of all the other things which armed forces do.

2. How have logistical factors helped or harmed the strategic performance of armed forces?

Logistics was a key area of vulnerability for both NATO and the Warsaw Pact. This does not mean that either alliance was unable to supply its forces on paper – it means that, in war, both sides would have had the opportunity to disrupt each other's support systems. Supplies have been both the means and the ends in many campaigns – the resources which made it possible for operations to take place, and also the target of those operations. To the victor go the spoils, and the side which dominated the land or air due to superior weapons or superior tactics would have gained a much greater scope for interfering with enemy logistics, while also gaining the opportunity to use captured supplies for its own purposes.

Prudence warns us not to assume that any one factor will determine the course of an entire war. The armed forces of a major nation can be remarkably resilient and the human mind can be remarkably inventive. Even if the Warsaw Pact had successfully caught NATO's armies in a position where they could not form into an effective fighting force and broken through to the Channel coast, there is no guarantee that the United States would not have attempted some sort of return to Europe, just as it did in the Second World War. Likewise, even if NATO had adopted a doctrine akin to FOFA or Air-Land and successfully disrupted the movement of Pact units, this would not necessarily have compensated for their own weaknesses, nor would it necessarily have prevented the WTO armies from overcoming Western defenders through simple numerical superiority.

Finally, in any discussion of war between NATO and the Warsaw Pact, one must consider the role of nuclear weapons. Logistics matters in nuclear war. Warsaw Pact commanders, for instance, hoped to overrun NATO nuclear depots before Western countries could deploy the weapons in those facilities, and both sides would have hoped to keep their air, sea and ground forces operating throughout the course of the nuclear exchange.[124] Nevertheless, the existence of nuclear weapons multiplies the number of possible outcomes for a war between East and West by a huge but unknowable factor. The effective use of a few low-yield nuclear weapons or the crushing blow of an all-out nuclear strike could have reversed the course of the war at almost any phase. Furthermore, the staggering real and perceived effects of nuclear weapons might well have led to the psychological breakdown of one or both sides, or, alternatively, to a situation in which the opposing governments negotiated a settlement relatively early in the conflict.

To summarise, logistics might well have been the decisive factor in a war between NATO and the Warsaw Pact, but only because of its role in supporting other factors. Much would have depended upon the will and creativity of the opposing commanders. Either side could have struck a potentially fatal blow against its enemy's logistical system. Victory would have gone to the side which managed to strike more surely, follow up on its successes more vigorously, sidestep its opponent's attacks with more agility and manage such partial unknowns as the military and political effects of nuclear weapons most effectively. Therefore, one must study logistics in the context of all the other things which affect strategy.

3. What factors have given particular forces advantages in logistics?
Both NATO and the Warsaw Pact had worked out ways to support their own forces, but neither side seemed to be dramatically more proficient at this task than its opponent. The opposing alliances did, however, have peculiar advantages in their ability to attack enemy logistical networks. These advantages were the same advantages which shaped most other aspects of the two sides' war plans. The WTO relied on the size of its forces and the aggressive strategy of its commanders at the highest levels. The Western Alliance, for its part, relied on superior technology and the (presumably) superior ability of its unit commanders to act on their own initiative.

4. What logistical problems are associated with particular styles of warfare, and how have commanders addressed them?
The most deep-rooted military problems of NATO and the Warsaw Pact manifested themselves in the opposing alliances' logistical establishments. Although the Soviet Union and its allies had the political will to field large armies, they seem to have lacked the general technological sophistication of the West. Those who have followed the progress of the Soviet Union's weapons development programmes may note significant exceptions to this principle, but, at least, it seems safe to conclude that the Eastern Bloc countries were unable to equip the bulk of their forces with the same quantity of advanced equipment that one would have found among their Western opponents. Therefore, the Warsaw Pact came to rely upon a strategy of mass.

The people of the West, for their part, had no desire to live in a state of perpetual mobilisation. Furthermore, other assorted strategic debates made it easy for NATO forces to neglect logistical preparation. There were always people who held the opinion, either openly or tacitly, that Western ground forces should serve primarily as a 'trip-wire' for the American nuclear arsenal. Those who subscribed to this idea saw few reasons to maintain the logistical apparatus for large land armies. For these and other reasons, NATO allowed its forces to become 'hollow'.

In the 1980s, military thinkers in both alliances began to recognise the shortcomings in their armed forces, both logistical and otherwise. For both sides, reform meant a firming-up of what already existed. When one considers the fact that more general change could easily have entailed general military or even social adjustments, this is hardly surprising. Although Warsaw Pact doctrine had always emphasised shock, speed and surprise, the Eastern Bloc military thinkers of the 1970s and 1980s placed even greater emphasis on these factors and developed concepts such as that of the OMGs in the hopes of overwhelming Western defences before WTO shortcomings or NATO advantages could become important. Likewise, the Western Countries, particularly the United States, added some bulk to their forces during the 1980s, and also developed new doctrinal concepts designed to raise the value of their technological advantage to a new level.

CONCLUSION

The interplay between NATO and Warsaw Pact concepts of strategy illustrates the fact that logistical factors determine the type of war which an army can fight, and therefore the range of strategic options its leaders can pursue. This study also serves as a counterpoint to Van Creveld's attempt to place logistic matters beyond the realm of intentions and conscious strategy.[125] One of the key lessons of Cold War strategy is that leaders on both sides of the Iron Curtain saw logistics as a key element in their plans to defeat their enemies. Furthermore, those of us who study strategic affairs in the late 1990s do well to remember that the Cold War is not yet very far in the past. If a political situation should develop in which two or more large nations with relatively modern military forces confront each other in the near future, the same issues of readiness, blitzkrieg strategy and the viability of mass armies on high-tech battlefields may become critical again.

NOTES

1. Tao Hanzhang, *Sun Tzu's Art of War: The Modern Chinese Interpretation*, (trans.) Yuan Shibing (New York: Sterling Publishing, 1987), p. 99.
2. Ken Brower, *The Warsaw Pact – NATO Military Balance: The Quality of Forces* (Sandhurst: Soviet Studies Research Centre of the Royal Military Academy, 1988), p. 1.
3. See, for instance, Keith A. Dunn, 'Limits Upon Soviet Military Power,' *RUSI*, Vol. 124, No. 4 (Dec. 1979), pp. 43–4.
4. Brower, *The Warsaw Pact – NATO Military Balance*, passim.
5. Ibid.
6. John Paxton (ed.), *The Statesman's Yearbook 1979–1980* (London: Macmillan: 1979), pp. 1237 and 1421.
7. Ibid.

THE COLD WAR

8. IISS, *The Military Balance 1981–1982* (London: IISS, 1981), pp. 5–31.
9. Ibid.
10. Comparing the strength of NATO and the Warsaw Pact was once a popular sport. Those who desire an introduction to the academic side of this debate might consult Barry R. Posen, 'Measuring the European Conventional Balance: Coping With Complexity in Threat Assessment', *International Security*, Vol. 9, No. 3 (Winter 1984–1985), pp. 47–88, and John Mearsheimer, 'Assessing the Conventional Balance: The 3:1 Rule and Its Critics', *International Security*, Vol. 13, No. 4 (Spring 1989), pp. 54–89. For a splendid discussion of the factors which went overlooked throughout the entire debate, see Eliot A. Cohen, 'Toward Better Net Assessment: Rethinking the European Conventional Balance', *International Security*, Vol. 13, No. 1 (Summer 1988), pp. 50–89.

In this study of logistics, the author has chosen to employ a direct numerical comparison of primary military assets. This study compares NATO and Warsaw Pact force levels in 1981 and 1988 in order to capture the changes which took place between the conventional build-ups of the early 1980s and the last full year of Soviet power which preceded the fall of the Berlin Wall in 1989. IISS, *The Military Balance, 1981–1982*, pp. 1–39, and IISS, *The Military Balance 1987–1988* (London: IISS: 1987), pp. 5–31.

11. Brower,*The Warsaw Pact – NATO Military Balance*, pp. 5–6.
12. Ibid., pp. 4–5.
13. Ibid., p. 16.
14. Ibid., p. 7.
15. Malcom Chalmers and Lutz Unterseher, 'Is There a Tank Gap? Comparing NATO and Warsaw Pact Tank Fleets', *International Security*, Vol. 13, No. 1 (Summer 1988), pp. 7–23.
16. Ibid., p. 32.
17. Steven G. Zaloga, letter to the editor, *International Security*, Vol. 13, No. 4 (Spring 1989), pp. 184–5.
18. Zaloga, letter, p. 184.
19. Christopher N. Donnelly, *Soviet Army Logistics: The Themes for 1978–79* (Sandhurst: Unpublished report to the Soviet Studies Research Centre of the Royal Military Academy A35, 1979), pp. 1–9.
20. Dunn, 'Limits on Soviet Military Power', pp. 42–3.
21. Brower, *The Warsaw Pact – NATO Military Balance*, p. 20.
22. Ibid., p. 24.
23. Cohen, 'Toward Better Net Assessment', p. 50.
24. Ibid.
25. Ibid., pp. 85–8.
26. Richard W. Gutmann, *US Military Equipment Prepositioned in Europe: Significant Improvements Made but Some Problems Remain*, LCD-78-431A: B-146896 (Washington, DC: General Accounting Office report, 1978), p. 5. See also Brower, *The Warsaw Pact – NATO Military Balance*, p. 30.
27. Brower, *The Warsaw Pact – NATO Military Balance*, p. 30.
28. Ibid.
29. IISS, *The Military Balance, 1987–1988*, p. 23.
30. Committee on Merchant Marine and Fisheries, *Operation Desert Shield/Desert Storm: Sealift Performance and Future Sealift* (Washington, DC: US Government Printing Office, 1992), p. 58.
31. The numerous deletions in Gutmann, *US Military Equipment Prepositioned in Europe*, serve to indicate the type of information which the US government still chooses to keep classified. See also William Park, *Defending the West: A History of NATO* (Boulder, CO: Westview Press, 1986), p. 186.

32. Ibid.
33. Ibid.
34. Ibid.
35. Ibid.
36. Brower, *The Warsaw Pact – NATO Military Balance*, p. 63.
37. Richard A. Gabriel, *Military Incompetence* (New York: Hill & Wang, 1985), p. 26.
38. Ibid., p. 25.
39. Ibid.
40. Ibid., pp. 31–2.
41. Ibid.
42. Ibid.
43. Ibid. p. 28.
44. David C. Jones, *US Military Posture FY 1980* (Washington, DC: US Government Printing Office, 1980), p. 78; Gabriel, *Military Incompetence*, p. 80.
45. Gabriel, *Military Incompetence*, p. 29.
46. Ibid., p. 31.
47. IISS, *IISS Strategic Survey 1978* (London: IISS, 1979), p. 32.
48. Gabriel, *Military Incompetence*, pp. 27–8.
49. Gutmann, *US Military Equipment Prepositioned in Europe*, p. 27.
50. Jones, *US Military Posture*, p. 79.
51. Manuel De Landa, *War In the Age of Intelligent Machines* (New York: Zone Books, 1991) p. 104.
52. Gutmann, *US Military Equipment Prepositioned in Europe*, p. 1.
53. Brower, *The Warsaw Pact – NATO Military Balance*, p. 1.
54. See, for instance, A.A. Sidorenko, *The Offensive*, trans. US Air Force (Washington, DC: US Government Printing Office, 1970), *passim* and P.H. Vigor, *Soviet Blitzkrieg Theory* (New York: St Martin's Press, 1983), *passim*.
55. For detailed analysis, see *The Soviet Threat to Europe in the 1980s* (Sandhurst: Report to the Soviet Studies Research Centre of the Royal Military Academy, AA2, 1979), pp. 2–7.
56. Sidorenko, *The Offensive, passim*.
57. Ibid., p. 41.
58. James Sherr, *NATO's Emerging Technology Initiatives and New Operational Concepts: The Assessment of the Soviet Military Press* (Sandhurst: Soviet Studies Research Centre of the Royal Military Academy, 1987), *passim*.
59. Sidorenko, *The Offensive*, p. 1.
60. Ghulam D. Wardak, *The Voroshilov Lectures, Vol. 1* (Washington, DC: National Defense University, 1989), p. 67.
61. Ibid., p. 112.
62. Ibid., p. 273.
63. Ibid., p. 253.
64. Sidorenko, *The Offensive, passim*; V.D. Sokolovsky, *Military Strategy*, trans. Wright-Patterson Air Force Base (London: Pall Mall Press, 1963), *passim*.
65. Brower, *The Warsaw Pact – NATO Military Balance*, p. 33.
66. Ibid., p. 32.
67. William Baxter, *Soviet AirLand Battle Tactics* (Novato, CA: Presidio Press, 1986), p. 111.
68. Sidorenko, *The Offensive*, pp. 132–7.
69. Ibid., p. 21.
70. Sokolovsky, *Military Strategy*, pp. 14–15.
71. Baxter, *Soviet AirLand Battle Tactics*, pp. 94–6.
72. Ibid.

73. *The Soviet Threat to Europe in the 1980s*, p. 25.
74. David Isby, *Weapons and Tactics of the Soviet Army* (London: Janes, 1981), p. 35.
75. Brower, *The Warsaw Pact – NATO Military Balance*, p. 31.
76. Wardak, *The Voroshilov Lectures, Vol. 1*, pp. 242–3.
77. Ibid., p. 242.
78. Charles Dick, 'The Growing Soviet Artillery Threat', *RUSI Journal*, Vol. 124, No. 2 (June 1979), p. 67.
79. Wardak, *The Voroshilov Lectures Vol. 1*, p. 209.
80. Vigor, *Soviet Blitzkrieg Theory*, pp. 183–4.
81. Dick, 'The Growing Soviet Artillery Threat', p. 68.
82. Baxter, *Soviet AirLand Battle Tactics*, pp. 100–1.
83. Ibid.
84. Ibid., p. 256.
85. Joint Chiefs of Staff, *The American Revolution in Military Affairs*, (Washington, DC: JCS document, 1996) p. 2.
86. *The Soviet Threat to Europe in the 1980s*, p. 32.
87. Ibid., pp. 33–4.
88. Isby, *Weapons and Tactics of the Soviet Army*, p. 61.
89. Wardak, *The Voroshilov Lectures, Vol. 1*, p. 273.
90. Graham Turbiville, 'Soviet Logistic Support for Ground Operations', *RUSI Journal*, Vol. 120, No. 3 (September 1975), p. 64.
91. Ibid., p. 63.
92. Ibid., p. 64.
93. Baxter, *Soviet AirLand Battle Tactics*, p. 206.
94. Turbiville, 'Soviet Logistic Support for Ground Operations', p. 65.
95. Christopher N. Donnelly, *Rear Support For the Soviet Ground Forces* (Sandhurst: Report to the Soviet Studies Research Centre of the Royal Military Academy, A17, 1978), pp. 14 and 17.
96. Baxter, *Soviet AirLand Battle Tactics*, p. 208.
97. Baxter, *Soviet AirLand Battle Tactics*, p. 208; Donnelly, *Rear Support For the Soviet Ground Forces*, p. 17.
98. Isby, *Weapons and Tactics of the Soviet Army*, p. 24.
99. Ibid., pp. 22 and 24.
100. *The Army Field Manual, Volume II, Part 2: A Treatise On Soviet Operational Art* (London: MOD 1991), p. 11–17. The author of this study thanks the Royal Military Academy at Sandhurst for making it possible for him to view appropriate sections of this restricted document.
101. Ibid., p. 4.2.
102. Isby, *Weapons and Tactics of the Soviet Army*, p. 33.
103. Leo Heiman, 'Soviet Invasion Weaknesses', *Military Review*, Vol. 34, No. 8 (August 1969), p. 41.
104. Isby, *Weapons and Tactics of the Soviet Army*, pp. 32–3.
105. Ibid., p. 38.
106. Donnelly, *Rear Support For the Soviet Ground Forces*, p. 18.
107. John Mearsheimer, *Conventional Deterrence* (Ithaca, NY: Cornell University Press, 1983), p. 182; Vigor, *Soviet Blitzkrieg Theory*, pp. 183–4.
108. Heiman, 'Soviet Invasion Weaknesses', p. 41.
109. Donnelly, *Soviet Army Logistics*, p. 5.
110. Donnelly, *Rear Support For the Soviet Ground Forces*, p. 6; Baxter, *Soviet AirLand Battle Tactics*, p. 213.
111. *A Treatise On Soviet Operational Art*, p. 4.2.

112. Dick, 'The Growing Soviet Artillery Threat', p. 72.
113. Sherr, 'NATO's Emerging Technology Initatives', p. 8.
114. Bernard W. Rogers, 'The Atlantic Alliance: Prescriptions for a Difficult Decade', *Foreign Affairs*, Vol. 60, No. 5 (Summer 1982), p. 1152.
115. Bernard W. Rogers, 'ACE Attack of Warsaw Pact Follow-On Forces', *Military Technology*, Vol. 3, No. 5 (May 1983), p. 41.
116. See Robert A. Gessert, 'The AirLand Battle and NATO's New Doctrinal Debate,' *RUSI Journal*, Vol. 129, No. 2 (June 1984), pp. 53–4.
117. Donn A. Starry, 'Extending the Battlefield,' *Military Review*, Vol. 61, No. 3 (March 1981) p. 34.
118. Baxter, *Soviet AirLand Battle Tactics*, p. 254.
119. Ibid., p. 253.
120. Dunn, 'Limits on Soviet Military Power', p. 41.
121. Rogers, 'ACE Attack', pp. 45 and 47.
122. Ibid., see the sidebars on pp. 38–60.
123. Ibid.
124. Sidorenko, *The Offensive*, p. 59.
125. Martin Van Creveld, *Supplying War* (Cambridge: Cambridge University Press, 1977), p. 236.

6

The Revolution in Military Affairs

Some would argue that the problem of military logistics is about to become obsolete. As theorists consider the social and technological developments of the 1990s, many propose that the world is in the throes of a Revolution in Military Affairs (RMA), which will transform both the nature of military operations and the identity of the institutions which wage war. If the dominant conception of the RMA should become reality, information will replace men and materiel as the decisive factor in combat. By this logic, the logistical infrastructure which supports conventional armed forces of the twentieth-century variety must decline in importance.

This chapter attempts to separate sense from nonsense in the RMA debate. From that point, the chapter goes on to explore the RMA vision of future war as a final case study in the relationship between logistics and strategic options. Not only have supply and movement been the 'arbiters of opportunity' throughout history, they continue to play that role in speculative discussions of future war. In passing, this chapter also indicates ways that a heightened awareness of logistics can help military planners make sound judgements about hypothetical situations. Logistical studies cannot tell us what weapons to procure or what tactics to use, but they can help us to ask some of the right questions.

AN END TO LOGISTICS?

Since definitions of the RMA have been anything but consistent, those who use the term have an obligation to explain what they mean. This thesis does not rely on any one author's interpretation of the RMA. Rather, it draws on the ideas of numerous theorists in order to address as many potential scenarios for information warfare as possible. A summary of the RMA hypothesis runs as follows.[1]

The RMA consists, not of a single scientific breakthrough, but of three ongoing technological trends which combine to create a revolution in military efficiency. The first of these trends is the proliferation of sensors on the modern battlefield. Satellite imaging, acoustic detectors, synthetic-aperture radar, unmanned reconnaissance aircraft, geophones and a host of similar devices have greatly increased the ability of officers at all levels to monitor the activities of both their own troops and those of the enemy.

The second trend is the spread of communications equipment, along with computers which sort, filter, fuse and process the information which such devices transmit. Data-processing equipment can magnify the effects of the new sensors by combining data from many sources into a coherent picture of the operational area. Combatants who once had a worm's eye view of the battlefield have gained a fly's eye view instead.

Computerised communications also have the potential to transform the relationship between leaders and the led. Armed forces have traditionally organised themselves into hierarchies where leaders at the higher levels draw up plans for their subordinates to carry out. The drawback to hierarchical organisations, from the point of view of institutional effectiveness, is that the people who have the most first-hand information about a problem often have the least power to design and organise a solution. Those who are, both literally and metaphorically, 'in the trenches' are invariably at the bottom of the command structure. However, as technology gives the leaders of subordinate units more information, their commanders should trust them with greater independence.

Network-style communications, of which the civilian internet is the best-known example, allow any unit in an organisation to communicate with any other unit or combination of units. Therefore, as members of a network, individual units may co-ordinate their activities in a co-operative fashion, without the need for higher-level commanders to dictate all of their plans in advance. Decentralised organisations are also less vulnerable to attack than their traditional counterparts. When units are capable of making their own tactical decisions, they can continue to fight effectively even when they lose contact with their leaders. Since any member of a network can relay messages to any other, there is no way for the enemy to cut off the flow of information by destroying key communication nodes.

For reasons of both practicality and tradition, armies are unlikely to do away with the command hierarchy entirely.[2] The proper model for military leadership in the twenty-first century may be the *auftragstaktik* system of the *Wehrmacht*.[3] Under this system, the upper echelons of the command structure make high-level strategy and assign subordinate units objectives to capture, as usual. Higher commanders, however, take care to phrase their wishes in general terms, and the leaders of lower-level units have the freedom to achieve their goals in any way they see fit. The world may never see an army without generals, but network communications allow armed forces to carry the *auftragstaktik* concept farther than ever before.

The third trend in modern military technology is the appearance of precision-guided munitions (PGMs). Weapons of every variety have become 'smarter' and more accurate, from the guided anti-tank missiles which temporarily halted the Israeli armoured forces in the Suez War to the laser-guided bombs which received widespread media coverage during Operation Desert Storm. Whereas the US Army Air Forces of Second World War estimated that it took 2,500 bombs to hit a single target point, air forces of the Vietnam era required only 50 bombs for the same task, and the fliers of the Gulf War could perform such a mission with a single bomb.[4] Conservative strategists may observe that precision-guided munitions remain rare, expensive and occasionally temperamental, but believers of the RMA may counter that technology almost always becomes cheaper and more reliable over time.[5]

Not only have weapons become accurate, but the source of their accuracy has begun to change.[6] Once, all weapons required human gunners to aim projectiles at targets. The development of missiles which had the ability to home in on the radio, infrared or acoustic signatures of enemy vehicles eliminated the need for direct guidance. Today, advanced weapons can follow directions from sensors in remote locations and find their way to points upon an internal map. If the remote sensors report that the targets have moved, these munitions can adjust their trajectories accordingly. RMA theorists envision a future battlefield where any sensor can guide any projectile to any target. Therefore, weapons themselves become an integral part of the decentralised command and communications network described above. The entire military contingent becomes a single 'system of systems', to borrow Admiral William Owens' much-used expression.[7] If the RMA hypothesis is correct, the three trends discussed above will fuse to create an entirely new form of warfare. Like the hydra of legend, the RMA fighting machine has many pairs of eyes and many sets of jaws. Its parts fight with unified purpose, but it has no single head to be cut off.

On a battlefield where long-range precision weapons are common, both sides will have the power to destroy any enemy force they can detect. To quote the RMA enthusiast Martin Libicki, 'Victory used to be determined by who brought the most force to bear first. Today, conventional conflict is akin to hide-and-seek.'[8] Furthermore, although stealth technologies and other countermeasures will help armies protect their assets, the spread of relatively inexpensive sensors seems to ensure that technology will favour the seeker.[9] Some of the more visionary writers in this field have suggested that, within a decade, individual infantrymen will carry frisbee-sized reconnaissance drones as part of their standard gear.[10]

When sensors can guide long-range weapons directly to their destinations, commanders may concentrate fire against targets without taking the risk of massing large numbers of friendly forces at a given geographical location.

Meanwhile, as vehicles and weapon emplacements become more vulnerable, armies will seek to deploy more of them over a wider area. Network communications will allow disparate units to act together in a co-ordinated fashion. Therefore, theorists envision what Libicki refers to as 'fire-ant warfare', in which both armies rely upon vast numbers of small, dispersed and individually expendable sensor platforms and weapons installations, linked by redundant communication lines and organised so that every node in the system can support every other.[11]

In this environment, given enough time and data, a technologically sophisticated force can destroy anything its enemies put in the field. Numerical superiority loses much of its meaning, and large vehicles such as tanks become mere targets. Victory will go to the side which can gather, process and act upon information most swiftly.[12] Information itself will become the medium of warfare, and the computer networks which process this information – cyberspace, as some would put it – will become the decisive battlefield. In the electronic world, all things move at the speed of light, geography has no meaning, and there are no forces to require supplies.

A RESPONSE: THE UNBEARABLE HEAVINESS OF BEING

For the reasons discussed above, RMA theorists often echo Martin Libicki, who wrote that 'with enough information, warfare becomes sufficiently precise to obviate much of logistics'.[13] As a student of strategy, however, one must ask exactly what it is that information will 'obviate'. Contemporary trends clearly reduce the supply needs of military forces, while giving logisticians new and more flexible ways to move materiel. However, these trends do not change the fact that supplies are, as Julian Thompson put it, the lifeblood of war, nor do they remove the business of logistics from its position as the factor which enables armies to carry out their plans.[14]

Warfare, ultimately, must take place in the material world. No matter how sophisticated information technology may become, even RMA-era combat must involve real sensors to find targets and real munitions to destroy them. Libicki himself notes that 'fire-ant warfare' will require logistical systems to seed the battlefield with automated fighting machines.[15] One also notes that, for the foreseeable future, all of the weapons which are cheap and effective enough to serve as the principle tools of an armed force will require airfields, fuel depots, launch facilities, stocks of munitions and the infrastructure which supports these services. Logistics, in other words, will remain with us.

Furthermore, even if one wishes to discuss war on a purely theoretical plane, armed conflict is not merely a matter of firepower. The destruction of enemy armed forces is only one step in a larger process. Clausewitz would have us believe that the aim in war is to disarm the enemy, and that is what the precision munitions of RMA theory give technologically sophisticated armed forces an unprecedented ability to do.[16] The statement about disarming the enemy, however, is merely the fourth proposition in a series of points which combine to form a more subtle argument about the nature of war.

At its most abstract level, Clausewitz tells us, war is 'an act of force to compel our enemy to do our will'.[17] At the level of reality, where things such as chance, uncertainty, the motives of the participants and the intangibles of human creativity come into play, war becomes 'a continuation of policy by other means'.[18] The concept of war as an attempt to disarm the enemy is only a transitional phase between these two more general definitions.

When one considers modern military technology in the context of Clausewitz's other definitions, one sees new dimensions to the problem of logistics. As a student of strategy, one must ask who the combatants in a given war are and what they are willing to fight over. These are not perfunctory questions – information warfare theorists themselves predict that they will be the key issues of twenty-first-century military affairs. The futurists Alvin and Heidi Toffler express the point as follows:

> [T]he military revolution which lies ahead will be far deeper than most commentators have so far imagined. A military revolution, in its fullest sense, occurs only when a new civilization arises to challenge the old, when an entire society transforms itself, forcing its armed services to change at every level simultaneously – from technology and culture to organization, strategy, tactics, training, doctrine and logistics. When this happens, the relationship of the military to the economy and society is transformed, and the military balance of power on earth is shattered.[19]

Other writers, whose work focuses less upon technology and more upon social factors, have taken up the same theme. In *The Transformation of War*, the historian Martin Van Creveld asks 'by whom will war be fought, what will war be fought about, how will war be fought, what will war be fought for and why war will be fought'.[20] Van Creveld believes that the answers to all these questions have changed and that such a development would have greater implications for the future of armed conflict than any change in weapons technology. The answers to these questions indicate yet more reasons why logistics will continue to play its role as a great enabling factor in warfare.

Broad arguments about the future of politics and society lie beyond the scope of this thesis, but it is useful to consider some of the things which people might fight over in the information age. RMA theorists and less technologically oriented futurists have suggested the following possibilities.

- Law Enforcement. Martin van Creveld, among others, takes Reagan administration rhetoric about a 'war on drugs' literally, and adds that if the United States cannot halt what he terms its 'current economic decline', the crime 'that is rampant in the streets of New York and Washington, DC, may develop into low-intensity conflict by coalescing along racial, religious, social and political lines'.[21]

- Criminal Insurgency. Ralph Peters, writing in *Parameters*, notes that 'In Southeast Asia's Golden Triangle and in the Andean Ridge, druglord insurgencies have moved from defying laws to denying great tracts of territory to the state.[22] Peters means to imply, one presumes, that circumstances such as this may eventually require a full-scale military response.
- Spillover Conflict. The Tofflers write that 'Ethnic and religious violence outside [a nation's] borders can ignite parallel violence inside.'[23] Thus, they fear that even relatively stable societies may sink into internal warfare.
- Ethnic Separatism. Van Creveld tells us that the desire for ethnic self-government may lead to warfare even within Western Europe.

> Integration will probably strengthen regional pressures for independence on the part of Basques, Corsicans, Scots, and a whole host of other peoples ... Not all these movements will employ violence to gain their ends. Still, and also in view of the growing numbers of resident, non-European, non-Christian people, in the long run the possibility exists that low-intensity conflict will break out and sweep over at least part of the continent.[24]

- Trade Issues. The Tofflers tell us that 'The air is teeming with trade-war scenarios which could translate, if stupidly handled, into actual war between major trading nations.'[25]
- Clash of Civilisations. Peters, who acknowledges his intellectual debt to Samuel Huntington, tells us that competition between cultures may assume the role formerly held by competition between ideologies as the organising principle for large-scale warfare.[26]
- Immigration Control. The clash of civilisations may also be reversed, as people flee one civilisation for another. Alvin and Heidi Toffler suggest that some nations may shortly have to use warlike means to turn back tides of refugees.[27]
- Aftermath Instability. Peters tells us that veterans of other military clashes may themselves present a threat to international order.

> In the wake of high-level agreements to resolve conflicts, most broken states or territories cannot reabsorb the human detritus left behind by waves of violence ... For those who have become habituated to violence and its quick rewards, post-conflict societies often have nothing to offer that can wean these warriors back to constructive patterns of behaviour.[28]

Furthermore, people will undoubtedly continue to fight wars for more traditional reasons. Jomini offers a useful summary of what these reasons might be. As he says, a government goes to war:

1. To reclaim certain rights or to defend them.
2. To protect and maintain the great interests of the state, such as commerce, manufacture or agriculture.
3. To uphold neighbouring states whose existence is necessary either for the safety of the government or the balance of power.
4. To fulfil the obligations of offensive and defensive alliances.
5. To propagate political or religious theories, to crush them out or to defend them.
6. To increase the influence and power of the state by acquisitions of territory.
7. To defend the threatened independence of the state.
8. To avenge insulted honour.
9. From a mania for conquest.[29]

As one reviews these reasons for war, one must continually ask how the belligerent parties will secure their aims. Needless to say, combatants can never accomplish their goals as long as their enemies have the power to destroy them. Therefore, the firepower battle of force against force will always be crucial, and as Clausewitz and the RMA theorists agree, a key aim in warfare will always be to disarm the enemy. For a warfighter who merely wishes to fulfil treaty obligations or, as Jomini put it, to 'avenge insulted honour', the firepower battle may, indeed, be sufficient in itself. Likewise, those whose aims are purely defensive may achieve their goals merely by inflicting enough pain to cause attackers to turn back, although the foresighted may note that a strategy of this nature can never prevent the aggressor from returning at a later date.

In the other cases, however, belligerents will eventually have to get about the business of extracting wealth, pacifying the people in occupied territory, propagating various belief systems, enforcing their preferred codes of law, etc. These tasks require, as Admiral Wylie would put it, a man on the scene with a gun.[30] Furthermore, although one may cripple opposing armed forces with long-range bombardment, it will seldom be possible completely to neutralise the enemy's war-making ability until one occupies his territory.[31] Therefore, the 'men on the scene' must have enough training and heavy equipment to participate in the war proper. In other words, even if tanks, heavy infantry, armed helicopters and similar forces lose their place as arms of decision, they will retain a vital place in warfare, and they will continue to need logistical support.

Furthermore, military leaders would be foolish to place too much reliance on the reduced logistical requirements of new weapons. 'Just-in-time' may be a useful slogan for business management, but it is a dangerous philosophy for warfare. In combat, one almost always needs more than one expects and to fall short is to risk catastrophe. The failure of the German army to provide its troops with cold-weather clothing during Operation Barbarossa is a classic example of this point.[32] Armies which maintain the ability to supply themselves as rapidly and abundantly as possible may be able to exploit opportunities and achieve successes which a more parsimoniously managed force would have missed. Generous logistical support is one of the prime factors which helps troops to overcome the factor which Clausewitz calls friction in war.[33]

The problem of military logistics is not likely to vanish, but the day-to-day business of the logistician is almost certainly on the verge of change. As armed forces attempt new types of operations, they will require new kinds of support. Likewise, as technology provides solutions to old logistical problems, commanders will be able to push their forces to new limits and undertake missions which would have been impossible in the past. With these thoughts in mind, one can discuss the role of logistics in twenty-first-century war.

PERCEPTIONS OF FUTURE WAR

In each chapter, this study poses the question: how have military commanders perceived the problem of logistics? As of the late 1990s, the RMA remains largely an American phenomenon, and therefore it is appropriate for this section to focus on the writings of American experts.[34] The war planners of the US armed forces know what they want from the information revolution, and what they want is speed. American doctrine calls for fluid manoeuvre warfare, and the international political situation at the end of the twentieth century has put the United States in a position where it may need to deploy forces across intercontinental distances at short notice.[35]

Therefore, all branches of the US armed services must improve both their tactical and their strategic mobility. These problems are logistical in nature, and many American commanders look to RMA-era technology for a solution. Colonel Bob Killebrew of the US Army Training and Doctrine Command (TRADOC) has noted that, 'before land forces became so dependent on extended logistics superstructures, they were able to roll freely about a theater of operations ... Genghis Khan's invasion of Europe is a good example.'[36]

In order that the US Army might recover this mobility, Killebrew recommends: 'We [at TRADOC] think [more efficient] technology should get into fighting vehicles: weapons that don't rely on huge stocks of cased ammunition and communications equipment which is smaller and requires less power.'[37] Andrew Krepinevich of the US Center for Strategic and Budgetary Assessments has elaborated upon Killebrew's suggestions:

> As the Army places greater reliance upon precision munitions, it will need far fewer of them, and it may lead to a significantly smaller manoeuvre force. When you fire a projectile better at hitting its target, you may get by with fewer tanks or helicopters.[38]

Air Force enthusiasts think along similar lines. The air power expert Benjamin Lambeth notes that because precision weapons can strike at the most vulnerable points of an enemy building or vehicle, they do not always require massive explosive charges to destroy their targets.[39] Therefore, not only will gunners need fewer rounds of ammunition to hit their targets, but each of those rounds may be smaller as well. The same principle, of course, applies to bombs and other forms of munitions.[40] Lambeth looks forward to a time when 'microsensor-directed microexplosive bombs will be able to neutralise moving targets with just grams of explosive'.[41] He feels that, within the near future, improvements in weapon accuracy will cause 'the explosive effectiveness per unit of mass' to 'grow by a factor of at least ten over current precision munitions'.[42]

Naval officers have noted that the US Army's vision of rapid strategic deployment is, by necessity, a vision of amphibious warfare. Before the Army can 'roll freely about a theater of operations' it must sail to get there. During Operation Desert Shield/Desert Storm, Coalition armed forces had months to transport forces into the theatre, and the Saudi Arabians were able to provide their ships with prebuilt shore infrastructure.[43] In future wars, the problems of maritime transport may be more troublesome. Commander Terry C. Pierce of the US Navy won honourable mention in the Colin S. Powell Joint Warfighting Essay contest with an article in which he warned RMA supporters not to neglect the importance of sealift.[44]

The branches of the US armed forces which specialise in logistics have also embraced the goal of lightning operations through information technology. General Leon E. Salomon of the US Army Materiel Command, for instance, has written at length on this subject.[45] The small, fast-moving and PGM-armed combat units of an RMA-era force will place new demands on the ability of logisticians to deliver supplies to the right place at the right time at short notice.[46] In the Gulf War, labelling problems forced supply officers to open fully half of the 40,000 bulk containers shipped into the theatre in order to determine their contents.[47] There will be no time for such mistakes in the future, and Salomon, among others, looks to 'information and digital technologies' as a means of preventing them.[48]

RMA warfare demands new levels of efficiency from logisticians, and information technology provides them with the means to acquire it. Salomon writes of the need for quartermaster services to adopt the same computerised information-management techniques used in the business world, and looks forward to a day when the digitisation of the battlefield will allow information to flow unimpeded 'from factory to foxhole'.[49] In order to manage more information, logistical services will need more information to manage, and therefore they will require increased support from the intelligence services. The Military Intelligence Professional Bulletin has devoted an entire issue to this topic.[50]

The logistical advantages of PGMs and the logistical efficiencies of computerised resource management will certainly make it possible for forces to manoeuvre more effectively than ever before. Among RMA theorists, there is a school of thought which holds that this will give rise to a new style of warfare. James R. Fitzsimonds, writing in *Parameters*, drew on TRADOC documents to offer the following proposition:

> The ability to identify and destroy a significant portion of an enemy's critical system vulnerabilities faster than he can move, hide or react may lead to a new theory of victory: that of forcing the enemy's recognition of defeat not through sequential attrition, but rather by inducing massive systemic shock on his operating and control systems. Indeed, Jefferey Cooper suggests that a conceptual end state of the RMA may be the reduction of protracted war to a *coup de main* executed in a single main-force engagement.[51]

Colonel John Warden of the US Air Force has dubbed this style of combat 'hyperwar', and numerous authors have discussed its strategic implications. David Jablonsky, in another *Parameters* article, suggests that in this era of rapid warfare, such fundamental concepts as the division of combat into strategy, operations and tactics may be out of date.[52] For a variety of reasons, the hyperwar theory may fail, but one must note that, once again, logistical developments have made it possible for military leaders to contemplate a new way of fighting. Whether or not current concepts survive the test of battle, advances in logistics will give commanders new strategic options.

SOURCE OF ADVANTAGE

When this study identifies a fighting force which has possessed an advantage in logistics, it routinely asks what factors permitted that military organisation to achieve superiority. In discussions of the RMA, all advantages are hypothetical, and the answers to this sort of question are a matter of opinion. That being said, this line of inquiry reveals clear distinctions between the concerns of soldiers and the writings of theoreticians. Libicki, the Tofflers and other civilian authors tend to emphasise social changes and the synergy between assorted technological developments. Military officers such as Salomon and Lambeth emphasise the miniaturisation of munitions and the appearance of technology to deal with the specific problems they face in their work.

There need not be any contradiction between these points of view. The practical developments which interest military writers may well interlock to form the general trends which interest theoreticians. Nevertheless, as one reviews the RMA literature, it is helpful to remember that different authors have different perspectives. Furthermore, this discrepancy may be symptomatic of the gap between theory and practice which affects all literature on the subject of strategic affairs. Once one learns to look for the broader implications of specific, practical issues, one has taken an important step toward understanding the relationship between logistics and strategy.

MODES OF WARFARE

In the historical case studies, this thesis examines the styles of warfare which various countries have pursued and asks what logistical challenges those methods of fighting entailed. Obviously, one cannot know what form of combat a nation will adopt in a war which has not happened yet. One can, however, examine the forces which are likely to play a role in future battles. If one knows how these forces operate, one can make reasonable propositions about the type of support they will require in a hypothetical war.

As we consider scenarios for information warfare, the key question will always be: how far will the revolution go? RMA theorists tend to write as if every piece of new technology will inevitably develop until it reaches its ultimate potential.[53] This process, however, will take many decades, and experience suggests that it will not follow a neatly marked path from start to finish. Guilio Douhet was, arguably, a succesful prophet of modern air combat, but air forces have never evolved into the all-bomber forces he envisioned.

Whatever the distant future may hold, the experience of Western armies in the 1990s indicates that high-technology weapons still have limits. In Operation Desert Storm, for instance, the United States brought its high-technology arsenal to bear, launching 1,100 sorties by F-117 Stealth fighter-bombers, firing over 60 per cent of the Tomahawk cruise missiles available in the theatre and testing a variety of munitions which have not yet officially appeared in the inventory.[54] The Coalition supplemented its precision weapons with a full-scale air offensive of a more conventional sort, which featured 110,000 sorties by aircraft ranging from the A-10 to the B-52.[55] Nevertheless, Iraq's Republican Guard divisions managed to survive the war in fighting condition, and Scud missiles continued to fly from the first day of the war to the last.[56]

To the strategist, and hence, to the logistician, the important issue is not what new technology might someday be like, but the details of what it is like at a given moment in time. This, combined with the objectives and circumstances of a particular war, will determine what options commanders will find themselves wishing to pursue. Therefore, in addition to considering what information warfare may be like in theory, it is important to consider what military technology can actually do at the moment, and how this is likely to advance in the foreseeable future.

MILITARY LOGISTICS AND STRATEGIC PERFORMANCE

In order to illustrate this study's conclusions about the nature of war, the following two subsections discuss selected operational issues in some detail. The first subsection covers air warfare, while the second covers infantry combat with an emphasis on special operations. These topics were chosen to show that the arguments of this thesis remain valid even in different combat environments and different technological mileus. The role of the air forces seems likely to mushroom in the era of information warfare while the role of ground forces seems likely to shrink, but the principles which relate logistics to strategy hold true at both ends of the technological curve.

THE BOMBARDMENT STYLE OF WARFARE

Proponents of air power suggest that aerial bombardment has come into its own as a distinct style of warfare.[57] These strategists argue that this method of fighting is the ideal tool for those who wish to put the RMA into practice. As they observe, no other branch of the armed services can strike as wide a range of targets over as large an area as air and missile forces. Furthermore, flying reconnaissance platforms can typically see more of the battlefield than surface-bound sensors. Therefore, those who wish to develop RMA capabilities must pay attention to what their air forces are logistically able to do.

Compared to land forces, air forces have always had relatively low requirements for fuel and ammunition. Indeed, air commanders can usually satisfy their needs with their own cargo aircraft.[58] Air units can also reach distant areas of operations faster than any other branch of the armed forces. In 1985, Colonel John Pickett (Now Lieutenant-General, retired) moved a wing of F-111 bombers, their crews and the crews' families from the United States to England in six hours.[59] Aircraft do, however, require secure places to land and take off. The availability of airstrips constrains aerial warfare in much the same way that the availability of logistical support constrains operations on land.

To wage a war of bombardment, one must maintain bases within range of one's targets. One must secure these bases against enemy attack and ensure that they are numerous enough to sustain operations of the intensity which one's strategy demands. Even under forgiving conditions, these are not trivial problems. In the Cold War, for instance, the NATO alliance consisted of the most technologically advanced and air-oriented military organisations in the world, and it had over 40 years in which to develop support facilities for its air forces. Nevertheless, as noted in Chapter 5, there were doubts about NATO's ability to keep planes in the skies during a war with the Soviet Union.[60]

Airbases not only provide support, they require support. Air commanders must have the ability to protect their facilities from enemy raids. This means that they need to devote some of their fighters to defensive patrols, and it also means that they need gun and missile systems, along with the appropriate personnel. As fans of the movie Dr Strangelove may recall, an air force installation also needs a contingent of infantry soldiers to protect the base from any terrorists, guerrillas, army units or special forces which attack it from the ground. This fact should remind those who believe that bombers will become the sole arm of decision in future wars must remember that air forces will always need at least a picket line of ground troops to keep the land forces of the enemy from overrunning friendly airfields. All of these ground units and air defence systems require logistical upkeep.

Nations which wish to deploy air forces throughout the world will often have to use bases in allied countries. Likewise, these nations will frequently need to send aircraft through foreign airspace. For these reasons, the problem of aerial logistics may often be a problem of diplomacy and public relations. (Land and naval forces, of course, may incur similar political difficulties when they attempt to find bases overseas.) One recalls the incident in 1986 when the Reagan administration in the United States resolved to retaliate for terrorist attacks upon its citizens and military personnel by launching an air raid against Libya. France refused to go along with this plan, and therefore, US bombers were forced to fly a circuitous route from Britain to their targets.

Commanders who suffer from a shortage of airbases have numerous options. The most obvious way to increase one's airfield capacity is to construct more airfields. American forces in Vietnam, for instance, built five strips capable of handling jet aircraft, along with numerous smaller facilities for use by propeller-driven planes.[61] In peacetime, however, it may be difficult to secure the political commitment to spend money and appropriate land for such projects and in wartime, the construction of modern airfields may simply take too long, especially if the enemy has the ability to stage air or missile strikes against the work sites.

For nations which can afford them, aircraft carriers serve as mobile offshore bases. Armed forces can also build air contingents around machines which require a minimum of support facilities. The Harrier fighter, with its vertical short take-off and landing capability, has given fine service in the British, Italian, Spanish and US forces.[62] Aircraft engineers can also design aircraft to operate at longer ranges, so that bases near the area of operations become less necessary.

Air Force supporters typically attempt to downplay the issue of basing, and seek technological solutions for the problem. The United States Air Force (USAF), for instance, has committed itself to the concepts of 'global attack' and 'global engagement'.[63] These terms imply that the USAF hopes to carry out many of its operations from bases in the continental United States, no matter where a given war happens to take place. There is nothing new about intercontinental bombing, but modern technology makes it economical for long-range aircraft to attack so-called tactical targets in the heat of battle.

America's air forces have already begun a programme to upgrade conventional munitions, so that B-52 bombers can undertake a broader range of combat missions. The USAF has also conducted exercises to demonstrate the ability of the B-2 bomber to destroy tank formations with precision-guided munitions.[64] The assortment of radar countermeasures known as 'stealth' technology make the use of such bombers in tactical roles far more feasible, since they increase the odds that the expensive aircraft will return from their bombing runs undamaged. Supporters of 'global reach' are free to note that aircraft operating from the United States can now carry out missions which would previously have required whole squadrons of short-range fighter-bombers based in the area of operations.

In the twenty-first century, technology may offer armed forces new ways to project power by air. The Scientific Advisory Board of the US Air Force wishes to develop a type of pilotless fighter-bomber which it calls the Uninhabited Combat Air Vehicle (UCAV).[65] Since UCAVs would need no cockpits, no manual controls, no display screens, no ejection seats, no life-support equipment nor other amenities for the pilot, they could be considerably lighter, faster, stealthier and longer-ranged than aircraft today.[66] Benjamin Lambeth envisions a day when large transport aircraft might carry clusters of smaller UCAVs into war zones in order to achieve 'intercontinental stand-off attack capability'.[67] UCAVs could conceivably travel at speeds of Mach 12–15, and therefore, they could be at their targets within minutes.[68] Needless to say, UCAVs and their flying aircraft carriers would still be rare and expensive. Lambeth states that they would be useful against 'high value' targets and leaves the question of whether or not air forces will still need short-range tactical aircraft unanswered.[69]

Until technology becomes considerably more advanced, there will be important restrictions on what global air forces can do. First, long-range bombers cannot sustain a protracted campaign against enemies who maintain effective air-defence systems. The B-2, for instance, is notoriously costly, and since the US Air Force fields only 26 of them, the loss of one would be a serious blow.[70] Only the most optimistic can believe that 'stealthy' aircraft will remain immune to anti-aircraft missiles forever. Furthermore, in a major war, the airfields from which such aircraft operate may make attractive targets for PGMs, nuclear weapons and, perhaps, commando raids. Even if such attacks were only marginally successful, they could cause great damage against an air force which has put all of its resources into a few highly valuable aircraft.

Second, airpower supporters have yet to demonstrate that global air forces can meet the needs of the ground troops. Tactical bombardment remains one of the most vital tools that land-bound commanders have at their disposal.[71] Soldiers need the ability to call on aircraft whenever and wherever the tactical sitiuation demands it, and it seems unlikely that air forces can provide this support across intercontinental distances. No matter how much firepower a B-2 armed with PGMs happens to possess, it can only be in one place at a time, and if it has to cover thousands of miles on its trips to and from its base, it cannot linger in the war zone for long.

Third, fighter aircraft tend to operate at much shorter ranges than bombers, and since they must operate in relatively large numbers, it is correspondingly more difficult to sustain them with aerial refueling.[72] If the enemy has the ability to put substantial numbers of fighters into the air, a purely global air force may find itself at a disadvantage in the battle for the skies. Lambeth's flying aircraft carriers may ameliorate this sitiuation somewhat, but they will always be more expensive and more difficult to deploy than ground-based fighters of the conventional variety.

As the RMA takes shape, makers of defence policy have a great deal of freedom to decide what the air forces of the twenty-first century will look like, and what their logistical requirements will be. Those who wish to pursue the concept of global engagement will be able to realise their vision more fully than ever before. This will allow them to avoid the problems of overseas basing but it will also limit their ability to support ground operations, and to conduct sustained air combat against a dangerous foe. The price of simplified logistics will be limited strategic opportunities.

THE HUMAN ELEMENT

If theoretical writings on the RMA are accurate, the day will come when human soldiers no longer deliver the mass of an army's firepower. Aircraft, artillery and miniprojectiles can do that job better, and the spread of PGMs may make it impossible for large infantry formations to survive. However, when military operations require judgement, creative thinking and the ability to make reasoned decisions, they will require human beings.[73] To appropriate a bit of jargon, one might observe that human beings remain the most cost-effective weapons platforms available for missions which require a broad range of skills.[74]

For the foreseeable future, even high-technology armies will rely on soldiers to find targets for their PGMs. Electronic sensors may be invaluable for reconnaissance and perimeter security purposes, but despite the claims of RMA theorists, they cannot yet serve as automatic sharpshooters. US commanders in Vietnam controlled the skies and had experimental infrared sensors at their disposal, but they found that infantry engagements were the only sure way to bring enemy troops under fire.[75] Remote sensing technology improved dramatically in the two decades after Vietnam, but even in the 1991 Gulf War, US commanders attempting to find targets in the Iraqi rear suffered from a 'dearth of eyes'.[76] Sensors are simply not as accurate as human observers. Satellite imagery and the high-flying U-2 aircraft, or its more modern TR-1 variant, provided some useful images, but only to an accuracy of 400 metres at best. To be effective, the Army Tactical Missile System requires a location error of not greater than 100 metres.[77]

The US Army has fielded sensor systems which may overcome these problems, but as of the late 1990s, none of them has reached maturity. Remotely Piloted Vehicles (RPVs), for instance, proved their ability to direct fire in the Gulf, but only against 'static, passive targets'.[78] The Joint Surveillance Target Attack Radar System (JSTARS) also earned great praise for its ability to locate enemy formations, but this system only managed to direct fire against Iraqi vehicles on two occasions.[79] In both instances, the enemy units had given away their positions by moving onto major highways.

Even if sensors eventually replace human observers, armies will still need living soldiers to cope with the myriad of unique circumstances which develop in the course of every war. The following list suggests aspects of warfare in which human troops will remain essential.

- Humans will carry on the fight in areas where radio jamming, computer viruses, electromagnetic pulses or simple mechanical failure have disabled the electronic 'system of systems'.
- Humans will operate in cities, mountains, dense jungles and other areas where armed forces cannot use their advanced technology to its full effect.
- Humans will carry out missions which require cunning and native intelligence, such as complex raids and deception operations.
- Humans will hunt down criminals and guerrillas who have managed to hide among the civilian populace.
- Humans will deal with other humans, as bodyguards, propagandists, hostage rescue teams and trainers for local militia forces.

As one considers the final two points, one should recall that, according to Van Creveld, Ralph Peters and many other respected authors on this subject, the importance of urban combat, guerrilla warfare and highly politicised operations other than war is likely to increase manyfold in the RMA era.[80]

Since automated systems can perform routine combat tasks less expensively and more effectively, commanders will rely on human troops to display a great deal of individual initiative. There will also be little room for error on missions which involve people. The destructive power of RMA-era weapons means that any mistake could be fatal. Survival will mean concealment, and missions will routinely depend on the element of surprise. Furthermore, in a media-driven 'information society', public relations may play a greater role than ever before.[81] In other words, combat missions involving human soldiers will resemble twentieth-century special operations (SO).[82]

For the next few decades, at any rate, land combat will almost certainly involve large numbers of troops and machines, and it will almost certainly require relatively large volumes of supplies. One should not take the commando analogy too far. However, like the special forces of today, these troops will need to operate on a battlefield where they are inherently vulnerable. One may use contemporary SO programmes as a model to determine what the logistical requirements of human troops in the information age might be. Furthermore, as normal forces become more like special forces, the importance of actual SO may well increase dramatically.

Commando forces are small by their very nature, and therefore they do not require a great volume of supplies. The main logistical challenge in special warfare is that of getting both the commandos and their equipment into the area of operations. Equally important is the challenge of getting the commandos out again. Since the success of special operations typically depends upon their stealth, logisticians must be prepared to perform these tasks unobtrusively. For forces which are not prepared to support themselves with captured weapons and supplies, these problems are largely problems of technology.

Airborne descents behind enemy lines and amphibious landings on hostile beaches are routine features of special operations. Even in instances where special forces infiltrate enemy lines on foot, they cannot rely on land-bound supply convoys. Therefore, SO forces usually rely on aircraft and small boats to meet their logistical needs. These vehicles must have the ability to penetrate deep into hostile territory, even in cases when enemy air defence systems are active.

Special forces use a variety of tools for these purposes. During the Vietnam War, United States forces equipped C-130 transport aircraft and H-3 helicopters with electronic warfare devices in order to make them suitable for SO purposes.[83] These modified aircraft evolved into the MC-130 Combat Talon and the HH-53 Pave Low helicopter, which have remained the standard means of transportation for US special forces up to the present day.[84] Seaborne commandos also use specialised vehicles, notably minisubmarines and swimmer delivery vehicles such as the US Subskimmer.[85] The Soviet Union and its allies maintained tracked submarines which carried special forces and crawled along the ocean floor.[86]

The technology of moving and supplying special forces continues to advance. The British defence corporation Avpro, for instance, has recently patented an amphibious assault craft known as the Marauder, which would use a pair of jet engines to cruise over water at speeds of up to 400 miles per hour.[87] This vehicle looks like a cross between an aeroplane and a speedboat, and its short wings would allow it to fly up to 20 feet above the water, thereby rendering it immune to the effects of rough seas.[88] The Marauder could carry up to eight soldiers, and a larger craft, known as the Manta, could transport up to 40 tons of equipment.[89] Russian designers have tested a similar vehicle, known as the Caspian Monster, which can cruise at up to 46 feet above the waterline and carry 900 troops.[90] Avpro has billed the Marauder as a new tool for Britain's Special Air Services (SAS), and vehicles of this nature clearly have great potential for special operations.[91]

There are a variety of less dramatic ways in which twenty-first-century technology may simplify the logistical problems of special operations. The Global Positioning System, (GPS) has obvious applications for commando teams. Since SO troopers must often carry their gear on their backs, any miniaturisation of equipment will be an advantage for them. RMA era communications equipment should simplify the problem of resupplying SO forces by air. SO forces may also choose to abandon cumbersome weapons such as mortars and anti-tank missiles in favour of equipment which will allow them to direct precision fire from distant aircraft or artillery at their targets.

These new capabilities do, however, saddle troops with new vulnerabilities as well. As commandos come to depend upon the support of the information-warfare network, their enemies become able to neutralise them by jamming their communications. The question of how fully to embrace information-warfare technology may soon become a major point of debate for those interested in the doctrine and tactics of special operations. As always, the key issue would seem to be the extent to which technology develops and the amount of confidence it inspires in troops.

Almost any military organisation can field the equipment for deploying special forces if it chooses. In the past, however, the logistics of special operations has seldom been a top priority for defence planners, and SO forces have often suffered from shortages of vital transportation equipment, even in major Western armies. In 1979, for instance, the Carter Administration determined that US special forces needed 12 new MC-130 aircraft. Despite the 'second' Cold War of the 1980s, the special forces had great difficulty getting these aircraft inserted into the Air Force budget.[92] If the RMA takes shape as predicted, such priorities may have to change.

The role of ground troops depends upon the shape which the RMA has taken at a particular time. Also, the more information technology reduces the role of ordinary forces, the more important unconventional units will become. The presence of living soldiers allows commanders to conduct operations which automated systems do not allow for, it allows armies to fight enemies who have managed to overcome the 'system of systems' and it smooths the transition from high-intensity combat to the phase of warfare in which the victors impose their own vision of a more desirable peace. Paradoxically, an army's ability to deploy human troops may be one of the major factors which determines its operational flexibility in the RMA era.

CONCLUSION

The proposition that the RMA will eliminate the problem of logistics rests on an overly credulous view of technology and an overly narrow understanding of warfare. This point appears most obvious at the level of practice, but it is valid even at the level of theory. Therefore, no one should be surprised to learn that although military professionals are hardly ignorant of information technology, they continue to recognise logistics as the factor which determines what their forces can do. Likewise, an appreciation for logistics can help one recognise important points in debates over operational issues. There is no single rule for identifying these crucial factors, but those who have educated themselves about supply and movement are likely to notice them.

As the German experience in Russia indicates, commanders who believe that their supply reserves are sufficient for the operations they contemplate must ask whether the nature of those operations might change. As Commander Pierce observed, those who wish to deploy forces to distant theatres of operations must ask about port infrastructure. Countless issues of this nature have come up in the RMA debate, as they do in every discussion of military issues. These are the questions which connect things such as strategic theory, defence policy, military budgeting and battlefield operations. Everyone who studies strategic affairs is familiar with the truism that details matter, and logistical savvy is often the intellectual asset which allows one to determine how and why.

NOTES

1. For more details on these ideas, readers might consult: John Arquilla and David Ronfeldt, 'Book Reviews', *Comparative Strategy*, Vol. 14, No. 3 (July–September 1995), pp. 331–41; James R. Fitzsimonds, 'The Coming Military Revolution Opportunities and Risks', *Parameters*, Vol. 32, No. 2 (Summer 1995), pp. 30–6; David Jablonsky, 'US Military Doctrine and the Revolution in Military Affairs', *Parameters*, Vol. 24, No. 3, (Autumn 1994), pp. 18–36; Martin Libicki, 'The Emerging Primacy of Information', *Orbis*, Vol. 40, No. 2, (Spring 1996), pp. 261–73 and William Owens, 'The Emerging System of Systems', *Military Review*, Vol. 75, No. 3 (May–June 1995), pp. 15–19.

2. There are many practical reasons why military organisations will need to remain hierarchical. No matter how well technology allows military units to communicate, troops may become so preoccupied with their own problems that they overlook vital bits of information which a high-level commander, with a more objective point of view, might have noticed. Furthermore, on the battlefield, an army may have to sacrifice some of its units in order to achieve its overall objectives. One cannot expect soldiers voluntarily to make decisions which may cost them their lives. For this reason alone, armies need commanders who have the authority to decide that certain units and certain missions are more important than others.

There is also an important distinction between management and military command. A victorious military strategy is more than a system which allows all the units of the armed services to function at maximum efficiency. To defeat a dangerous opponent, one must direct the efforts of one's fighting forces toward some objective which will compel the enemy to do one's will. (The allusion to Clausewitz is, of course, intentional.) In order for the whole, as well as the parts, to fight effectively, military leaders must plan their operations so that they lead, step by step, toward the ultimate goal.

Furthermore, one must ask what phrases such as 'compel the enemy to do one's will'

mean in practice. No algorithim can answer such questions – military leaders must rely upon experience and judgement. Therefore, it is unlikely that the collective mind of a network organisation can answer such questions spontaneously. Strategy requires a strategist, and strategists are most effective when they have the authority to give unequivocal orders.
3. See Franz Uhle-Wettler, 'Auftragstaktik: Mission Orders and the German Experience', in Richard D. Hooker (ed.), *Maneuver Warfare: An Anthology* (Novato, CA: Presidio Press, 1993), pp. 236–47.
4. Libicki, 'The Emerging Primacy of Information', p. 262.
5. See, for instance, Martin Libicki, *The Mesh and the Net: Speculations On Armed Conflict In an Age of Free Silicon* (Washington, DC: National Defense University, McNair Paper, 1994), p. 6.
6. Ibid., p. 263.
7. Owens, 'The Emerging System of Systems', *passim*.
8. Libicki, 'The Emerging Primacy of Information', p. 263.
9. Ibid.
10. James Adams, 'The New Spies', *RUSI Journal*, Vol. 142, No. 1 (February 1997), p. 17.
11. Libicki, 'The Mesh and the Net', p. 14.
12. A concept made popular by Colonel Boyd. Owens, 'The Emerging System of Systems', p. 17.
13. Libicki, 'The Emerging Primacy of Information', p. 261
14. Julian Thompson, *The Lifeblood of War: Logistics in Armed Conflict* (London: Brasseys, 1991), *passim*.
15. Libicki, 'The Mesh and the Net', pp. 16–17.
16. Carl Von Clausewitz, *On War* (trans. and ed. Michael Howard and Peter Paret) (Princeton, NJ: Princeton University Press, 1976), p. 77.
17. Ibid., p. 75.
18. Ibid., p. 87.
19. Alvin and Heidi Toffler, *War and Anti-War: Making Sense of Today's Global Chaos* (London: Warner, 1994), p. 34.
20. Martin Van Creveld, *The Transformation of War* (New York: Free Press, 1991), pp. 192–224.
21. Ibid., p. 196.
22. Ralph Peters, 'The Culture of Future Conflict', *Parameters*, Vol. 25, No. 4 (Winter 1995–1996), p. 24.
23. Alvin and Heidi Toffler, *War and Anti-War*, p. 101.
24. Van Creveld, *The Transformation of War*, p. 196.
25. Alvin and Heidi Toffler, *War and Anti-War*, p. 101.
26. Peters, 'The Culture of Future Conflict', p. 25.
27. Alvin and Heidi Toffler, *War and Anti-War*, p. 110.
28. Peters, *The Culture of Future Conflict*, p. 24.
29. Antoine Jomini, *The Art of War* (trans. G.H. Mendell and W.P. Craighill), (Philadelphia, PA: J.B. Lippincott & Co., 1868), p. 14.
30. J.C. Wylie, *Military Strategy: A General Theory of Power Control* (Annapolis, MD: Naval Institute Press, 1989), p. 72.
31. For further discussion of this issue, see Benjamin Lambeth, 'The Technology Revolution in Air Warfare', *Survival*, Vol. 39, No. 1 (Spring 1997), pp. 65–6.
32. See Martin Van Creveld, *Supplying War* (Cambridge: Cambridge University Press: 1977), p. 174.
33. Some writers have argued that RMA technology will eliminate friction in warfare. For a discussion and refutation of their arguments, see Barry D. Watts, *Clausewitzian*

Friction and Future War (Washington, DC: National Defense University, McNair Paper No. 52, October 1996), *passim*.
34. For a discussion of the American role in the development of RMA theory, see Joint Chiefs of Staff, *The American Revolution in Military Affairs* (Washington, DC: Joint Chiefs of Staff documents, 1996), *passim*.
35. For a discussion of the connection between the RMA concept and US Army manoeuvre doctrine, see Alvin and Heidi Toffler, *War and Anti-War*, pp. 7–11. For a discussion of force projection and the strategic posture of the United States, see J.H. Binford Peary, 'Building America's Power Projection Army', *Military Review*, Vol. 74, No. 7 (July 1994), pp. 4–15.
36. George I. Seffers, 'US Army Study: Reduce Force Logistics, Improve Mobility,' *Defense News* (16 December 1996), p. 1. Sticklers for historical accuracy may note that Genghis Khan did not actually lead his armies much farther west than Khwarezm, in what is now northern Iran. His successors, however, did indeed invade Europe.
37. Ibid.
38. Ibid.
39. Lambeth, 'The Technology Revolution in Air Warfare', p. 69.
40. Ibid.
41. Ibid.
42. Ibid.
43. Terry C. Pierce, 'Voodoo Logistics Sink Triphibious Warfare', *Proceedings of the US Naval Institute*, Vol. 122, No. 9 (September 1996), p. 74.
44. Ibid., pp. 74–7.
45. Leon E. Salomon, *Transforming Logistics For the 21st Century* (posted to internet site http://204.7.227.67:1100/infonet/per-log/logistics/articles/log-arts.html in 1996).
46. Pierce, 'Voodoo Logistics', *passim*.
47. Ibid., p. 77.
48. Salomon, 'Transforming Logistics', p. 4.
49. Ibid.
50. *Military Intelligence Professional Bulletin*, Vol. 20, No. 4 (October–December 1994), *passim*.
51. Fitzsimonds, 'The Coming Military Revolution', p. 31.
52. M. Clodfelter and J.M. Fawcett Jr., 'The RMA and Air Force Roles, Missions and Doctrine', *Parameters*, Vol. 25, No. 2 (Summer 1995), p. 23; Jablonsky, 'US Military Doctrine and the Revolution in Military Affairs', pp. 18–36. Thanks to David J. Lonsdale for research assistance.
53. See, for instance, Libicki, *The Mesh and the Net*, pp. 6–7.
54. See Robin Russell, Humphrey Crum-Ewing, David Wiencek, and David Bodset, 'Cruise Missiles: New Theories, New Thinking', *Comparative Strategy*, Vol. 13, No. 3 (June–September 1995), pp. 76–7 and *Soviet Analysis of Operation Desert Storm and Desert Shield* (trans. W.A.B.) (Washington, DC: Defense Intelligence Agency, 1991), p. 76.
55. *Soviet Analysis of Operation Desert Storm and Desert Shield*, *passim*.
56. Anon., 'Chronology of Events', *Military Review*, Vol. 61, No. 9 (September 1991), pp. 72 and 77.
57. See Lambeth, 'The Technology Revolution in Air Warfare', p. 66.
58. Personal Interview with Lieutenant-Colonel Gerald Samos, November 6 1993.
59. Ibid.
60. IISS, *Strategic Survey 1978* (London: IISS, 1979), p. 32.
61. William C. Westmoreland, *A Soldier Reports* (New York: Da Capo Press, 1980), p. 186.
62. Phil Coulson (ed.), *Proud Heritage* (Fairford: RAFBFE Publishing, 1995), p. 88.
63. Lecture by General R.R. Fogleman, US Air Force Chief of Staff, at the University of Birmingham, England, April 4 1997.

64. NAFB with DoD voiceover, *1st B-2 GATS/GAM Live Weapons Demonstration*, Northrop Grumman, Product No. 9610320 Reel No. 1 DM 40619 (10/08/1996).
65. Lambeth, 'The Technology Revolution in Air Warfare', p. 67.
66. Ibid.
67. Ibid.
68. Ibid., p. 68.
69. Ibid.
70. IISS, *The Military Balance 1997–1998* (London: Oxford University Press, 1997), p. 18.
71. For a detailed discussion, see Robert H. Scales Jr., *Firepower in Limited War* (Novato, CA: Presidio Press, 1995), p. 113.
72. The B-52 bomber, for instance, has a normal combat radius of 16,000 km, and even the lighter F-111 bomber has a range of 2,000 km. An F-15 fighter, by comparison, has a range of only 990 km and the F-16 has a range of only 900 km. There are, of course, many variants of these aircraft, each of which have slightly different performance statistics. James F. Dunnigan, *How to Make War: All the World's Weapons, Armed Forces and Tactics* (New York: Quill Press, 1983), p. 108.
73. One can, of course, speculate about the possibility of artificial intelligence. Sentient android soldiers, however, lie beyond the scope of this discussion.
74. RMA theorists affirm that military planners will find it most economical to design information warfare automatons for highly specialised roles. See Libicki, 'The Mesh and the Net', p. 9.
75. Scales, *Firepower in Limited War*, p. 112 and 115–16.
76. Ibid., p. 260.
77. Ibid., pp. 260–1.
78. Ibid., p. 261.
79. Ibid.
80. Peters, 'The Culture of Future Conflict', p. 26.
81. See, for instance, Alvin and Heidi Toffler, *War and Anti-War*, p. 202–13.
82. For these purposes, one can define special operations as '[s]mall-scale clandestine, covert or overt operations of an unorthodox and frequently high-risk nature, undertaken to achieve significant political or military objectives in support of foreign policy.' Colin S. Gray, *Special Operations – What Suceeds and Why: Lessons of Experience, Phase 1* (Washington, DC: National Institute for Public Policy, 1991), pp. 9–10.
83. Ross S. Kelly, *Special Operations and National Purpose* (Lexington, MA: Lexington Books, 1989), p. 23.
84. Ibid., p. 8.
85. Terry White, *Swords of Lightning* (London: Brasseys, 1992), p. 92.
86. Ibid., p. 93.
87. Hugh McManners, 'Wave-skimmer Will Smuggle SAS Past Enemy Radar At 400 MPH', *Sunday Times* (16 February 1997), p. 7.
88. Ibid.
89. Ibid.
90. Ibid.
91. Ibid.
92. Susan L. Marquis, *Unconventional Warfare: Rebuilding US Special Operations Forces* (Washington, DC: Brookings Institute Press, 1997), pp. 129–30.

Conclusion:
The Foundation of Strategy

This study began with a paradox and a proposition. The paradox was the discrepancy between scholarly theory and practical experience concerning the importance of logistics in warfare, which is vast even by the standards of the social sciences. The proposition was that supplies and transportation assets derive their full military significance, not from their tangible value on the battlefield, but from their intangible value as factors which increase the number of strategic options available to commanders. This study went on to test its general argument against the specific circumstances of three military campaigns, a cold war and an ongoing strategic debate. In each case, the empirical details bore out the previously stated hypothesis.

The significance of this study's central proposition lies, not in the mere fact that it is correct, but in its value as a starting point for strategic analysis. In the course of making its argument, this study articulates the reasons why experienced commanders throughout history have emphasised the importance of logistics. The case studies illustrate what these ideas mean in practical terms. It is in this way that this study goes beyond stating the obvious point that logistics is vitally important. It rescues key concepts about the relationship between logistics and strategy from the limbo of common wisdom (which, as the literature review in the first chapter indicates, is not nearly as common as it should be).

This study transforms vague sensibilities into explicit and carefully explained principles. Thus, it allows both scholars and practitioners to appreciate the logic behind those principles and then, when they deem it appropriate, to apply those principles in a conscious and well-considered fashion. This does not, however, mean that this study brings logistics into the fold of social science theory. Rather, this study identifies a fallacy in contemporary academic methods, and suggests that scholars adopt a more flexible approach to the study of strategy and politics.

THE SCIENCE OF THE POSSIBLE: THE CASE STUDIES IN REVIEW

An understanding of logistics provides foundation stones for a more general understanding of strategy, warfare, and, by extension, all aspects of human relations which involve the possibility of organised violence. If politics is the art of the possible, logistics is the corresponding science. When one investigates the way in which armed forces supply themselves, one accumulates information about the measurable, objective and, hence, scientific side of military operations. There are also immeasurable, subjective and fundamentally artistic aspects to warfare, but in strategy, material and immaterial factors are linked. Therefore, our studies of objective considerations will provide us with clues which lead to a fuller knowledge of subjective matters, and vice versa.

Carl von Clausewitz addressed this issue in Book Two, Chapter Three of *On War*. 'The object of science is knowledge', Clausewitz writes, 'and the object of art is creative ability'.[1] Although one may distinguish between the concepts of art and science for intellectual purposes, one may not separate them in practice.[2] The art of painting, for instance, involves a science of perspective, and even such a scientific endeavour as mathematics becomes an art when one applies its principles to solve complex problems.

Clausewitz goes on to tell us that war is more of an art than a science, but contains elements of both.[3] Furthermore, as an art form, warfare involves special problems.

> [W]ar is not an exercise of the will directed at inanimate matter, as is the case with the mechanical arts, or at matter which is animate but passive and yielding, as is the case with the human mind and emotions in the fine arts. In war, the will is directed at an inanimate object that *reacts*. [Emphasis in original.][4]

When we study the way in which armed forces supply themselves, we develop an appreciation for what those forces can and cannot do. Therefore, we begin to see what the 'inanimate object' of *On War* is like, and how it might 'react' to various dangers and opportunities. This, in turn, helps us to make judgements about the way in which commanders might deploy this force, the political significance of its existence and all the other factors which Clausewitz implies when he refers to the 'exercise of will'. A review of the case studies demonstrates how logistics can form the link between the innumerable other factors which influence military operations.

Each case study considered the question of how practising military commanders have perceived the relationship between logistics and strategy. The most universal answer – that professional war-fighters have invariably seen a link between the two – not only adds weight to this study's central argument, it is significant for its own sake. A force which seems to enjoy a robust logistical system will have a far greater psychological effect upon both

CONCLUSION

its allies and its enemies than one which appears poorly supplied. Furthermore, opposing commanders will seek ways to take advantage of each other's logistical situation. Logistics is both an end and a means in war; a factor which can influence operations and a factor which can be influenced by operations.

All the case studies support these points to one degree or another. The chapter on the Cold War provides a particularly clear example of how enemies attempt to exploit the vulnerabilities of each other's supply networks. This chapter also illustrates the importance of perceptions in this sort of jockeying for position. Likewise, American commanders in Vietnam made extensive studies of the Communist logistical system, and many believe that US forces should have focused their operations on disrupting this supply network.

The second routine question asked how logistical factors have helped or harmed the overall performance of armed forces. When one summarises the answers to this question, one finds that both 'logistical factors' and 'performance' mean different things in different types of campaigns. Slim used aerial transportation to conduct highly flexible campaigns in the Burmese jungle, thereby seizing the operational initiative from his Japanese enemies. American commanders in the Pacific used mobile bases, long-range submarines, amphibious techniques and a variety of other methods to bring their superior force to bear promptly, despite their early losses of ships and bases. The Vietnamese Communists used the Ho Chi Minh Trail to sustain irregular and semi-irregular forces in a fierce war of attrition. The NATO and Warsaw Pact countries used routine late-twentieth-century means to support two different types of armies, one of which depended on technology while the other depended on mass, and RMA theorists seek to develop forces which can deliver firepower precisely enough to achieve results without a substantial logistics tail.

The details of these chapters are entirely different. There are, however, fundamental principles which resurface in every case study. Logistics is, as Chapter 1 stated, an arbiter of opportunity. The fact that both logistics and opportunity can appear in many guises merely means that those who wish to understand strategic affairs must learn to look beneath technical facts and interpret military operations in terms of what commanders might hope to do (opportunity) and how they might assemble the means to do it (logistics).

The third routine question asks what factors have given countries logistical advantages. Again, the case studies provide a variety of answers, but, once again, an insightful reader will notice common themes. In Burma, Cold War Europe and the hypothetical battlefields of the information age, the key variable would seem to be technology. Diplomatic, psychological and geographical considerations made it possible for the Vietnamese Communists to build their logistical network. The US armed forces won the Pacific War by introducing a happy combination of innovative equipment and innovative doctrine, and by using the lessons they learned in both exercises and early battles to perfect their techniques.

The theme which unites these case studies is that, for armed forces to benefit from a potential logistical advantage, they must wed their logistical assets to the more general demands of their order of battle and their strategy. Just as new weapons are seldom decisive unless one can deploy them in large numbers, logistical advantages are seldom significant unless they benefit a significant proportion of one's forces. The case study on the Pacific War emphasised the fact that logistics is a large-scale enterprise. The comparative value of raids, larger operations such as those mounted by the Chindits and full-scale battles in the Burma campaign remain a matter of controversy, but one must observe that Slim did not defeat the Japanese decisively until he fought them in major engagements at Kohima and Imphal.

Furthermore, logistic success is a matter of preparation and organisation. One Viet Cong guerrilla observed that without such legwork, 'all units would get lost in the immense forest', and there is a great deal of truth in this observation, both literally and metaphorically.[5] The case study on the Pacific War discusses this issue in some detail, and the chapter on Vietnam notes that the same rule applies even to intangible logistical advantages, such as motivated troops and a potentially supportive civilian population. Hanoi made the people of North and South Vietnam support its war effort, not through its ephemeral grasp on the national aspirations of the population, but through a network of overt and covert institutions which enforced political conformity and mobilised civilian labour. One should also note that the Pacific War chapter contains a direct rebuttal to Van Creveld's argument that preparation is of secondary importance.

Finally, each case study investigates the particular problems of supporting particular styles of warfare. Here, one encounters a variety of trade-offs and grim realities, some of which have become classic problems of strategy. For instance, larger armies have more cumbersome logistical tails. The armies of the USSR offer a clear example of this principle in action. 'Leaner' armies can move and strike more efficiently, but may shatter under a sharp blow. The Soviet Union hoped to exploit this fact to defeat NATO, just as Japan once hoped to take advantage of this principle to make the United States government accept a negotiated end to the Second World War. In the same vein, aerial resupply and other forms of high-speed, high-technology transportation allow armed forces to conduct highly flexible campaigns, as Slim's exploits in Burma demonstrate, but only until opposing forces develop the means to shoot down the aircraft or otherwise neutralise the transportation resources. Those who believe that information technology will lead to a revolution in the speed with which armies can manoeuvre do well to remember this fact.

As the chapter on the Pacific War explains, different branches of one's forces

CONCLUSION

may raise different logistical problems and open different operational possibilities. To understand the implications of these advantages and disadvantages, one must examine the way that these branches work together within the framework of a larger strategy. Once again, this is an important lesson for those who place their faith in information warfare – the shape of any future RMA depends on the precise technological advances which take place and the type of war which the technologically advanced armed forces find themselves fighting.

As one examines the relationship between logistics and strategy, one inevitably encounters other principles of armed conflict, some of which are nearly universal. To understand Communist logistics in Vietnam, for instance, one must explore the role of timing in warfare. To understand why aerial transportation meant so much to Slim's campaigns in Burma, one must examine the concept of initiative. The Pacific War demonstrates the importance of co-ordinating all the different levels of military operations, from tactics to grand strategy. Readers are free to pick the lessons which they consider most relevant to their own interests, but one will note that, in most cases, logistics is the factor which allows commanders to apply these ideals in practice.

To summarise the findings of the case studies, an inquiry into logistics inevitably touches upon many different issues, which involve many different aspects of warfare. At first glance, these issues seem united only by their diversity. However, the simple fact remains that studies of one issue – logistics – reveals new insights into all these other matters as well as showing that logistical studies are invaluable to those who wish to gain a comprehensive understanding of war. Logistics is the key to many doors. Furthermore, our studies of supply and movement allow us to see the underlying structure which connects these other factors which affect the outcome of armed struggle.

'A weapon of the keenest is in the forging,' Colonel G.C. Shaw wrote in 1938, on the subject of mechanised warfare, 'but its temper will depend on supply.'[6] This metaphor sums up the importance of logistics quite nicely. One studies logistical capabilities because they pervade the 'weapon' of armed forces; because they lend strength and resilience to the other factors which lead to advantage in war. '[Supply] forms the basis on which rests the whole structure of war; it is the very foundation of Tactics and Strategy.'[7]

THE NEXT STEP: A GUIDE FOR FUTURE RESEARCH

The author hopes that readers will be able to apply his logic and ideas to studies of their own and to gain useful insights from the effort. However, this will never be an automatic process. To understand logistics and its implications for a particular case, one must use one's own intelligence, imagination and judgement. Each researcher must decide for himself or herself which sources of information are relevant and which ones are of secondary importance; which facts are clear and which are subject to multiple interpretations; which military problems are insurmountable and which are merely minor obstacles.

Those who wish to refine the art of strategic analysis must follow the method which the philosopher Ludwig Wittgenstein described in the following passage:

> Corrector prognoses will generally issue from the judgements of those with better knowledge of mankind.
>
> Can one learn this knowledge? Yes; some can. Not, however, by taking a course in it, but through 'experience'. Can someone else be a man's teacher in this? Certainly. From time to time he gives him the right tip. This is what 'learning' and 'teaching' are like here. What one acquires here is not a technique; one learns correct judgements.
>
> There are also rules, but they do not form a system, and only experienced people can apply them right. Unlike calculating rules.
>
> What is most difficult here is to put this indefiniteness correctly and unfalsified into words.[8]

What Wittgenstein describes as 'experience' need not be acquired firsthand. Historical readings may provide similar benefits. Indeed, in the study of military operations, they must do so, for even those who have personally been in combat see only a tiny fraction of the vast and complex enterprise which is war. Scholars may discover some of the 'tips' which Wittgenstein mentions in written sources as well.

Some would find the absence of what Wittgenstein calls a 'system' unsatisfactory. Wittgenstein's method of analysis depends upon what is known as inductive logic, which is to say that the researcher gathers information first, and forms conclusions only after s/he has had an opportunity to see how the facts fit together. This approach has a bad reputation in contemporary social science. The anthropologist Levi-Strauss referred to it as 'the inductivist illusion', and Kenneth Waltz, the founder of the neo-realist school of thought and a key figure in the development of contemporary international relations theory, tells us that observation and experience never lead directly to knowledge.[9]

Waltz goes on to observe:

> Today's students of politics nevertheless display a strong commitment to induction. They examine numerous cases with the hope that connections and patterns will emerge and that those connections and patterns will represent the frequently mentioned 'reality that is out there'. The hope apparently rests on the conviction that knowledge begins with certainties and that induction can uncover them. But we can never say with assurance that a state of affairs inductively arrived at corresponds

CONCLUSION

to something objectively real. What we think of as reality is itself an elaborate conception constructed and reconstructed through the ages. Reality emerges from our selection and organisation of materials [i.e. raw information] which are available in infinite quantity. How can we decide which materials to select and how to arrange them? No inductive procedure can answer the question, for the very problem is to figure out the criteria by which induction can usefully proceed.[10]

Waltz advocates a different method of accumulating knowledge. He feels that we must base our research upon theories and models. A theory, by his definition, is a 'concept' or 'assumption' which purports to explain some relationship between facts, and a model is an intellectual construct which deliberately oversimplifies some phenomenon in order to limit the number of factors which might complicate our understanding.[11] Waltz takes pains to emphasise that theories and models come before empirical work – in other words, one develops one's explanations for phenomena first and observes them afterward.

'[Theoretical notions] are neither true nor false,' Waltz tells us.[12] 'Theoretical notions find their justifications in the success of the theories that employ them.'[13] Waltz goes on to say that the most useful theories are those which generalise most broadly, incorporating the greatest number of phenomena and making the fewest allowances for specific cases. The power of Newton's theory of universal gravitation, Waltz writes, 'lay in the number of previously disparate empirical generalisations and laws that could be subsumed in one explanatory system ...'[14]

Later, Waltz emphasises the following point: 'Explanatory power, however, is gained by moving away from 'reality', not by staying close to it. A full description would be of least explanatory power; an elegant theory, of most.'[15]

In other words, those who subscribe to Waltz's position feel that theories and models should be as abstract and as pared down as possible. Waltz takes care to note that departing from reality is not an end in itself, unless one can do so in 'some clever way', but quotes James Conant, who defined science as an 'undertaking directed to lowering the degree of empiricism in solving problems' and goes on to state that we should be looking for 'suggestive ways' to depict the theory, 'and not the reality it deals with'.[16]

Waltz cites numerous authorities from assorted branches of the social sciences to support his propositions, and at the level of metaphysics, his arguments about the nature of knowledge and reality may carry considerable weight. For those who wish to understand military affairs, however, Waltz's ideas are not particularly useful, and nowhere is this more apparent than in the study of logistics. Van Creveld did not offer the kind of theories which Waltz advocates, but nevertheless, his failure illustrates the reasons why more formalised approaches must fail as well.

The principles of logistics and strategy refuse to be pinned down. Although this body of work has traced them through five diverse historical case studies, they manifest themselves in different ways every time. Anyone who attempted to apply one general theory to each case would quickly become lost. Hence, Van Creveld found little evidence to confirm his implicit hypothesis that, if logistics affected the outcome of battles, the commanders who devoted the greatest amount of effort to prediction, administration and stockpiling would reap the greatest rewards. The effects of logistics are infinitely more subtle and varied than that.

The more simplifications, generalisations and abstractions we accept about the relationship between logistics and strategy, the more frequently we will fail to see the way in which that relationship operates. Furthermore, to gain useful information about such matters, we must gather specific facts about particular cases, and this means that, Conant's formulation notwithstanding, we must increase, rather than reduce, the amount of empiricism in our work. We must study each case on its own terms. We must look at why politicians and military commanders do the things they do, and what material factors make it possible for them to act as they do.

This study has proposed that logistics is an arbiter of strategic opportunity. In one sense, this is a theoretical statement. It does, after all, explain a relationship in simple, general terms. However, to make this proposition meaningful, one must translate it into specific terms and apply it to specific cases – one must see 'logistics' as transport aircraft and 'opportunity' as the chance to outflank enemy units through the jungle; 'logistics' as the fleet train and 'opportunity' as an industrial base which allows one to build a materially superior navy; 'logistics' as jungle highways through a neutral country on your enemy's flank and 'opportunity' as a long-term strategy to erode your enemy's will to fight – or whatever else the situation happens to involve. This study's theoretical statement is the beginning, not the end, of productive inquiry.

This method of analysis relies upon judgement. One does not, however, wish to rely upon guesswork, and that is why the study of logistics is particularly valuable. If we understand how a given military force supplies itself, we have a basis for making informed inferences about its capabilities. Logistics is the bridge between the things which armed forces physically can do and the things which their commanders might want them to do. When military forces make material preparations, it is because their leaders intend them to achieve something, and the type of preparations they make may indicate what those leaders have in mind.

There are innumerable other clues which may reveal a government or military leader's plans, which range from the philosophical tenets of certain political movements to the nuances of diplomatic symbolism. As one learns to interpret these clues, one learns how to think like a practitioner of international relations. Eventually, one learns to think like a *good* practitioner of international relations. Thus, one develops a sense for what these clues

CONCLUSION

mean, and eventually, one gains the ability to assemble them into a cogent, coherent synthesis.

Kenneth Waltz described such methods of analysis with some derision: 'The belief that the pieces can be added up, that they can be treated as independent variables whose summed effects will account for a certain portion of a dependent variable's movement, rests on nothing more than faith.'[17]

One might be tempted to respond that a man, who feels that reality is no more than 'an elaborate conception constructed and reconstructed through the ages' and who advises us not to worry about whether or not our theories resemble the picture of that reality which our senses provide for us, has no business chiding others for their willingness to rely on faith. Furthermore, if this process of analysis and synthesis is faith, it is at very least a form of faith which has a basis in our knowledge of international politics.

Strategy and statecraft are not unconscious forces of nature, but practices which originate in the human mind. It is both reasonable and pragmatic to assume that individual people can come to understand at least a healthy proportion of their own thoughts, and that most *homo sapiens* have at least a substantial number of thought processes in common. Therefore, it is not extreme to propose that war, politics and other human practices are intelligible, and that one can match deeds, such as material preparations for combat, with the ideas and intentions which inspire them. If one accepts these notions, then a knowledge of logistics is an excellent stepping stone to a broader understanding of the use of force in international relations. Contrary to Van Creveld, this author concludes that the best instrument for waging war, and therefore the best instrument to understand it, is the human intellect after all.[18]

NOTES

1. Carl Von Clausewitz, Michael Howard and Peter Paret (trans.), *On War* (Princeton, NJ: Princeton University Press, 1976), p. 148.
2. Ibid.
3. Ibid., p. 149.
4. Ibid.
5. L.P. Holliday and R.M. Gurfield, *Viet Cong Logistics* (Santa Monica, CA: RAND, 1968), p. 48.
6. G.C. Shaw, *Supply in Modern War* (London: Faber & Faber, 1938), p. 26.
7. Ibid.
8. Jon Tetsuro Sumida, *Inventing Grand Strategy and Teaching Command: The Classic Works of Alfred Thayer Mahan Reconsidered* (Washington, DC: The Woodrow Wilson Center Press, 1997), p. 99.
9. Kenneth Waltz, 'Laws and Theories', in Robert Keohane (ed.), *Neorealism and Its Critics* (New York: Columbia University Press, 1986), p. 30.

10. Ibid., p. 31.
11. Ibid., pp. 27–8 and 33.
12. Ibid., p. 32.
13. Ibid.
14. Ibid., p. 33.
15. Ibid., p. 34.
16. Ibid.
17. Ibid., p. 30.
18. 'It is perhaps fitting that the present study – starting, as it did, with the determination to avoid 'vague speculations' and concentrate on 'concrete figures and calculations' should end with an admission that the human intellect alone is not, after all, the best instrument for waging war and, therefore, understanding it'. Martin Van Creveld, *Supplying War* (Cambridge: Cambridge University Press, 1977), p. 236.

Bibliography

BOOKS AND MONOGRAPHS

Allen, Louis, *Burma: The Longest War 1941–1945* (London: J.M. Dent & Sons Ltd., 1984).
The Army Field Manual, Volume II, Part 2: A Treatise on Soviet Operational Art (London: Ministry of Defence [MOD], 1991).
Ballantine, Duncan S., *US Naval Logistics in the Second World War* (Princeton, NJ: Princeton University Press, 1949).
Baxter, William, *Soviet AirLand Battle Tactics* (Novato, CA: Presidio Press, 1986).
Bond, Brian, *Liddell Hart: A Study of His Military Thought* (London, Cassell, 1977).
Boulding, Kenneth E., *Conflict and Defense: A General Theory* (New York: Harper Brothers, 1962).
Bowersox, Donald J. and David J. Closs, *Logistical Management: The Integrated Supply Chain Process* (New York: McGraw-Hill, 1996).
Brower, Charles F., *Strategic Reassessment in Vietnam: The Westmoreland 'Alternate Strategy' of 1967–1968*, (Newport, RI: Naval War College, 1990).
Brown, Kenneth N., *Strategics* (Washington, DC: National Defense University Press, 1987).
Buckley, Thomas H., *The United States and the Washington Conference: 1921–1922* (Knoxville, TN: University of Tennessee Press, 1970).
Callwell, C.E., *Small Wars* (East Ardsley: EP Publishing, 1976).
Carter, Worrall Reed, *Beans, Bullets, and Black Oil* (Washington, DC: US Government Printing Office, 1953).
Chesneau, Roger (ed.), *Conway's All the World's Fighting Ships 1922–1946* (London: Conway Maritime Press, 1980).
Clausewitz, Carl von, *On War*, trans. and ed. Michael Howard and Peter Paret (Princeton, NJ: Princeton University Press, 1976).
Costello, John, *The Pacific War* (London: William Collins & Sons, 1981).
Coulson, Phil (ed.), *Proud Heritage* (Fairford: RAFBFE Publishing, 1995).
De Landa, Manuel, *War in the Age of Intelligent Machines* (New York: Zone Books, 1991).

Duiker, William J., *The Communist Road to Power in Vietnam* (Boulder: CO Westview Press, 1981).
Dunnigan, James F., *How to Make War: All the World's Weapons, Armed Forces and Tactics* (New York: Quill Press, 1983).
Dupuy, Trevor N, *International Military and Defense Encylopedia* (Washington, DC: Brasseys, 1993).
Eccles, Henry E., *Logistics in the National Defense* (Harrisburg, PA: The Stackpole Company, 1959).
Friedman, Norman, *US Submarines Through 1945: An Illustrated Design History* (Annapolis, MD: Naval Institute Press, 1995).
Gabriel, Richard A., *Military Incompetence* (New York: Hill & Wang, 1985).
Gibson, William, *The Perfect War: Technowar in Vietnam* (Boston, MA: The Atlantic Monthly Press, 1986).
Griffith, Samuel, *Peking and People's Wars* (London: Pall Mall Press, 1966).
Hannah, Norman B., *The Key to Failure: Laos and the Vietnam War* (New York: Madison Books, 1987).
The Ho Chi Minh Trail (Hanoi: Red River Foreign Language Publishing House, 1985).
Huston, James A, *The Sinews of War 1775–1955* (Washington, DC: US Government Printing Office, 1966).
Ike, N. (ed.) *Japan's Decision for War: Records of the 1941 Policy Conferences* (Stanford, CA: Stanford University Press, 1967).
IISS, *IISS Strategic Survey 1978* (London: IISS, 1979).
——, *The Military Balance 1981–1982* (London: IISS, 1981).
——, *The Military Balance 1987–1988* (London: IISS, 1987).
——, *The Military Balance 1997–1998* (London: Oxford University Press, 1997).
Isby, David, *Weapons and Tactics of the Soviet Army* (London: Janes, 1981).
Isely, Jeter A. and Philip A. Crowl, *The US Marines and Amphibious War: Its Theory, and its Practice in the Pacific* (Princeton, NJ: Princeton University Press, 1951).
Jomini, Antoine, *The Art of War*, trans. G.H. Mendell and W.P. Craighill (Philadelphia, PA: J.B. Lippincott & Company, 1868).
Jones, David C., *US Military Posture FY 1980* (Washington, DC: US Government Printing Office, 1980).
Karnow, Stanley, *Vietnam – A History: The First Complete Account of Vietnam at War*, (New York: Penguin Books, 1984).
Keegan, John, *Churchill's Generals* (New York: George Weidenfeld & Nicolson, 1991).
Kelly, Ross S., *Special Operations and National Purpose* (Lexington, MA: Lexington Books, 1989).
Kirby, S. Woodburn, *The War Against Japan, Volume II: India's Most Dangerous Hour* (London: Her Majesty's Stationery Office, 1958).

BIBLIOGRAPHY

———, *The War Against Japan, Volume III: The Decisive Battles* (London: Her Majesty's Stationery Office, 1961).
Kolko, Gabriel, *Anatomy of a War: Vietnam, the United States and the Modern Historical Experience* (New York: The New Press, 1985).
Krepinevich, Andrew F. Jr., *The Army and Vietnam* (Baltimore, MD: Johns Hopkins University Press, 1986).
Krulak, Victor H., *First to Fight: An Inside View of the US Marine Corps* (New York: Simon & Schuster, 1991).
Lanning, Michael Lee and Dan, Cragg, *Inside the VC and the NVA: The Real Story of North Vietnam's Armed Forces* (New York: Ivy Books, 1992).
Leighton, Richard M. and Robert W. Coakley, *Global Logistics and Strategy 1940–1943*, (Washington, DC: US Government Printing Office, 1955).
Libicki, Martin, *The Mesh and the Net: Speculations on Armed Conflict in an Age of Free Silicon* (Washington, DC: National Defense University, McNair Paper, 1994).
Lorelli, John A., *To Foreign Shores: US Amphibious Operations in World War II* (Annapolis, MD: Naval Institute Press, 1995).
Lynn, John A., *Feeding Mars: Logistics in Western Warfare from the Middle Ages to the Present* (Boulder, CO: Westview Press, 1993).
Macdonald, Peter, *Giap: The Victor in Vietnam* (London: Warner, 1993).
Mao Tse-Tung, *Problems of War and Strategy* (Peking: Foreign Languages Press, 1954).
———, *Selected Military Writings of Mao Tse-Tung* (Peking: Foreign Languages Press, 1968).
Marcus, Geofrey, *Quiberon Bay* (London: Hollis & Carter, 1960).
Marquis, Susan L., *Unconventional Warfare: Rebuilding US Special Operations Forces* (Washington, DC: Brookings Institute Press, 1997).
Mearsheimer, John, *Conventional Deterrence* (Ithaca, NY: Cornell University Press, 1983).
Miller, Edward S. *War Plan Orange: The US Strategy to Defeat Japan, 1897–1945* (Annapolis, MD: Naval Institute Press, 1991).
Millett, Allan R., *Semper Fidelis: The History of the United States Marine Corps* (New York: The Free Press, 1991).
Mrozek, Donald J., *Air Power and the Ground War in Vietnam* (London: Pergamon–Brasseys, 1989).
Nobutaka Ike, (ed.) *Japan's Decision For War: Records of the 1941 Policy Conferences (*Stamford, CT: Stamford University Press).
Pagonis, William G., *Moving Mountains* (Boston, MA: Harvard Business School Press, 1992).
Palmer, Bruce Jr, *The Twenty-Five Year War: America's Military Role in Vietnam*, (Lexington, MA: University Press of Lexington, 1984).
Paret, P. (ed.) *Makers of Modern Strategy from Machiavelli to the Nuclear Age* (Princeton, NJ: Princeton University Press, 1986).

Park, William, *Defending the West: A History of NATO* (Boulder, CO: Westview Press, 1986).
Partington, Angela (ed.) *The Oxford Dictionary of Quotations* (Oxford: Oxford University Press, 1992).
Paxton, John, *The Statesman's Yearbook 1979–1980* (London: Macmillan, 1979).
Phillips, Thomas R., *Roots of Strategy* (London: John Lane at the Bodley Head, 1943).
Pike, Douglas, *PAVN: People's Army of Vietnam* (New York: Da Capo Press, 1986).
Rood, Harold W., *Kingdoms of the Blind* (Durham, NC: Carolina Academic Press, 1980).
Rooney, David, *Burma Victory: Imphal, Kohima and the Chindit Issue, March 1944 to May 1945* (London: Arms & Armour Press, 1992).
Romanus, Charles F. and Riley, Sunderland, *Stilwell's Mission to China* (Washington, DC: Department of the Army, 1953).
Scales, Robert H. Jr, *Firepower in Limited War* (Novato, CA: Presidio Press, 1995).
Shaw, G.C., *Supply in Modern War* (London: Faber & Faber, 1938).
Sidorenko, A.A., *The Offensive*, trans. US Air Force (Washington, DC: US Government Printing Office, 1970).
Slim, Sir William, *Defeat Into Victory* (London: Cassell, 1956).
Sokolovsky, V.D., *Military Strategy*, trans. Wright-Patterson Air Force Base (London: Pall Mall Press, 1963).
Southeast Asia Command, *The Campaign in Burma* (London: Her Majesty's Stationery Office, 1946).
Spector, Ronald H., *Eagle Against the Sun: The American War With Japan* (New York: The Free Press, 1985).
Stanton, Shelby L., *Vietnam Order of Battle* (Washington, DC: US News Books, 1981).
Sumida, Jon Tetsuro, *Inventing Grand Strategy and Teaching Command: The Classic Works of Alfred Thayer Mahan Reconsidered* (Washington, DC: Woodrow Wilson Center Press, 1997).
Summers, Harry G. Jr., *On Strategy: A Critical Analysis of the Vietnam War* (New York: Dell Publishing, 1984).
Tao Hanzhang, *Sun Tzu's Art of War* trans. Shibing, Yuan (New York: Sterling Publishing, 1987).
Taylor, David (ed.), *Global Cases in Logistics and Supply Chain Management* (London: International Thomson Business Press, 1997).
Thayer, Carlyle A., *War By Other Means: National Liberation and Revolution in Viet-Nam 1954–60* (Boston: Allen & Unwin, 1989).
Thompson, Julian, *The Lifeblood of War: Logistics in Armed Conflict* (London: Brassey's, 1991).
Thorpe, George C., *Pure Logistics* (Washington, DC: National Defense University Press, 1986).

BIBLIOGRAPHY

Toffler, Alvin and Heidi Toffler, *War and Anti-War: Making Sense of Today's Global Chaos* (London: Warner, 1994).

US Navy, *Naval Logistics* (Philadelphia, PA: National Technical Information Services, 1995).

Vagts, Alfred, *Landing Operations: Strategy, Psychology, Tactics, Politics from Antiquity to 1945* (Harrisburg, PA: Military Service Publishing Company, 1952).

Van Creveld, Martin, *Supplying War* (Cambridge: Cambridge University Press, 1977).

——, *Command in War* (Cambridge, MA, Harvard University Press, 1985).

——, *The Transformation of War* (New York, Free Press, 1991).

Van Dyke, Jon M., *North Vietnam's Strategy for Survival* (Palo Alto, CA: Pacific Books, 1972).

Vigor, P.H., *Soviet Blitzkrieg Theory* (New York: St Martins' Press, 1983).

Wardak, Ghulam D., *The Voroshilov Lectures, Vol. 1* (Washington, DC: National Defense University, 1989).

Watson, Mark S., *Chief of Staff Prewar Plans and Preparations* (Washington, DC: US Government Printing Office, 1950).

Watts, Barry D., *Clausewitzian Friction and Future War* (Washington, DC: National Defense University, McNair Paper No. 52, October 1996).

Westmoreland, William C., *A Soldier Reports* (New York: Da Capo Press, 1980).

White, Terry, *Swords of Lightning* (London: Brassey's, 1992).

Wylie, J.C., *Military Strategy: A General Theory of Power Control* (Annapolis, MD: Naval Institute Press, 1989).

REPORTS

Brower, Ken, *The Warsaw Pact – NATO Military Balance: The Quality of Forces* (Sandhurst: Soviet Studies Research Centre of the Royal Military Academy, 1988).

Committee on Merchant Marine and Fisheries, *Operation Desert Shield/Desert Storm: Sealift Performance and Future Sealift* (Washington, DC: US Government Printing Office, 1992).

Donnelly, Christopher N., *Rear Support For the Soviet Ground Forces* (Sandhurst: Report to the Soviet Studies Research Centre of the Royal Military Academy, A17, 1978).

——, *Soviet Army Logistics: The Themes for 1978–79* (Sandhurst: Unpublished report to the Soviet Studies Research Centre of the Royal Military Academy, A35, 1979).

Gray, Colin S., *Special Operations – What Succeeds and Why: Lessons of Experience, Phase 1* (Washington, DC: National Institute for Public Policy, 1991).

Gutman, Richard W., *US Military Equipment Prepositioned in Europe: Significant Improvements Made but Some Problems Remain*, LCD-78-431A: B-146896, (Washington, DC: General Accounting Office report, 1978).

Holliday, L.P. and R.M. Gurfield, *Viet Cong Logistics* (Santa Monica, CA: RAND, 1968).

Joint Chiefs of Staff, *The American Revolution in Military Affairs* (Washington, DC: JCS document, 1996).

North Vietnam Personnel Infiltration into the Republic of Vietnam (Military Assistance Command, Vietnam: Office of the Assistant Chief of Staff – J-2, 16 December 1970).

Pande, M.C., *Allied Air Logistic Supply and Air Transport Operations During the Burma Campaign (1944–45)* (Upavon: Tactical Doctrine Retrieval Cell, 1994).

Rodgers, S.P., *The Influence of Combat Service Support on Operations During the Burma Campaign 1944–45* (Upavon: Tactical Doctrine Retrieval Cell, 1994).

Sherr, James, *NATO's Emerging Technology Initiatives and New Operational Concepts, The Assessment of the Soviet Military Press* (Sandhurst: Soviet Studies Research Centre of the Royal Military Academy, 1987).

Soviet Analysis of Operation Desert Storm and Desert Shield, trans. W.A.B. (Washington, DC: Defense Intelligence Agency, 1991), p. 76.

The Soviet Threat to Europe in the 1980s (Sandhurst: Report to the Soviet Studies Research Centre of the Royal Military Academy, AA2, 1979).

Staff Group 10C, *Imphal–Kohima – Encirclement: 14th British Army and 15th Japanese* (Ft. Leavenworth, KS: USACGSC, 1984).

Supply Lines through Laos and Cambodia Into South Vietnam (Military Assistance Command, Vietnam: Office of the Assistant Chief of Staff – J-2, 28 February, 1969).

VC/NVA Logistics Study (Military Assistance Command, Vietnam: Combined Intelligence Center, Vietnam, 1971).

ANTHOLOGY CHAPTERS

Holborn, Hajo, 'The Prusso-German School: Moltke and the Rise of the General Staff' in Peter Paret (ed.) *Makers of Modern Strategy from Machiavelli to the Nuclear Age* (Princeton, NJ: Princeton University Press, 1986), pp. 281–95.

Uhle-Wettler, Franz, 'Auftragstaktik: Mission Orders and the German Experience', in Richard D. Hooker (ed.), *Maneuver Warfare: An Anthology* (Novato, CA: Presidio Press, 1993), pp. 236–47.

Waltz, Kenneth, 'Laws and Theories', in Robert Keohane (ed.), *Neorealism and Its Critics* (New York: Columbia University Press, 1986), pp. 27–46.

BIBLIOGRAPHY

PERIODICALS

Adams, James, 'The New Spies', *RUSI Journal*, Vol. 142, No. 1 (February 1997), pp. 17–20.

Anon. 'Chronology of Events', *Military Review*, Vol. 61, No. 9 (September 1991), pp. 64–112.

Arquilla, John and David Ronfeldt, 'Book Reviews', *Comparative Strategy*, Vol. 14, No. 3 (July–September 1995), pp. 331–41.

Ballance, E., 'The Ho Chi Minh Trail', *The Army Quarterly & Defence Journal* (April 1967), pp. 105–10.

Beaumont, Roger A. 'Beyond Tooth and Tail: The Need For New Logistical Analogies', *Military Review*, Vol. 60, No. 3 (March 1985), pp. 2–11.

Chalmers, Malcom and Lutz Unterseher, 'Is There a Tank Gap? Comparing NATO and Warsaw Pact Tank Fleets', *International Security*, Vol. 13, No. 1 (Summer 1988), pp. 5–49.

'Chronology of Events', *Military Review*, Vol. 61, No. 9 (September 1991), pp. 64–78.

Clodfelter, M. and J.M. Fawcett Jr, 'The RMA and Air Force Roles, Missions and Doctrine', *Parameters*, Vol. 25, No. 2 (Summer 1995), pp. 22–9.

Cohen, Eliot A., 'Toward Better Net Assessment: Rethinking the European Conventional Balance', *International Security*, Vol. 13, No. 1 (Summer 1988), pp. 50–89.

DePuy, William E., 'Vietnam: What We Might Have Done and Why We Didn't Do It', *Army* (February 1986), pp. 23–40.

Dick, Charles, 'The Growing Soviet Artillery Threat', *RUSI Journal*, Vol. 124, No. 2 (June 1979), pp. 66–73.

Dunn, Keith A., 'Limits Upon Soviet Military Power', *RUSI Journal*, Vol. 124, No. 4 (December 1979), pp. 38–45.

Fitzsimonds, James R. 'The Coming Military Revolution Opportunities and Risks', *Parameters*, Vol. 32, No. 2 (Summer 1995), pp. 30–6.

Gessert, Robert A., 'The AirLand Battle and NATO's New Doctrinal Debate', *RUSI Journal*, Vol. 129, No. 2 (June 1984), pp. 52–60.

Gilmore, Kenneth O., 'Along the Infamous Ho Chi Minh Trail', *Reader's Digest* (October 1970), pp. 163–8.

Heiman, Leo, 'Soviet Invasion Weaknesses', *Military Review*, Vol. 34, No. 8 (August 1969), pp. 38–45.

Hine, Patrick, 'Concepts of Land/Air Operations in the Central Region: II', *RUSI Journal*, Vol. 129, No. 3 (September 1984), pp. 63–6.

'How To Win the War in Vietnam: Admiral Sharp's Prescription', *US News and World Report* (2 October 1967), p. 22.

Jablonsky, David, 'US Military Doctrine and the Revolution in Military Affairs', *Parameters*, Vol, 24, No. 3 (Autumn 1994), pp. 18–36.

Kelley, Richard L., 'Applying Logistics Principles', *Military Review*, Vol. 57,

No. 9 (September 1977), pp. 57–63.
Lambeth, Benjamin, 'The Technology Revolution in Air Warfare', *Survival*, Vol. 39, No. 1 (Spring 1997), pp. 65–83.
'Laos: More Troublesome Trail', *Time* (17 December 1965), pp. 28–9.
LePore, Herbert P., 'Contribution to Victory: The Distribution and Supply of Ammunition and Ordnance in the Pacific Theater of Operations', *Army History*, Issue No. 34 (Spring/Summer 1995), pp. 31–5.
Libicki, Martin, 'The Emerging Primacy of Information', *Orbis*, Vol. 40, No. 2 (Spring 1996), pp. 261–73.
McManners, Hugh, 'Wave-skimmer Will Smuggle SAS Past Enemy Radar At 400 MPH', *Sunday Times*, (16 February 1997), p. 7.
Mearsheimer, John, 'Assessing the Conventional Balance: The 3:1 Rule and Its Critics', *International Security*, Vol. 13, No. 4 (Spring 1989), pp. 54–89.
Military Intelligence Professional Bulletin, Vol. 20, No. 4 (October–December 1994), *passim*.
Muckerman, Joseph E. II, 'L is For Logistics', *Joint Forces Quarterly*, No. 16 (Summer 1997), p, 121.
Owens, William, 'The Emerging System of Systems', *Military Review*, Vol. 75, No. 3 (May–June 1995), pp. 15–19.
Pagonis, William G. and Harold E. Raugh, 'Good Logistics is Combat Power', *Military Review*, Vol. 71, No. 9 (September 1991), pp. 28–41.
Peary, J.H. Binford, 'Building America's Power Projection Army', *Military Review*, Vol. 74, No. 7 (July 1994), pp. 4–15.
Peters, Ralph, 'The Culture of Future Conflict', *Parameters*, Vol. 25, No. 4 (Winter 1995–1996), pp. 18–27.
Pierce, Terry C, 'Voodoo Logistics Sink Triphibious Warfare,' *Proceedings of the US Naval Institute*, Vol. 122, No. 9 (September 1996), pp. 74–7.
Posen, Barry R., 'Measuring the European Conventional Balance: Coping With Complexity in Threat Assessment', *International Security*, Vol. 9, No. 3 (Winter 1984–1985), pp. 47–88.
Rogers, Bernard W., 'The Atlantic Alliance: Prescriptions for a Difficult Decade', *Foreign Affairs*, Vol. 60, No. 5 (Summer 1982), pp. 1145–56.
——, 'ACE Attack of Warsaw Pact Follow-On Forces', *Military Technology*, Vol. 3, No. 5, (May 1983), pp. 38–60.
Russell, Robin, Humphrey, Crum-Ewing, David Wiencek, David Bodset, 'Cruise Missiles: New Theories, New Thinking', *Comparative Strategy*, Vol. 13, No. 3 (June–September 1995), pp. 255–76.
Seffers, George I., 'US Army Study: Reduce Force Logistics, Improve Mobility', *Defense News*, (16 December 1996), p. 1.
Singer, J. David, 'International Conflict: Three Levels of Analysis', *World Politics*, Vol. 12, No. 3 (April 1960), pp. 453–61.
Starry, Donn A., 'Extending the Battlefield', *Military Review*, Vol. 61, No. 3 (March 1981), pp. 31–50.

BIBLIOGRAPHY

Turbiville, Graham, 'Soviet Logistic Support for Ground Operations', *RUSI Journal*, Vol. 120, No. 3 (September 1975), pp. 63–9.

Wohlstetter, Albert, 'Illusions of Distance', *Foreign Affairs*, Vol. 46, No. 2 (January 1968), pp. 242–55.

Zhang Xiaoming, 'The Vietnam War, 1964–1969: A Chinese Perspective', *Journal of Military History*, Vol. 60, No. 4 (October 1996), pp. 731–62.

Zaloga, Steven G, letter to the editor, *International Security*, Vol. 13, No. 4 (Spring 1989), pp. 180–7.

INTERVIEWS AND LECTURES

Interview with Lieutenant-Colonel Gerald Samos, USAF, 6 November 1993.

Lecture by General R.R. Fogleman, USAF Chief of Staff, at the University of Birmingham, England, 4 April 1997.

INTERNET DOCUMENTS

Salomon, Leon E., *Transforming Logistics For the 21st Century* (Posted to internet site http://204.7.227.67:1100/infonet/per-log/logistics/articles/log-arts.html in 1996).

VIDEOTAPE

NAFB with DoD voiceover, *1st B-2 GATS/GAM Live Weapons Demonstration*, Northrop Grumman, Product No. 9610320 Reel No. 1 DM 40619 (10/08/1996).

MASTER'S THESIS

Gregory Banner, 'The War For the Ho Chi Minh Trail' (Fort Leavenworth, KS: Thesis presented to the US Army Command and General Staff College, 1993).

Index

AirLand Battle, 140–2
Akyab Island, 18–19
Allen, Louis, 25, 28, 32–5, 181
Arab–Israeli Wars, 125
Arakan Campaign, 18–19, 21–2, 28
Auftragstaktik, 150, 168

Badger, O.C., 58
Ballantine, Duncan S., 39, 59, 70–4, 76
Barnett, George, 42
Bartlett, Dewey F., 128
Basic Readiness Plan, 40
Binh Ba (villlage), 95
Binh tram, 90
Bonaparte, Napoleon, xii, 7, 87
Booz, Allen and Hamilton, 58–9
Bora-Bora, 50–1, 57, 64, 66; *see also* Operation Bobcat
Boulding, Kenneth E., 3, 13, 181
Boyd, John, 9
Bradley, Omar, xii, 2
Brower, Charles F., 109, 144–7, 185
Brower, Kenneth, 127, 181
Brown, Kenneth N., 4, 13, 181
Burma Road, 16, 18

Callwell, C.E., xii, 13, 181
Carter, James, 166
Carter, Worrall Reed, 40, 47, 70–3, 75–6
Central Office of South Vietnam (COSVN), 82, 98, 100, 105–6
Chiang Kai-Shek, 22
Chindits, 16, 22–6, 28–32
Chinh, Truong, 87
Churchill, Winston, 23
Clausewitz, Carl von, xii, 6, 10, 13, 68, 78–9, 117, 152–3, 155–6, 167–8, 172, 179, 181
Combined Action Platoons, 102
Conant, James, 177–8
Conolly, R.L., 62
Coontz, Robert E., 42
Cooper-Church Ammendment, 113

Cooper, Jefferey, 158
Coral Sea, Battle of, 48–9, 57, 59, 65, 68
Craig, Malin, 45
Cunningham, A.C., 40

Dardenelles Campaign, 44; *see also* Gallipoli Campaign
Dau tranh, 89
Dick, Charles, 139, 147–8, 187
Diem, Ngo Dinh, 80
Dien Bien Phu, 31–2, 104
Dong, Pham Van , 80, 82
Donnelly, Christopher N., 138, 145, 147, 185
Douhet, Guilio, 159
Duan, Le, 87–8
Dung, Van Tien, 81
Dunn, Keith, 140, 144, 187
Dupuy, Trevor, 5, 13
Dyer, George, 56

Eccles, Henry E., 4–5, 13, 182
Ellis, Earl, 43
Encounter Battles, 133
Engels, Donald, 4,

Fabius, 78
Feeding Mars, 13–14, 36
Fire Ant warfare, 152
Fitzsimonds, James R., 158, 167, 169, 187
FOFA (Follow-On Forces Attack), 139–42
Frederick the Great, xii, 5
French Nickel Company, 56
Frunze, M.V., 133

Gallipoli Campaign, 42; *see also* Dardenelles Campaign
Gerow, Leonard T., 6
Giap, Nguyen Vo, 83–6, 88, 101, 103–4, 107
global attack, 161
global engagement, 161
Greene, Nathanael, 2
Gropman, Allan, 4, 13

Guadalcanal Campaign, 45, 51–7, 59–60, 64, 66–8

Halsey, William, 58
Hannah, Norman B., 108–10, 122, 182
Hannibal, 78
Higgins, Andrew J., 43
Hine, Patrick, 126
Historic Encounter, 87
Ho Chi Minh, 80, 82–4, 86, 94, 104
Ho Chi Minh Trail, 77, 79, 89–94, 96–7, 101–2, 104, 106, 108–15, 173
Ho Chi Minh Trail, The, 109–10, 116, 119, 122, 182
House Appropriations Committee, 129
Huntington, Samuel, 154

Ia Drang, Battle of, 101–2, 104, 111
Illusions of Distance, 3
Imphal, 15, 26–
Irwin, Noel, 19
Isby, David, 136, 147, 182

Jablonsky, David, 158
Johnson, Lyndon, 104
Jomini, Antoine, xii, 2, 13, 36, 154, 168

Khe Sanh, Battle of, 104
Khoi nghai, 85, 88, 107
Killebrew, Robert, 156
Kimmel, H.E., 40
King, Ernest J., 51, 56, 58, 64
Kohima, 29, 31
Krupchenko, 135

Lambeth, Benjamin, 157–8, 162, 168–9, 170, 187
Lejeune, John A., 42–3
Lentaigne, W.D., 24
Libicki, Martin, 151–2, 158, 167–9, 183, 188
Local (Provincial) Forces, 99–100
Lynn, J., xii, 13, 36, 67, 70, 76, 183

MacArthur, Douglas, 49, 51–2, 64
Magruder, John, 15
Mao Zedong, 84–5, 89, 183
Marshall, George C., 45, 64–5
McNamara, Robert S., 104
Michalak, Wojcieh, 136
Midway, Battle of, 51, 65
Mikawa, Gunichi, 54–5
Miller, Ellis, 43
Moltke, Helmut von, 7
Moses, Emile P. , 43
Mountbatten, Louis, Lord, 17, 24, 29

Nimitz, Chester A., 47–9, 52, 58–9, 68
Nixon, Richard, 107

Normandy Campaign, 67–8
Nunn, Samuel, 128

Ogarkov, Nicolai, 135
Okinawa, Battle of, 63–4
On Strategy, 109, 122; see also Summers, Harry
Operation Barbarossa, 67, 155
Operation Bobcat, 50–1, 62; see also Bora-Bora
Operation Desert Shield, 4, 128
Operation Desert Storm, xii, 4, 141, 151, 159
Operation Galvanic, 59–60; see also Tarawa, Battle of
Operation Iceberg, 63–4; see also Okinawa, Battle of
Operation Longcloth, 23–4
Operation Nifty Nugget, 130
Operation Sledgehammer, 51
Operation Thursday, 23–4, 26
Operational Manoeuvre Groups (OMGs), 136, 144
Operations Plan 712, 43
Our Military Tradition, 82
Owens, William, 151, 167–8, 188

Pagonis, William G., xii, 4, 13, 183, 188
Palmer, Bruce, 109, 118, 120–1, 183
Palmer, David. R., 85–6, 88,
Patton, George S., xii
PAVN, 89
Peters, Ralph, 154, 164, 168, 170, 188
Pickett, John, 160
Pierce, Terry C., 72, 74, 157, 167, 169, 188
Pike, Douglas, 89, 117–18, 184
PMT-100 Pipelayer, 137
POMCUS, 128, 132
Popular Forces, 102–3

Ready Reserve, 128
Reagan, Ronald, 153, 161
Rear Services Group 83, 95
REFORGER, 128
Regional Forces, 102–3
Richardson, J.O., 40
Roebling, Donald, 43
Rogers, Bernard, 127–8, 139–40, 141, 148, 188
Rommel, Erwin, xii, 7, 68
Rooney, David, 30, 32–5, 184
Roosevelt, Franklin, 23, 40, 42, 64–5

Sakurai, Shozo, 28
Saloman, Leon E., 157–8, 169, 188
Sanders, Carl H., 50
Savkin, V. Ye, 134
Scoones, Geoffry, 26
Shaw, G.C., 175, 179
Siderenko, A.A., 131, 146, 184
Slim, William Sir, 17–22, 24–35, 173–5

192

INDEX

Smith, Holland M., 44–5, 52, 61
Sokolovsky, V.D., 133, 146
Spruance, R.A., 41, 65
Stalingrad, Battle of, 31
Stark, H.R., 40
Starry, Donn A., 140, 148, 188
Stilwell, Joseph, 18, 24
Submarine Flotilla Board, 41
Sugiyama, Haijime, 37
Summers, Harry S., 108–10, 116, 122, 184
Sun Tzu, 20, 77, 116, 124, 144, 184
Supplying War, 6–8, 67, 76, 148, 168, 180; *see also* Van Creveld, Martin
'Sweep' operations, 102

Tarawa, Battle of, 52, 60–1, 66, 68, 76
Task Force Smith, 2
Tazoe, 24
Tentative Manual for Landing Operations, 43–4
Tet Offensive, 88, 104–5, 107–8
Thai, Hoang, Van, 82
Thanh, Nguyen Chi, 88, 101–2
Tho, Le Duc, 82, 88
Thoi co, 87
Thompson, Julian, 152, 168, 184
Thorpe, George C., 5, 7, 13, 184
Tin, Bui, 85
Toffler, Alvin, 153–4, 158, 168–70, 184
Toffler, Heidi, 153–4, 158, 168–70, 184
Tomahawk Cruise Missile, 159
Tra, Tran Van, 109
Training and Doctrine Command (TRADOC), 156, 158
Transformation of War, The, 153, 168, 184; *see also* Van Creveld, Martin

Tsushima, Battle of, 70
Tung, Hoang, 87
Turner, Frank, 54–5, 67
Turner, Kelly Richmond, 52, 61

Udar, 133
US Army War College, 140
US Naval War College, 41

Van Creveld, Martin, 2, 6–8, 12–13, 32, 36, 67–9, 76, 141, 144, 148, 153–4, 164, 168, 174, 177–80, 184; *see also Supplying War* and *The Transformation of War*
Vandegrift, Alexander, 54, 56
Vanguard Youths, 91
Vegetius, xii, 13
Victualing sloops, 39
Viet Minh, 80
Voroshilov Military Academy, 132, 134

Waltz, Kenneth, 176–7, 186
War Plan Orange, 39, 45
Warden, John, 158
Washington, George, 2
Washington Naval Accords, 41, 46
Wavell, Archibald, 22–3
Wehrmacht, 9–10, 58, 150
Westmoreland, William, 101–9, 111, 113, 120–2, 169, 184
Wingate, Orde, 15, 17, 20, 22–8, 30–2
Wittgenstein, Ludwig, 176
Wohlstetter, Albert, 3, 13, 188
Wylie, J.C., 155, 168, 184

Zhou Enlai, 80